EXPERIENTIAL LEARNING DESIGN

Experiential Learning Design comprehensively demonstrates the key theories and applications for the design of experiential approaches to learning and training. Learning is gradually moving away from management and delivery of content, and toward experiences that encourage learners to engage and take greater responsibility for their own progress. This book's empirically sound, multi-disciplinary approach balances technical-rational and artistic-intuitive design elements to accommodate the complex, fluctuating capacities of human learning. In-depth chapters cover design principles, social and environmental factors in learning, the importance of senses and emotions, and links between body and brain. This bold, unique perspective shift will enrich the work of learning scientists, instructional designers, educational technologists, and beyond.

Colin Beard is Professor of Experiential Learning at Sheffield Hallam University, UK. He is a National Teaching Fellow, an innovative thinker, and an experienced practitioner in experiential learning. As owner of *Experience – The Difference*, he works with many individuals, organisations, and governments across the globe.

EXPERIENTIAL LEARNING DESIGN

Theoretical Foundations and Effective Principles

Colin Beard

NEW YORK AND LONDON

Cover image: Getty Images | metamorworks.

First published 2023
by Routledge
605 Third Avenue, New York, NY 10158

and by Routledge
4 Park Square, Milton Park, Abingdon, Oxon, OX14 4RN

Routledge is an imprint of the Taylor & Francis Group, an informa business

© 2023 Taylor & Francis

The right of Colin Beard to be identified as author of this work has been asserted in accordance with sections 77 and 78 of the Copyright, Designs and Patents Act 1988.

All rights reserved. No part of this book may be reprinted or reproduced or utilised in any form or by any electronic, mechanical, or other means, now known or hereafter invented, including photocopying and recording, or in any information storage or retrieval system, without permission in writing from the publishers.

Trademark notice: Product or corporate names may be trademarks or registered trademarks, and are used only for identification and explanation without intent to infringe.

ISBN: 978-0-367-46756-2 (hbk)
ISBN: 978-0-367-46653-4 (pbk)
ISBN: 978-1-003-03086-7 (ebk)

DOI: 10.4324/9781003030867

Typeset in Bembo
by Apex CoVantage, LLC

CONTENTS

List of Figures	*vii*
List of Design Illustrations	*ix*
Acknowledgements	*xi*

1 Introducing Experiential Learning Design	1
2 Design Basics: Becoming an Architect of Experiential Learning Design	26
3 The Holistic Experiential Learning Design Model (HELM): A Complex Web of Interactions	58
4 Experience Design: Doing~Sensing	69
5 Experience Design: Sensing~Feeling	101
6 Experience Design: Feeling~Thinking	124
7 Belonging: Social Interactions in Social Spaces	150
8 Belonging: The Human Connection with the More-Than-Human World	176

vi Contents

9 *Being* – The Development of the Ontological Self 201

10 Back to the Drawing Board 217

References *235*
Index *251*

FIGURES

1.1	15 typical "features" that commonly underpin the design of experiential learning.	22
1.2	Another 15 typical "features" that commonly underpin the design of experiential learning.	24
2.1	The experiential wave.	41
2.2	Graphical primitives: letters and numbers.	49
2.3	Primary schools three-step math teaching sequence: hands, eyes, head.	54
3.1	A simplified history of dominant theories of how humans learn.	61
3.2	The five Hs: foundations of the Holistic Experiential Learning Model.	64
3.3	The origins of the Holistic Experiential Learning Model (HELM).	66
3.4	The Holistic Experiential Learning Model (HELM).	67
3.5	A simplified version of the Holistic Experiential Learning Model for use in design.	67
3.6	Other *representational formats* of the seven modes of experiencing: the learning combination lock.	68
4.1	Spatial layout and memory on a domino.	74
4.2	Numbers presented on ladybird wings.	75
4.3	Using mathematics manipulatives to subtract.	75
4.4	Classifying fixtures and fittings, sweets or stationary.	91
4.5	Plastic water bottle and a school skirt made form plastic bottles.	96
4.6	Radial relational patterns that show the increased value of recycled plastic due to increased demand.	97
4.7	Using a guiding code (HDOAC) for an experiential activity.	98
4.8	The web-like nature of the industrial ecology.	100

viii Figures

4.9	Signalling, sequencing, and relational connections.	100
5.1	The pervasive nature of emotions: the pleasure of learning at university.	117
6.1	The hot seat.	127
6.2	Seven adaptive developments that have influenced the human ability to learn from experience.	134
6.3	Design implications of multiple "intelligences."	139
6.4	A simplified representation of the major processing ("thinking") areas of the brain.	140
6.5	Points of view: Language as a design clue.	143
6.6	Basic multi-media design principles.	145
7.1	Education and *edutainment*.	159
7.2	The design of touchpad awareness cards.	163
8.1	Deciding on digital technology use.	185
8.2	Systems thinking and the spider's web.	197
9.1	*Being*: Towards integration and coherence.	203
9.2	The 3 Cs of conscious awareness, conditioning, and conduct.	206
9.3	21st Century Competences aligned with the Holistic Experiential Learning Model (HELM).	215
10.1	Learning Experience Design (LED): notes on the structural framework (3 distinct phases).	226
10.2	The changing emphasis on peer relations in the three phases.	230
10.3	Structure, choreography, and navigation.	233

DESIGN ILLUSTRATIONS

1	Explaining experiential learning: fingertips, cups, and a giraffe.	22
2	The significance of layout.	34
3	Designing creative structures: digital learning journey maps as "routes."	36
4	Mapping experiences, the experience gap, and experience "touchpoints."	38
5	Design structure, shape, and flow.	42
6	Visual cueing–communication using equations, icons, signs, signals, and symbols.	50
7	Text, icons, and "widgets."	51
8	Behavioural sensitisation using physical or digital touch cards.	53
9	*Doing* maths: "lost and found in space."	74
10	Authentic, experiential assessment of learning.	84
11	Doing it for real.	88
12	Sensory experiences: touching, moving, observing, categorising, and creating a classification chart.	90
13	Using the hands to explore complex concepts.	94
14	Sensory design vignettes.	106
15	The emotional climate – fun, fear, and magic.	111
16	The Everest experience.	118
17	Liberating introductions.	126
18	Recall, Reflection and Refiring potential.	141
19	The development of higher thinking skills – a simple depictive representation.	142
20	Thinking through alignment and association.	146
21	Thinking through word weaving.	147

x Design Illustrations

22	Moments of collaboration.	152
23	Geometric psychology – conversations about "difference."	159
24	Starting out – acknowledging power and control.	160
25	Self-authorship, internal authority and self-awareness.	164
26	Designing the experiencescape.	169
27	Finding a special solo space: the reading experience of *coffee and papers*.	171
28	Action for change in the design of programmes and conferences.	181
29	Digital memories.	186
30	Finding space and time to connect.	188
31	Making connections.	193
32	Self-awareness, audit, and action.	199
33	Developing feedback skills – bespoke designs.	208
34	Flying broomsticks and experiences within experiences.	217
35	Micro-design – understanding the design of a "How to Pack a Rucksack" session.	220
36	A simple 30-point checklist for *experiencescape* design.	224

ACKNOWLEDGEMENTS

I would like to thank my family for their amazing patience and understanding. I would especially like to thank Maggie, my wife, for her continual support, and for helping me to remain positive and focused.

Friends have also helped me, including: Dr. Roger Greenaway for his words of wisdom and for asking insightful questions about the manuscript; Professor Andy Martin from New Zealand for his comments on an early draft; and Dr. Julie Vaudrin-Charette from Canada, for her advice on Chapter 8.

For recreating and digitising the many graphics and illustrations, I would like to thank my friend Richard McCarter, and my friend Jason Ruffell for overseeing the digitisation process.

1

INTRODUCING EXPERIENTIAL LEARNING DESIGN

Porpoises and Snakes

The teachers said *you could hear a pin drop!* It was the late 1970s and I was practising the fine art of gaining the attention of hundreds of fidgety young children. I had been invited to speak to a large audience of children about the rainforests, and my 1975 zoological expedition to the Amazon. They were seated in a grand Town Hall, and more were arriving up in the balcony. Accompanied by rainforest sounds I showed pictures and told stories about porpoises, vultures, sloths, monkeys, snakes, and bird-eating spiders: all the beautiful and exotic wildlife they could wish to see. It was going well. But eventually the high level of attention dropped, and their imagination started to wane, until that is, a 'hook' came into play – a story that was designed to take them to their next level of *imagination*, to rekindle *attention*.

It was night-time, in a dense jungle area in the heart of Brazil, near the Rio Taruma. Our circle of hammocks centred around a fire that we were told must be kept going, as the *jaguar* had taken the dog of our local guide a few days previously. That night he gestured and told us about his hunting methods, and other stories, as we sat by the fire, eating monkey and tortoise. None of us could speak Portuguese, though one of our team could speak Spanish. We settled into our hammocks late that night. My hammock was slung closest to the stream. The sound of nocturnal wildlife was almost deafening. I pulled a thin sleeping bag that had been sewn together from a cotton sheet over my head. I remember thinking that the stream near me might be where the jaguar would come to drink. I was the nearest to the stream! I fell asleep. The next morning I woke to find my sleeping bag soaked in blood . . . that was the moment you could hear a pin drop!

DOI: 10.4324/9781003030867-1

2 Introducing Experiential Learning Design

Was this experiential learning? What did the children experience and what did they go away with? Did I inspire these children and show them the beauty of the rainforests, or did I scare them? Who were the learners on that day? I learnt a lot from this experience, and I asked myself many other questions, including how I might create presentations that were less passive to avoid *habituation*, and I pondered over the role of *emotions* in *engagement, attention, interest,* and *memory retention*. There is a lot to interpret if the story is critically *unpacked*. I wanted to design great *learning experiences*, so I was engaging in *design thinking*. This raises an important question: to what extent can learning experiences, with predictable outcomes, be intentionally designed? The answer is the subject of this book.

As a young zoologist, I had been *inspired* to go to the Amazon after meeting with Professor Arthur Cain (1971), author of *Animal Species and Their Evolution*. He explained so many fascinating things to me, including the fact that the river Amazon is so wide that subspecies form on either side. Oh yes, the blood. I nearly forgot. Or did I? Margaret Parkin in her book *Tales for Trainers* (1998: 28), comments that starting a story and finishing it later arouses a "level of curiosity and intrigue."

There is more intrigue to this story of blood on my sleeping bag. Building on and continuing to learn from my initial experiences. I discovered, by reading *Red Gold: The Conquest of the Brazilian Indians* (Hemming, 1978) just three years after my return, that the name *Brazil* is derived from the Portuguese word *brasa*, meaning a fire's red embers: Brazil is the only Portuguese speaking country in South America. The book explains the invasion and colonisation of Brazil by the Portuguese in 1500, and one tree became a significant reason for the invasion. The wood of this tree is a creamy colour when first cut, but soon turns to a deep blood red: it was harvested by enslaved indigenous people, to be shipped back to Portugal for clothing dye. What was on my sleeping bag was not blood, nor was it connected with the jaguar. It was a bright red tree sap!

What Is the Book About?

Fast forward 45 years later and I have learned so much more about learning experience design, not only about anticipation and attention, but also engagement, interaction, assimilation and understanding, reflecting, remembering, application, and transformation. My experiences have included design work with local communities; delivering evening classes on the environment for the Workers Education Association; becoming a professional ornithologist; a biology teacher; a field officer and then director of a practical conservation charity; a director of a Wildlife Trust involving the management of many nature reserves; a consultant, facilitator, and trainer working with many corporate clients; a lecturer and professor of experiential learning; and work with local, national, and international governments. Yet, as I write this book, I am acutely aware that for me there is so much more to learn.

This book is for practitioners who want to know more about the foundational theoretical underpinnings of experiential learning design, and that includes anyone who has an interest in helping people to learn more effectively. Each of the book chapters features common components: (1) essential *foundational knowledge* and *references* to other sources; (2) *core design principles*; and (3) *creative illustrations* offering practical design ideas. Each chapter zooms in to focus on specific aspects of the complex flux of experiential interactions that occur in the processes of learning. Collectively the overlapping chapters offer an integrative approach to learning experience design. Breadth rather than depth of understanding is offered to create design ideas applicable to many levels, such as a programme, a session, a philosophy, or a method. In places I may fail to express the complex interconnectivity: in book format words march across the page in regimented linearity, section by section, making it difficult to expose the interconnectivity inherent in the many modes of experiencing. If any sections are difficult to understand, follow your gut feelings and return to it later.

This first chapter is a very brief introduction to the terms located in the title, notably *experience, learning, design,* and *experiential learning.* The second chapter introduces a wide range of foundational principles for experience design, including program layouts, storyboarding and infographics, navigational aids, journey maps, structures, and the sequencing and shape and flow of the *experiencescape.* Basic micro level design is first explored: the use of colour, signs, and symbols such as icons and widgets, movement, spatial-relational layout, touchscreens, and linguistic design clues. The third chapter creates the Holistic Experiential Learning Model (HELM). It embraces seven core *modes* of experiencing. The remaining Chapters 4 to 8 explore the ecology of outer-inner world interactions, with each chapter focussing on two *modes* of experiencing to explore their significance in experiential learning design. Chapter 9 concerns the complex nature of *being,* the search for a connected and balanced "self," and the constant battle with the habits of mind that control so much of what we do. Chapter 10 goes back to the drawing board to explore more complex designs. Each chapter takes a different theoretical orientation, presenting essential underpinning theoretical knowledge and practical design illustrations.

This book takes the view that experiential learning is holistic, as *embodied, embedded, enacted, relational,* and *extended,* and that learning is not only *socially* and *culturally* "constructed," but also *biologically, psychologically, emotionally, sensorially, cognitively, spiritually,* and *conatively* (intention to act/action/behaviours) constructed. Not all modes of experiencing and all foundational principles can be covered in a single book, and so selected core modes of interacting and experiencing the world are: *doing, sensing, feeling,* and *thinking,* that contribute to the human sense of self, as a person *belonging, becoming,* and *being* in the world.

Belonging, becoming, and *being,* are complex overarching modes of experiencing. The theoretical underpinnings to these human interactions are explored in sufficient detail so that practical design questions about *what, so what, now what,*

4 Introducing Experiential Learning Design

and *why not*, as well as the *who, why, when, where,* and *how* can be addressed in terms of experiential learning design. Each chapter introduces a comprehensive literature base for further reading, and the titles of many books are included in the main text when they are significant to outline important principles. An illustrative example on *embodied* learning is *The Hand, an Organ of the Mind: What the Manual Tells the Mental* (Radman, 2013).

Experience and *learning* are big topics: they are regarded as inseparable, and difficult to define. *Learning experience design* (LED) (Beard, 2018a) is an acronym and metaphor for this book. It is time to throw away the old, inefficient, incandescent bulbs that produce 96% heat, and just 4% light, and replace them with light emitting diodes. LED bulbs are more powerful (*learning*), energy efficient (less exhaustion than teaching by *telling*), and longer lasting (*memory*). This emerging design language is highlighted by an American Express advertisement for a Learning Experience Designer in 2019:

> We are looking for a highly creative, tech savvy, *Learning Experience Designer* with experience of working across multiple instructional delivery modalities. The learning experience designer will create and continuously improve our leadership learning experiences using an array of approaches that engage learners and drive high impact learning.

Ideas presented in the book will require adaptation to accommodate different learners, in different cultures, contexts, and circumstances. As Howard Gardner, founder of the theory of multiple intelligences, notes:

> Factoring in each person's genetic blueprint, we become capable of achieving different potentials, and our different family and cultural milieus ensure that we will eventually become distinct human beings as no two selves, no two consciousnesses, no two minds are exactly alike. Each of us is therefore situated to make a unique contribution to the world.
>
> *(Gardner, 2008: 132)*

The human capacity to learn has been influenced by over 3.5 billion years of evolutionary processes. The book chapters show how challenging environments have played a significant role in the enhancement of these capacities, including: active food searching and foraging, predatory lifestyles, honing of the senses, faster nerve processing, warm bloodedness, movement, upright posture, the crafting of tools, and intricate social and emotional interactions. These capacities continue to be important for learning, and they have been upgraded.

Whilst the book focus is on experiential learning design for adults and young adults, many principles apply to early years learning. Designs for formal and informal learning, indoors and outdoors, are included. The work is based on more than 40 years of practice, exploration, research, reading, and testing in face-to-face interactions and online experiences. My own learning is the result of working and interacting with many people across the globe: I have also learnt much from them. Originally trained in the natural sciences (zoology), I have learnt a great deal from the beautiful creatures in the world around me. The spirit of the book is one of creative inquiry and uncertainty: Wenger-Trayner and Wenger-Trayner (2020) argue that uncertainty is a safeguard against simplification, biases, and assumptions. Uncertainty is not the opposite of certainty; it is its critical friend. It is also important to note that much learning occurs by accident rather than design.

Becoming an Architect of Experiential Learning Design

> We won't meet the needs for more and better higher education until the professors become designers of learning experiences and not teachers.

This quotation is from a book on learning design (Fink, 2013: 1). Have you ever really considered yourself as a designer? If you are involved in working with people to develop learning in some way, are you a designer? In *Visible Learning and the Science of How We Learn* several principles about learning design are offered, the first of which argues that no matter what you might define as *natural ability*, *talent*, or *intelligence*, these notions are insufficient to explain learning and achievement. They suggest that "substantial investments of time, energy, structured tuition, and personal effort are all required to develop mastery in all knowledge domains" (Hattie & Yates, 2014: xiii).

Many people claim to possess knowhow about teaching and learning because they have experienced being taught!

> [B]efore anyone starts their formal training as a teacher, they have already experienced well over 10,000 hours as students in classrooms, making teaching the profession with the most intensive and lengthy apprenticeship of any. One consequence of this *experience* is that everyone in our society, including teachers, think they already know what an expert teacher is, without any serious consideration of the research.
>
> *(Stigler & Miller, 2018: 431) (italics added)*

Unfortunately, extensive research on the topic of "expertise" highlights that "despite the fact that teaching is one of the oldest and largest of human professions . . . we still lack a clear conception of what it means to be an expert teacher" (Stigler & Miller, 2018: 431). The relationship between *experience, learning,* and *expertise* is not straightforward. The design of experiences that influence learning is not an easy task, nor should it be taken up without recognising the responsibility it brings.

6 Introducing Experiential Learning Design

There are few if any books on the market that unpack the theoretical as well as the practical principles of the design of learning experiences, less so ones that embrace the diverse disciplines such as the social, historical, biological, technological, and psychological dimensions of learning. Practical books can be overly simplistic and formulaic, presenting "off-the-shelf" packaged activities, techniques, and methods, as "ready-made" recipes. Theoretical books, on the other hand, rarely embrace practical design issues: some adopt single disciplinary perspectives. This book, spanning numerous disciplines, presents a balanced approach to design theory and practice. Kelso and Engstrom (2006) use the ~ symbol to introduce the notion of *complementary pairs such as* yin~yang, body~mind, or nature~nurture, rather than polar 'opposites' (They present a substantial glossary of complementary pairs). Six chapters (4–9) explore two *complementary* aspects of experiential learning design, such as *doing~sensing*, or *feeling~thinking*. The last chapter (10) pulls together many of the design principles, illustrating one design involving a complex *web* of interactions that took many years to develop.

The Use of Verbs as Design Clues

Stella Collins, in *Neuroscience for Learning and Development*, comments on her Brain-Friendly Training the Trainer programmes (2016), where people are encouraged not only to borrow her ideas from the course, but to create their own. Her participants are asked to create a list of *methods* for learning. The "methods" that people come up with are relatively well known, and include quizzes, crosswords, anagrams and puzzles, producing variations on a radio or TV show, completing jigsaws, and creating or building models, and writing a song or poem. I have modified them and highlighted some of the important words:

1 *Produce* and a video, radio, or television program, or a podcast, *choreograph* a dance.
2 *Invite learners to teach:* a webinar, play, blog, *design* a slide presentation . . . to others.
3 *Fill in* the blanks, jigsaws, quizzes, crosswords, anagrams, *solve* puzzles . . .
4 *Draw* ideas, draw a cartoon strip, an image to represent . . .
5 *Practice* on mannequins, bake cakes, embroider information, bandage a volunteer, operate the machinery under safe conditions . . .
6 *Analyse and explore* case studies, real-life scenarios, *sort and categorise* information.
7 *Devise* questions to ask another team . . .
8 *Create–build* models, *build* a replica, body sculpture, *create* a game . . .

(Taken and adapted from Collins, S. (2016) Neuroscience for Learning and Development, London: Kogan Page.
Reproduced with kind permission of Kogan Page Ltd.)

Introducing Experiential Learning Design **7**

This list is not about methods as such: the italicised words are action-based *experiential* verbs that suggest being *active*, *moving*, and *engaged* in *doing* or *producing* some-*thing*, as *hands-on experiences* (see Chapter 4 for an extensive section on human hands and the role of movement). Other verbs expand doing beyond the *concrete*, and *active*. The following words from Blooms (1956) hierarchical taxonomy are also *doing*: (1) *knowledge and knowing* (such as knowledge of facts, conceptual knowledge, theoretical models, etc.); (2) *comprehension and understanding* (creating meaning); (3) *application* (the ability to apply knowledge and understanding to new situations, or a different context); (4) *analysis* (the ability to break material down into its constituent parts, and identify the relations and connections between them); (5) *synthesis* (the ability to reassemble the parts to form new and meaningful connections and relationships); (6) *evaluation* (the ability to judge the value of material using explicit criteria, either developed by the learner or derived from other sources). These active verbs provide important design ideas that are helpful in broadening the experience of learning in that they point to ways that learners can be more actively involved, to experience *doing* something, *knowing* something, *describing* something, *remembering* something, *associating* things, *constructing* things, *sensing* things, *developing* a skill, *changing* things, *solving* problems, becoming *sensitive* and *aware* of, or *acting* upon something. The *something*, the subject, topic, or skill for example, is also of central importance in experiential learning design.

The active–passive dualism is unhelpful: being in*active* and present in the moment can be a significant learning experience (explored later). Similarly *imagining, thinking, feeling, reflecting, talking with others, or sensory focussing* are all forms of *experiencing*, yet *experiencing* is often mistakenly thought to be synonymous with *doing*. Kolb et al. (1971) refer to learning as the process of extracting knowledge through the transformation of a concrete experience using reflection. This is a constructivist approach referring to the construction of meaning through reflective interpretations of concrete experiences. Learning is much more than knowledge extraction using the process of reflection. Kolb et al. (1971) use the term "*concrete* experience" to denote something *physical* and *real*, though these ideas need further investigation. Furthermore, the understanding of *reflection* as "on" an experience, to recapture, review, or revisit experience, portrays reflection as distinct and separate, emphasising a "looking back," with reflection not classified as "experience." Looking *back* excludes situations where reflection is spontaneous, *in* action, rather than *on* experience (see Schon, 1983). Ringer (2002: 99) suggests that "experiential educators need to pay attention to the quality of the lived experience . . . at a time when they are having the experience."

> Even in the case of "reflection-in-action" we "think about" the situation as it occurred a few seconds ago. We are the one reflecting, and there is an object of reflection. In this way, reflection slightly alienates us from the essence of our being in the here-and-now. . . . Hence, although reflection

8 Introducing Experiential Learning Design

is an important instrument in learning, there is a risk of missing the most valuable source for growth (i.e., our awareness for the here-and-now).

(Miller & Nigh, 2017: vii)

Finkel regards reflection as an experience, so "the line between experience and reflection is not hard and clear" (2000: 155). If people do not experience something *directly*, for themselves, then an experience is *imagined*, though the boundaries between hands-on experiences and those which are imagined are indistinct.

Reflection can involve looking forward to influence future experiences, for example reflecting on upcoming examinations. Reflection is enhanced by walking and talking, or conducting an interview, or by creating a review chart or map (for creative options for the design of the *experience* of *reviewing* or *reflecting*, see Reviewing.co.uk). Reflection can be continuous, and multi-layered, involving reflection on earlier reflections (see Moon, 2004). The experiential learning cycle, whilst beneficial as a rudimentary design template, has led to reflection being seen as predominantly a separate, afterwards process. Furthermore, the existence of a *procedural* (non-verbal) *memory* system implies that learning can occur without any form of post-experience reflection. Such an experience might be subconsciously occurring when "a young person who has recently completed a long arduous journey in a wet forest may learn – at a procedural level –that being in the forest is an intensely unpleasant experience" (Ringer, 2002: 98).

Reflection can thus be regarded part of a continuous, expansive, unfolding *flow of experiencing*, that enhances the recurring re-*construction* of self, others, communities, wider society, and the more-than-human world. Reflection, as an experience, has the potential to be equally immersive, engaging, and dynamic as any other kind of experience. Reflection can be of less, equal, or greater value than a previous experience revisited. Reflection can be forwards, backwards, or in the present moment.

The historical foundations underpinning the early thinking by Kolb and Fry are explored in their 1975 publication on experiential learning. It describes the human relations work by Lewin and his colleagues using action-research interventions and the reflective processes. They focused on the group cognitive and social-emotional processes inherent in their reflective discussions about their concrete experiences (practice). Lewin and his colleagues (as staff) provided interventions and they observed and facilitated the group (as trainees) reflections. Later staff explored the conceptual analysis of what occurred in separate meetings: the group conversations were considered as "data." The ability of staff to be detached was considered important in the development of abstract conceptualisations (theory). Confrontation and conflict occurred between *practice* and the development of *theory*, creating a dialectic (oppositional) tension. Reflection was changed when it became a joint process: staff and group reflections were amalgamated at an event in 1946 when group members asked to join the separate staff meetings that analysed the group data. This amalgamation of trainee-staff interpretations proved to be productive. These group

Introducing Experiential Learning Design **9**

processes were initially developed to enhance the development of *agency* and *action* in the prevention of racism. Reflection and action also occurred as an oppositional (dialectic) tension. In their chapter (Kolb & Fry, 1975) Lewin's Experiential Learning Model is virtually indistinguishable from the Experiential Learning Theory and Cycle presented by Kolb in 1984.

Kolb (1984) acknowledges how he extensively drew on the educational work of John Dewey (1938) who recommended that school students should reflect on their own *observations*, by testing their own *hypotheses* through the application of a rigorous, *scientific method* (which he believed would lead to a more *democratic* society). The four common stages of the scientific method thus contributed to the notion of *doing, reflecting, theorising*, and *acting/testing*.

In this book seven foundational *modes* of experiencing, rather than four, shape the foundational principles of experiential learning design. These seven modes are used to create a more comprehensive holistic design model for experiential learning. The seven modes are not presented as separate, nor linear nor cyclical, but as an interacting web in a constant state of flux: *experience* is after all complex, fluid, relational, embodied, enactive, and embedded.

Learning Design: Evolution or Revolutionary?

> The new field of learning design has the potential to revolutionize not only technology in education, but the whole field of teaching and learning through the application of design thinking to education. Learning Design looks inside the "black box" of pedagogy to understand what teachers and learners do together.
>
> *(Dalziel, 2016)*

This rather grand claim to *revolutionise* learning is taken from the back cover of *Learning Design: Conceptualising a Framework for Learning and Teaching Online*. Similarly, *The Learning Revolution* by Dryden and Vos (2001) makes *revolutionary* claims about making changes to how the world learns. Selling millions of copies, the book includes 16 trends that will shape tomorrow's world, 13 steps needed for a 21st-century learning society, and 20 steps to learning anything in a much better way! In the 21st century many books focus on learning design, and the following seven titles are illustrative: *Learning as a Design Science* (Laurillard, 2012); *Learning Design: Conceptualising a Framework for Learning and Teaching Online* (Dalziel, 2016); *Learning Design: Create Amazing Learning Experiences with Design Thinking* (Klang & Suter, 2019); *Higher Education by Design* (Mackh, 2018); *Rethinking Pedagogy for a Digital Age: Principles and Practice of Design* (Beetham & Sharpe, 2020); *Designing Experiences* (Rossman & Duerden, 2019); *Design for How People Learn* (Dirkson, 2015).

This wave of interest in experience design thinking has emerged with both positive and negative consequences. The growth and popularity of the digitally

10 Introducing Experiential Learning Design

connected world has encouraged the *physical* to become *digital*, with human face-to-face interaction becoming an expensive luxury. In addition, developments in neuroscience research on the human brain have contributed to a renewed interest in commercial applications of experience design within the "experience economy." This new knowledge has been applied to create consumer attention, and interaction, and, in some cases, addictive habits (Nyal, 2014). Within hospitality, tourism, and events a design shift has occurred, from *atmospherics* and *aesthetics* (lighting, colours, furniture, ambience, etc.), to the broader notion of *servicescape* design, and on to *experiencescape* design (the *whole experience*) (Pizam & Tasci, 2019). Other forms of *scape* have emerged including cyber*scape*, services*cape*, wine*scape*, ship*scape*, and performance*scape*.

Learning Design in Museums and Art Galleries

To learn about experience design, a trip to the best museums could prove productive. Go armed with a notepad and simply watch people. Consider what draws their attention, and what engages. What inspires and what gives pleasure? How are resources utilised to generate educational experiences? There has undoubtedly been a relatively recent shift from "museum education" to "museum learning" (Hein, 1998; Hooper-Greenhill, 1999; Hooper-Greenhill, 2007). In the past interactional experiences were difficult for museums and art galleries because of exhibits being rare or valuable: to place such items in glass cabinets or cordon them off was justifiable. In the early 16th century touching of the artefacts was allowed, as a form of manual investigation, as curators often received salaries out of the entrance fees, and this was an inducement to them to make their museums attractive to visitors and so they allowed visitors to physically interact with exhibits. In the 17th and 18th centuries visitors mostly just looked: occasionally touching was allowed. Art paintings were looked at, sculptures were touched. Except for particularly high value and/or rare pieces, the restricted ability to just look is now declining. *Hands-on* and *minds-on* interactive experiences are increasing. Museums have also capitalized on digital interactions known as "customer experience enhancement systems." They operate on touchscreen handheld devices with "stations" that offer interactive experiences, such as a carefully choreographed voice that simulates a curator talking to you about the exhibits. The Anne Frank and Van Gough Museums use these hand-held devices (see Chapter 2 to read more on museum designs and haptic experiences).

Museums are re-examining their educational role by scrutinising their experience designs as they have been criticised for endorsing repressive, authoritarian identities. Educational narratives in museums have been carefully *re*considered, *re*scripted, and *re*designed: for example, museums display ancestral artefacts of indigenous peoples, but the old, ill-informed colonial narratives that proport to help visitors understand can have a destructive impact (see "In My Blood It Runs," Chapter 8). The reflective opportunity to rewrite outdated colonial

Introducing Experiential Learning Design **11**

narratives is in itself a valuable learning experience. The museum experience is increasingly digitally integrated to engage wider audiences beyond those visiting the physical museum building. Digital and physical experiences have limitations:

> A lot of what matters is the power and the feeling of the experience. . . . But when you put something in a museum, or even on TV, you can see it alright, but you are really only looking at the shell.
>
> *(Barbara Smith, Navajo educator, quoted in Buhner,*
> The Lost Language of Plants, *2002: 77)*

The problems of the "shell" can negatively affect the visitor experience in museums and art galleries: Nina Simon in *The Participatory Museum* says, "I don't blame the participants. I blame the design" (2010: i).

The Titanic Museum in Northern Ireland is arguably one of the best museum experiences in the world, so what makes it so special? The *journey* of learning *moving* through the museum has been carefully choreographed. The making of the boat is the beginning of a learning journey. This is experienced in moving time pods with six visitors per carriage, rising up the steel face of the simulated ship's side. Voices of the workers can be heard in the shipyard, and images of red-hot glowing rivets from the embers of a fire being pounded into the holes on the side of the ship are projected onto the steel walls. Fitting the ship out, setting sail, the people on board, the emergency morse code messages – "we have hit an iceberg and we are sinking" – the survivors, the deaths, inequality, finding the ship on the bottom of the ocean 76 years later, and watching a film in the museum cinema of the submarine dive to locate this magnificent ship that had such a short life, are just some of the educational experiences. Even old sepia photographs come alive through a video clip of walking Victorians which is projected and superimposed on glass to *manipulate* the sense of *reality*.

The museum visitor experience has been choreographed in a similar way to the Titanic movie. The moment in the film that is highly emotionally charged is introduced in a large picture of actress Kate Winslet shivering and holding the hand of Jack in the ice-cold water below. The caption reads "I will never let you go Jack." The analysis of a movie can help to understand experience design principles. Film directors understand choreography and storylines. The emotional content, intrigue, and historical accuracy for example, are all important (more in later chapters).

If the *museum experience* is essentially a learning experience, then maybe there are insights to be gleaned for experiential learning design. In the concluding section of *Museums and Education* (2007: 187) Hooper-Greenhill comments that:

> From the evidence we can describe learning in museums, at its best, as immersive, embodied, holistic, and pleasurable which together lead to learners adopting an open-minded and receptive outlook. Museums can induce a "readiness to learn."

12 Introducing Experiential Learning Design

What Is Meant by the Term *Experience?*

The term "experience" is complex, vague, and contested, with different meanings within different cultures (see Fox, 2008: Jay, 2005). The word derives from the Latin *experiri*: to *try*, and it is also the root of *experience, experiment,* and *expertise*. Experience alone does not necessarily lead to learning, and the relationship between experience and expertise is complex. Something has to happen to the experience/s: there has to be attention, intention, engagement, and a readiness to grasp and transform the experience in some way and at some point, in order to learn from it, and reviewing and reflecting *in* or *on* experiences are part of these processes. Throughout the book many other interactional processes are highlighted.

Whilst the four stages of doing, reflecting, creating new thinking, and testing out represents "scientific" investigative approaches, these stages present a relatively unsophisticated design framework for experiential learning. Experience is a multi-dimensional phenomenon, involving individuals, groups, organisations, and societies *interacting* with the world, to mutually influence continuous change as a result of unfolding layers of *interpretation* involving the personal, social, biological, cultural, conscious, and subconscious to name a few layers of interaction. Past experiences shape present and future experiences: the term experience has a sense of *continuity* (Dewey, 1938), and each layer forms part of another layer, and some layers have greater significance at any one time. We also function within large networks of experiences, and we negotiate norms and values, and attend to relationships, involving power and politics, within societal and historical frames. *Experience* is a term that, as historian Martin Jay suggests in his book *Songs of Experience*, "exceeds concepts and even language itself" (2005: 5).

The more we know about experience, the more we recognize that there is much more still to understand, and the more we participate in experiential learning, the more we learn by experiencing it for ourselves. Whilst the book is about design, the complex flux of interactions that unfold through experiencing cannot be fully steered or influenced. No *learning experience* can be disconnected from the contextual *relevance* and *reality* of an individual personal life experience, or individual abilities, or motivations to learn. When experience is *planned* other *unplanned* experiences will *emerge*: the ability to maximise these opportunities differs widely in individuals (Megginson, 1994). *Life experience*, described through simple but significant metaphors, is so very different for every individual:

> We experience ourselves and the world as a constant flow of thoughts and sensations . . . according to one influential theory, consciousness is like a theatre –a "spotlight of attention" shines a bright beam onto certain neural processes, and those that are lit up enter the "stage" of conscious awareness.
>
> *(Costandi, 2013: 76)*

The term *flow*, as in a *river*, is a metaphor often used by philosophers because life, in many ways, is like a river flowing past us. Experience is constantly being reconfigured, and so it is also impossible to dip our toes into the same water (experience) twice, as the Greek philosopher Heraclitus remarked. A river does have *currents, flow, eddies*, and *backwaters*. Roberts, in *Beyond Learning by Doing* (2012), uses the notion of theoretical currents with eddies and backwaters to create the themes of his chapters on experiential education. The river metaphor can also be misleading, as it suggests "the flow of a river is almost entirely out of our control" (Godfrey-Smith, 2016: 81). This metaphor separates the human experience from the river, yet we are integrated and part of the river (world).

Equally experiences can be likened to a *film*. Developing the habit of *noticing* makes learning experiences "*visible*" to self and others. Indeed, therapeutic work acknowledges that we write our own life scripts and capture our own "screenshots," to construct our own unique memories, life stories, and biographies. Exploring these life scripts and associated images, in terms of how they are remembered, is central to therapeutic practice. Deconstruction and reconstruction of personal films offers individuals opportunities to re-examine the debilitating impact that specific experiential interpretations can cause. The brain possesses an enormous capacity to store long sequences of experiences as opposed to a collection of separate shots:

> [I]n our brains, the extra capacity is so excessive that the pictures run together to be nearly continuous. The resulting "episodic" memory is prevalent in us: we think back to events and can reconstruct them almost like a movie. Using our vast memories, we can call up long sequences, rearrange them, add to them. We can also recall them almost as if they were happening in the present time: we reactivate sensory images so strongly that we can practically hallucinate them.
>
> *(Lynch & Grainger, 2008: 159)*

Designing Experiences

Humans have a long history of design expertise. Definitions of *expertise* refer to someone who is skilful and well informed, suggesting a movement from novice to expert, requiring a period of apprenticeship. As the many layers of understanding are developed through practice a shift from novice to high levels of competence and proficiency occurs. The expert designer can call on a vast repertoire of familiar experiences and circumstances. In *The Cambridge Handbook of Expertise & Expert Performance*, Cross suggests we all *design* when we plan to do something new, whether we are cooking or rearranging the living room: "*everyone can – and*

14 Introducing Experiential Learning Design

does – design" (2018: 372). Design is a process that has considerable impact on our lives. Design is associated with professions such as architecture, involving building design, structural design, and soft furnishing design. Architects create drawings and plans, with explanatory text. They include formal and measured drawings of structures as well as rough sketches of garden areas, or interior designs. Drawings and sketches make ideas *visible*. Sketches move what is inside the head to the outside, and sketches are particularly useful to enable spatial, relational, and/or functional issues to be visualised and explored. Drawings are an external memory, to deposit design ideas: we have cognitive limits (cognitive load) to the amount of information that can be held mentally.

Sketches are not just about drawing, they also include annotations, icons, and symbols, which are all explored in more detail in Chapter 2. The design of infographics, storyboards, and maps are also considered as they are now widely used in the experience economy for customer experience enhancement maps, for example. All these designs formats are also called *external representations*, and much research has been conducted on their design and use (see also Kalbach on *Mapping Experiences*, 2016). The use of design drawings for experiential learning is explored in Chapter 2, and the design of more advanced external representations is covered in Chapter 10.

In *Designing Experiences* (2019: 14) Rossman and Duerden suggest that "experience design is the process of intentionally orchestrating experience elements to provide opportunities for participants to co-create and sustain interactions that lead to results desired by the participants and the designer." An overarching notion of an "event experience," that could equally apply to experiential learning design, suggests:

> participation and involvement; the state of being physically, mentally, socially, spiritually and emotionally involved; the changing knowledge, skill, memory or emotion; a conscious perception of having intentionally encountered, gone to live through an activity or event; and effort that addresses a psychological need.
>
> *(O'Sullivan & Spangler, 1999: 23)*

Design involves problem-solving methods which include empathising with the problem, defining, ideating, the development of a prototype, and subsequent testing (see Jonassen, 2022, for a comprehensive account of designing problem-solving learning environments). Learning design deals with ill-defined or ill-behaved problems, which tend not to follow any exacting rules or procedures. Experiential learning design is regarded as a skill requiring a slightly different approach to problem solving, notably the art of developing questions for problem *finding* (see *The Cambridge Handbook of Expertise & Expert Performance* by Ericsson et al.,). Studies on expert design note that "the more expert designers move rapidly to early solution conjectures and use these conjectures as a way of exploring and defining *problem*-and-*solution* together" (Cross, 2018: 377). A form of "generative reasoning" is used rather than deductive reasoning. If the problem cannot be fully understood, then the problem cannot be considered in isolation from potential solutions, and so there is something of a *creative bridge* between the solution and the problem, with the focus of attention often rapidly alternating between the two (see Cross, 2018: 379). Cross refers to research that highlights:

> the importance of rapid alternation between different modes of activity, facilitated by external representations: drawing sketches, representing the visual field in the sketches, perceiving visuo-spatial features in sketches, and conceiving of design issues or requirements are all dynamically coupled with each other.
>
> *(Cross, 2018: 379)*

In learning design art and science merge: it is an iterative process, involving identifying and resolving challenges through design cycles of creativity, user feedback, and ongoing investigation. Early research on design processes involved exploring *expertise* in leading chess players, and research into animation design, by asking designers to "think aloud," to make their internal processing visible. This type of research however utilised "laboratory" style experiments that were carried out in simulated conditions. For experiential learning design, the idea of asking participants to "think aloud" during their experience holds promise, to externalise internal thinking.

"Experiential" Learning

Experiential learning embraces a vast field of practice, and a very basic understanding of experiential learning is necessary at this stage of the book, as more will follow in subsequent chapters. *Experiential* learning is a *category* or *type* of learning, where the "experience" of learning has high design significance. One simple principle underpinning experiential learning is to "let the learners do the learning," by acknowledging the rich resources that reside in the learners themselves, and in their *interactions* with each other. This "*learner-experience-centred*" approach involves spending more time on the design of the learning experience, so that the learner becomes *engaged* by actively participating in a discovery process of "finding out" (for themselves). Experiential learning foregrounds experience through *acquaintance with* rather than *knowledge about* something (Stapely, 2004).

When a word or concept like *experience* is examined in some detail it becomes apparent just how elusive its meaning is, and the closer we look the more indistinct and taken for granted the concept is. *Experience* and *learning* are perhaps two of the most complex but fascinating words in a dictionary – both words are fundamental to human life; indeed language may be insufficient to communicate and clarify complex terms like *learning* or *experience*. These two ideas are so intimately intertwined that there is no learning without experience. The concept of

16 Introducing Experiential Learning Design

experiential learning resists categorisation in that there is little agreement on the defining parameters and boundaries and for this reason Malinen (2000) is critical about notions of experiential learning in the 20th century:

> Adult experiential learning is a complex, vague, and ambiguous phenomenon, which is still inadequately defined, conceptually suspect – and even poorly researched . . . its theoretical and philosophical foundations are fragmented and confusing. . . . There are too many interpretations and priorities among the theorists and practitioners so that no single, clear definition of these foundations could be constructed.
>
> *(p. 15)*

It might be that we learn to accommodate these conceptual difficulties because experience, and learning, are not static phenomena. They are shifting, multimodal, and subject to continuous reflective reconstructions. Critical feminist Elana Michelson suggests there is a *fruitful incoherence* to experiential learning, as its roots lie in alternative, liberatory practice. It is unstable and provisional, collective, and not individual, always containing an element of insurgency that "*resists categorisation and management*" (1999: 142). Similarly, Kayes (2007), in *The Handbook of Experiential Learning and Management Education* notes "experiential learning tends to be defined by diversity rather than homogeneity, complexity rather than simplicity, and disagreement rather than consensus." Kayes notes the "postmodern belief that to name (or define) experience is to undermine its very definition" (p. 426).

There have been numerous attempts to define experiential learning, and these can be used to construct several foundational characteristics, despite the concerns of Malinen (2000). One comprehensive 150-word definition by Itin (1999) captures some of the practical aspects of experiential education as:

> a holistic philosophy, where carefully chosen experiences are enhanced by reflection, critical analysis, and synthesis, are structured to require the learner to take initiative, make decisions, and be accountable for the results, through actively posing questions, investigating, experimenting, being curious, solving problems, assuming responsibility, being creative, constructing meaning, and integrating previously developed knowledge.
>
> *(p. 93)*

Nearly a decade later I "attempted" to define experiential learning in a broad, multi-disciplinary and holistic perspective as:

> a sense making process involving *significant experiences* that, to varying degrees, act as the source of learning for individuals, groups, societies, and organisations. These *experiences inter*-actively immerse, and reflectively

Introducing Experiential Learning Design **17**

engage the inner world of learner(s) as whole beings (including physical-bodily, intellectually, emotionally, psychologically, and spiritually) with the intricate "outer world" environment (the more-than-human world of space, place, and planet, and the human world of the social, cultural, and political milieu) to create memorable, rich, and effective experiences for and of learning.

(adapted from Beard & Wilson, 2018: 3)

Each of these contemporary definitions outline different *layers* and *modes* of "experiencing." The first definition focuses on the micro layers, whilst the second definition focuses on macro layers. They both highlight the centre stage role that experience plays in learning. Together these definitions also reveal how *experience* engages the *whole person/s* in an interactional dynamic with their environment. Whilst outdoor education, expeditionary learning, adventure learning, service learning, and adventure therapy represent some of the more popular physical activity-based forms of experiential learning, experiential learning can, in contrast, be a small component of a session or programme. In this way experiential learning resists being interpreted as an *all or nothing* concept. This is important because of frequent, often unfounded concerns that experiential learning takes more time. It can, but it doesn't need to: what experiential learning does is to provide engagement, participation, inclusion, a reduction in cognitive load, and depth to understanding, as will be shown in later chapters. Experiential learning can be formal or informal, or form part of a community change project, or a personal development initiative. What is common to all varieties of experiential learning is that the *experience* is regarded as the foundation *of*, and the stimulus *for*, learning.

A third definition of experiential learning, created by Boud et al. in their book *Using Experience for Learning* (1993: 8), further develops these underpinning principles:

> We found it to be meaningless to talk about learning in isolation from experience. Experience cannot be bypassed; it is the central consideration of all learning. Learning builds on and flows from experience: no matter what external prompts to learning there might be – teachers, materials, interesting opportunities –learning can only occur if the experience of the learner is engaged, at least at some level. These external influences can act only by transforming the experience of the learner.

In this definition the word *experience* is portrayed in two very different but interwoven ways. Firstly, that the experience is purposefully provided, or pointed to by a facilitator or teacher, to become raw material for learning. Secondly, the learner brings their own experience to the table, and so the experience of learning becomes more significant for the learner when it builds on what is already

18 Introducing Experiential Learning Design

known. In this way engagement is likely to occur, with the potential for transformation (change).

A suitable or significant experience for learning can be either intentionally planned and designed, as in formal programmes, or such experiences can occur in a more informal or emergent way (See Megginson, 1994, for an exploration of *planned* and *emergent* learning). Design, as in experiential learning design, is not just about the design of things for learners to do and the provision of resources. There are two major design considerations: the design of the experience *for* learning, blended carefully with an understanding of *how people learn*, that is, the processes *of* learning.

Experiential learning and experiential education are often used synonymously. Their historical roots intertwine and separate. Experiential education is rooted in progressive ideas about school education. The phylogenetic and ontogenetic difference between *learning* and *education* is significant. In terms of the way we develop and grow from babies to adults (*onto*genetically) learning precedes education, and in evolutionary terms (*phylo*genetically) learning precedes education.

Emerging Core Principles

Experiential learning, as a concept, is still evolving. Several foundational principles appear from the three definitions above: (1) *experience design* is important to the learning process, taking "centre stage"; (2) the *experiential* dynamic has multiple layers in that (a) the experience *of* and (b) *for* learning are both important in the design of experiential learning; (3) that learning affects the "whole" person in terms of (a) *inner* experiences (cognitive, affective, etc.) and (b) *outer* world experiences (spaces, power, culture, interactions with others and materials, etc.); (4) there is a certain *quality* to the experience so as to *engage* the learner in meaning making; (5) that the experience should be *memorable;* (6) that *conditions* for learning, such as *motivation, engagement,* and *immersion* are important; (7) that the richest resources originate within the learner/s; and (8) that the *experience* of learning has transformative potential for the "self" and others. In adopting these core principles of experiential learning, this book embraces a broader conceptualisation of experience, highlighting its interactive and ecological form in a way that moves beyond seeing "concrete" *doing* as synonymous with *experiencing*. By embracing more than just four modes of learning found in the learning cycle, other *modes of experiencing* are regarded as equally important to the concept of experiential learning. The time has come to reconsider the popularist notion that *experiencing* is *doing*.

Experiential Learning: A Brief History

Perhaps the concept of experiential learning will never be fully explained. Moon (2004) argues that any search for unanimity might be impracticable, and that its core meaning is derived from "all those who have contributed to the literature" (p. 107). As to who the main contributors are is controversial, because, as Moon

Introducing Experiential Learning Design   **19**

comments, across many disciplines the "views of experiential learning differ widely" (p. 110). At this stage it might be productive to briefly explore some of the core philosophical foundations, whilst recognising that longstanding Western narratives should be opened up for unpacking and rescripting.

Designing experiences for learning is a unifying yet neglected thread that runs through the long and complex evolution of experiential learning. Its early origins are said, in predominantly Western accounts, to lie in ancient philosophical debates about how we experience the world, and how we might come to "know" and make meaning from it. From the East, Confucian and Tao philosophers contributed to foundational thinking, and the translated saying *I hear I forget, I see I remember, I do I understand*, is an inadequate Western translation of the Chinese Confucian aphorism, which underpins the *"Tell-Show-Do"* Instructional Triangle developed by Dale in the 1960s. Early Western philosophical contributions are significant; indeed Aristotle is said to have developed early ideas about learning from experience (Stonehouse et al., 2011). It was not until the 19th century that additional foundations underpinning experiential education and experiential learning arose due to concerns about methods of schooling. At this time harsh discipline, and basic methods of teaching, involving rote, repetition, and regurgitation gave rise to calls for more "progressive" approaches. Published material suggests that calls for change surfaced simultaneously in the USA and across parts of Europe, including the UK. In the UK progressive educationalists proposed the Heuristic Method (meaning *discovery*), which had clear similarities to the "scientific discovery methods" proposed by John Dewey in the US (see Curtis, 1963). Both involved the systematic use of observation, hypothesis, experiment, and testing. Whilst numerous educationalists sought to liberate and *progress* education, to remove oppressive and inequitable conditions, Dewey is regarded as making a particularly important contribution to forms of education that he felt would be needed to develop a more democratic society. Though he did not use the term experiential learning, he expressed concerns about design of teaching methods, calling for the experience of the learner to be valued, advocating *discovery* through "scientific" enquiry. Dewey felt that a sound philosophy of *experience* was much needed (see Beard, 2018b).

Experiential learning continued to evolve with new ideas built upon the work of peers and predecessors. In the 20th and the early 21st centuries the most popular theory of experiential learning, accompanied with a simple and easily remembered experiential learning cyclical model, was that developed by Kolb, Rubin, and McIntyre during the 1970s, and further developed by Kolb (1984). Kolb's 1984 publication remains the most frequently cited experiential learning theory (ELT), undoubtedly helping to spread ideas about experiential learning across the globe in a way that no other author has been able to achieve. Moon (2004) regards the model by Kolb in 1984 as a "teaching" model rather than a "learning" model. Kolb acknowledges that his ideas were derived from the contributions of several predecessors, including several cognitive and developmental

20 Introducing Experiential Learning Design

psychologists whose preceding work provided much underpinning theoretical basis to the later work of Kolb. Lewin, Piaget, and Dewey were particularly influential in this respect.

It has been speculatively suggested (Seaman et al., 2017) that the term "experiential" *learning* was first used in T-Group (training group) workshops that were designed to investigate human relations interactions, pioneered by Kurt Lewin and others. The T-Group method was originally based on small groups of people *revisiting* and *reflecting* on their community experiences (e.g., racial tensions). Their social *interactions* and *human relations* abilities were explored and facilitated by specialised researchers in the fields of psychology and social science (again we see that experiential learning has a history of confronting social inequality). These experiential methods essentially took the form of *conversations*, followed by an analysis of the *interactions*. These socio-emotional approaches were said to be "experiential." These processes clearly underpin Kolb's *experience-reflect-learn* constructivist model.

It does not matter a great deal when the words *experiential* and *learning* were first joined together. Experiential learning has been the way of humans for thousands of years but no one called it that. What does become clear from the recent history of experiential learning, however, is that concerns about the design of experiences have been at the forefront of all the lines of enquiry.

Time to Rethink Design

In 2008 Jayson Seaman published a paper that was critical of simple experiential learning cycles. It was titled: *Experience, Reflect, Critique: The End of the "Learning Cycles" Era.* Unsophisticated experiential learning theories have tended to separate and privilege the social from the psychological, the "human" from the "natural," mind over body. The notion that the body simply *does*, and the mind *thinks* will be frequently challenged in this book. Kidner (2001: 10) refers to:

> (a problematic) interlocking system of overlapping dualisms that guide our thought and actions in environmentally significant ways; and these include civilised/wild, modern/primitive, culture/nature, mind/body, and so on. In each case, the first term of each pair represents a preferred state or entity, whereas the second indicates something that we try to distance ourselves from, composing a value system that gives the impression of being based on "factual" distinctions.

Pepper (1984: 6) argues that prejudicial filters present the "world" as synonymous with "social," "experience" as synonymous with "environment," as though somehow "they were the same wherever one happens to be." Benton and Redclift critically examine the heritage of social theory in relation to the natural environment, arguing that sociology has made a slender contribution to the study of the environment:

Introducing Experiential Learning Design **21**

culture, meaning, consciousness and intentional agency differentiated the human from the animal, and effectively stemmed the ambitions of biological explanation. . . . In one move the opposition between nature and culture (or society) made room for social sciences as autonomous disciplines distinct from the natural sciences, and undercut what were widely seen as the unacceptable moral and political implications of biological determinism.

(Benton & Redclift, 1994: 3)

This book approaches experiential learning design in ways that reconnect these dualisms, acknowledging the essential *integrative complexity* of experience. Experiential learning is both a philosophy and a method, and the preceding paragraphs make clear the rejection of the view that experiential learning is merely "a method or technique that any teacher might employ to meet certain instructional objectives" (Roberts, 2012: 4). All terms, like experience, design, practice, experiential learning, and experiential education are problematic. When these terms are considered in isolation they lose the essential fluidity of meaning, to become divorced from the complexity of the constant state of flux of holistic connectedness.

The Foundations of Experiential Learning Design

Some of the current foundational features that underpin experiential learning design (explored in this book) are briefly listed in Figure 1.1.

Fifteen more typical features of experiential learning are listed in Figure 1.2 after the story of the Fingertips, the Giraffe, and the Cup.

It is important to point out that there are of course criticisms of experiential learning. Most relate to the lack of clear defining boundaries, and the use of simplistic modelling and theorising, and in particular the dominance of rational, brain-based cognitive processing perspectives where experience is reduced to mental constructions (sometimes referred to as a *cephalocentric* approach – the octopus is a cephalopod – *ceph* means brain, *pod* means foot). The notion of *experience* cannot be understood through the lens of a single discipline. *Experience* is more than the product of our *biology* (biologically determined) or *social* interaction (social determined), or mental processing (cognition/cephalocentric focus).

Complexity in Experiential Learning Design

The way learning is understood has continually changed. Peter Jarvis in his book *Towards a Comprehensive Theory of Human Learning* (2006: 12) in a candid admission, comments that "while I am confident that learning is a combination of processes, I now realise that I did not: manage to capture its complexity; depict the person in the world, rather their relationship with the world; relate reason and the emotions."

22 Introducing Experiential Learning Design

> 1. The experience is central to the learning process, and in experiential forms of learning experience is the foundation and stimulus for learning, and in this way the experience takes centre stage.
> 2. A strapline is: 'Let the learners DO the learning themselves!' (see what is 'delivered' and redesign so participants *do* more for themselves).
> 3. Experiential Learning typically involves meaning making processes that involve active, and reflective learning through discovery, leading to a finding out for one's self, that results in a deeper understanding.
> 4. In experiential learning there is a strong focus on self-authorship, adopting a critical interpretation of external authority to enhance the development of internal authority. Experiential Learning is typically low on prescription.
> 5. Experiential learning uses a balance of description and depiction (representations).
> 6. The experience typically should engage the whole person – holistically. This requires a transdisciplinary approach.
> 7. Experience is recognised as a complex composite made up of information and feedback (energy) flows, derived from the constantly interacting flux between the inner world of the individual self, and the outer world involving other humans and the more-than-human world.
> 8. There should ideally be a certain quality, to arouse and engage in ways that create memorable experiences.
> 9. In experiential learning there is a shift in emphasis on relational learning, moving away from the notion of distance in facilitator/teacher-dominated teaching, towards more learner-centred experiencing with learners involving co-dependent and co-productive learning relationships.
> 10. Others contribute to the social construction of knowledge: their voices are heard through relational dialogue.
> 11. Experiential learning focuses especially on episodic memories (experience based) that can enhance semantic (explicit factual) memory
> 12. The body is freed to play its vital part in learning (embodied learning).
> 13. Experiential forms of learning (such as experiential learning, experiential education, adventure learning) derive from a common heritage/history.
> 14. Experiential learning design requires a fourfold consideration: experiences (1) of and (2) for learning, affecting the whole person, their (3) inner and (4) outer world experiencing.
> 15. The outer world experience embraces human interactional experiences (social/cultural), as well as interactional relationships with the more-than-human world (e.g. natural world, and physical world).

FIGURE 1.1 15 typical "features" that commonly underpin the design of experiential learning.

When I am asked what experiential learning is, I often simply tell a story about two very different experiences of a giraffe, as told in Design Illustration 1.

 DESIGN ILLUSTRATION 1 EXPLAINING EXPERIENTIAL LEARNING: FINGERTIPS, CUPS, AND A GIRAFFE.

A senior official in the US Government (Foreign Service Institute) introduced me to an audience before a keynote speech and said that she had done her homework and had come across the interesting idea of "*The Giraffe Effect*." In speeches I have often been asked to explain and define experiential learning, but I don't usually have sufficient time to explain it in much detail. I simply show a picture of a giraffe and explain two experiences I have had with them. The stories translate

Introducing Experiential Learning Design   **23**

as *conceptual metaphors* that explain experiential learning. Before I tell the audience about the two experiences of a giraffe, I create a short experience involving fingertips. I ask people to face another person and to hold their fingertips above those of their colleague. When I give the go-ahead, they then gently touch the fingertips of another person. When they experience this, they realise that there is no sense of one's own fingertips until they touch something or someone. You can also try this using your own two hands and fingertips. The experience explains *reciprocity*: that there is no sensory experience of the fingertips without the interaction with *something*, or *someone* else (Merleau-Ponty refers to this as a *double sensation*, where each hand is experienced as both perceiver and perceived). This illustrates that there is no *self* without *other* (self~other).

In experiential learning there are many modes of experiencing besides the sensory experience: these modes all interconnect with each other. For example, there is no thinking (brain) without sensing (body), and vice versa. *Modes of experiencing* are all intricately intertwined in an interactional dynamic that exists in a continuous state of flux. For an understanding of the way that the multiple modes of experiencing are integrated, pick up a cup from above with your fingertips spread evenly around the rim. Although you can see the fingers make contact around the lip of the cup in different places, the experience is one that is unified, as a single experience of a cup. This is a physical metaphor highlighting how we experience the world: although we sense, think, move, talk with others, and so on, the experience is not separated into its component parts. Experience occurs in a state of constant flux, yet it appears as connected and unitary (see Ratcliffe, 2013).

Different experiences of interactions with a giraffe are then introduced. The first experience took place on the plains not far from Nairobi. I was running an executive management training programme for Intercontinental Hotels. The hotel paid for a wildlife safari trip, and we were all taken out on the back of a truck to spot the animals on the savannah. The powerful sun created a shimmering haze, and as we moved along a dusty track I spotted, through my binoculars, that leggy gait of three giraffes way off in the distance. There were other spectacular animals that day too, and for me as a zoologist, this was a fantastic experience.

The second experience involved our family going to a wildlife safari park. On this occasion a giraffe leaned down and popped its head into our car. The smell of urine was strong, the head moved slightly as we stroked it and we could sense the enormity of the beast, its large black eyes, surrounded by enormous eyebrows that would be the envy of many women, were looking at us. I felt the gaze. The long rasping tongue then came out to eat the food from my daughter's hand which soon became smothered in saliva. Despite being out of its natural habitat, this giraffe experience was quite remarkable: we could sense it, smell it, touch it, and engage with its movement and witness its beauty close-up. The experience is quite hard to describe: this *experience* of a giraffe was powerful and memorable, "experiential learning" at its best. The binocular experience of a giraffe on the other hand reminded me of sitting at the back of a class, seeing and hearing the teacher or facilitator from a *distance*.

This story metaphorically explores a few principles underpinning experiential learning. When an experience touches you, you touch it: there is no "self" without the "other," no inner world without the outer world. The encounter is experienced as fluid, ever changing. The direct encounter with the giraffe involves looking into its eyes, and to sense it: the experience *moves* you, and you reflect on it as a powerful, close-up experience of yourself *interacting* and experiencing *acquaintance* with this beautiful creature. Figure 1.2 lists 15 more typical features that underpin the design of experiential learning.

1. The inner world includes consideration of the sensorial, emotive, cognitive, psychoanalytic, and spiritual elements of the experience of learning.
2. The experience of learning, when of a certain quality, has potential for the transformation of the 'self', and others.
3. The continuous nature of change is such that we are always in a state of 'becoming'.
4. The conditions for learning include motivation, awareness-attention, active engagement, and immersion. These are important for design.
5. Learning experiences are continuous, building on previous experiences. In this sense all learning might be considered as relearning.
6. When participants are engaged in doing things for themselves then the facilitator or teacher can devote more time to the development of the relationship with the learners.
7. Experiences are recognised as continually constructed and reconstructed, changing and flowing (like a river, or a film in which individuals narrate and script).
8. Each film is a complex, internal composition that results from interactions with the outside world.
9. Experience acts as the bridge unifying typical dualisms such as action and thought, doing and knowing, body and mind, nature and person, practice and theory.
10. Teachers, university lecturers, and facilitators are increasingly spending more time designing experiences for the learner, as opposed to simply designing specific content to 'teach'.
11. The learner, and their experience of the world, is highly valued: people are like seeds that can grow and bear fruit, not containers for filling.
12. Teaching by telling uses words. Words spread across a page in linear form and exit the mouth one at a time. Language is linear in form. Language is permeated with spatial and conceptual metaphors that help understanding: experiential learning utilises concrete spatial designs.
13. Experiential learning has a long history of confronting social inequalities.
14. Where possible the learners are involved in designing their own learning.
15. Our understanding of the complex nature of human learning experiences continues to expand, to further inform experiential learning (in both positive and negative directions).

FIGURE 1.2 Another 15 typical "features" that commonly underpin the design of experiential learning.

Experiential learning is a short-hand expression for a category of learning, and it means different things to different people. The term can represent a concept, a philosophy, a theory, a method, or a practice. In the beginning there was only experiential learning. As it continues to evolve and re-spread across the globe in its many forms, what has happened so far may well prove to be only the

Introducing Experiential Learning Design **25**

beginning, as new and more integrative, holistic, and "ecological" approaches emerge. I take comfort from the movie *The Best Exotic Marigold Hotel*. There is a lovely saying: *"it will be alright in the end and if it is not alright, then it is not the end."*

Dewey (1938) argued that the methods that focus on the learner-experience are harder to design than "traditional" approaches. The increased effort required in *experience design* is more than compensated for by the instruction and delivery being transformed into facilitation and guidance. The energy is redirected towards *supporting* learners in *their* learning, as an experiential guide.

This book is my "story." Written in just over 18 months during a global pandemic, it was always going to be an ambitious project. I know it will always be incomplete, always a work in progress. There are several bits I am still unhappy with, and the compromise with depth is necessary due to the holistic breadth. There is always more for me to learn, and my points of view will change.

2

DESIGN BASICS

Becoming an Architect of Experiential Learning Design

Becoming an Architect of Design

The art and science of design is fundamental to the professions of architecture, fashion, textiles, art, furniture, graphics, service, and products. Art and science underpin the design of this book also. The words of Martin Ringer (2002: 267) may be helpful in this respect: "because visual art is a language that uses symbolism as a medium, the quality of communication achieved by art is fundamentally different from the quality of communication achieved by the rational use of spoken or written prose."

In *Designing and Facilitating Experiential Learning*, Brooks-Harris and Stock-Ward (1999) suggest that design is like building and furnishing a new house, which involves both an architect and an interior designer, involving the integration of hard and soft design skills. These interrelated tasks are the topic of this chapter, that is, (1) the creation of overall learning *structures*, and (2) the design of specific *learning experiences* (big-picture~detail).

Design language differs across professions. In digital design the term UX means "user experience," and terms like *storyboarding* or *wireframing* are frequently used (architects' line sketches look like a wire frame – templates are free online). In event design, which includes everything from Olympic games to weddings and music festivals, the notion of "*Imagineering*" hybridises *engineering* and *imagination* (Richards et al., 2014). Lundborg notes that Swedish architect Arne Branzell regards the "exploratory sketch" as a creative first step, and that the "silent knowledge, creativity and improvisational abilities of the hand are of utmost importance before premade computer programs become too involved in the process" (2014: 141).

Design is seen by some as a form of problem solving, though research suggests that expert designers challenge the traditional rules of problem solving, because

DOI: 10.4324/9781003030867-2

Design Basics **27**

"unlike normal problem-solving, in a design project it is often not at all clear what 'the problem' is" (Cross, 2018: 377). Some designers focus more on solution conjecturing, using generative rather than deductive reasoning in problem analysis, so that problems and solutions co-evolve at the same time. Experienced architects rapidly shift their attention between hard structures and creative imagination by using different *representational* formats such as sketches: they visualise their thinking. Sketching and thinking are dynamically coupled: sketching assists both cognition and conversation, by reducing internal cognitive (mental) load: "the activity of sketching, drawing or modelling provides some of the circumstances by which designers put themselves into the design situation and engage with the exploration of both the problem and solution" (Cross, 2018: 380). A drawing becomes a memory device to make design ideas visible.

Traditionally *content* is utilised to drive design: content is seen as material to be assimilated, consumed, and learnt. An integrated and holistic approach counteracts narrow, knowledge-focussed learning objectives, which focus on capacities to *know, think*, and *remember* (see Sterling, 2001). Experiential learning can be integrated within *traditional* content designs: as mentioned earlier, experiential learning is not an *all or nothing* approach, and small changes can be productive.

Design sketching has increasingly made use of multi-media in the form of external *representations* to communicate ideas. These include maps, graphs, figures, charts, icons, objects, and other depictions. Communication through description alone (speech or text) is problematic, in part due to its inherent linearity. That is why language utilises spatial and conceptual metaphors to enhance understanding. *Importance* for example is *represented* by *size*, time by *space*, and similarity by *closeness*. The use of representations for design is explored in more detail later.

What Do Experiential Learning Designers Do?

Long ago Dewey (1938: 90) noted how experience design is a demanding occupation: "there is no discipline in the world so severe as a discipline of experience subjected to the tests of intelligent development and direction." He noted that the path of education based on experience "is not an easier one to follow than the old one." It is, he says "more strenuous and difficult." The calls for more attention to be paid to experience design are also found in the digital world. Whitton (2014: 3), in *Digital Games and Learning*, believes that gaming experiences, whether digital or traditional, can provide a way "to move the focus of our schools, colleges and universities to more active, experiential and student-centred models of teaching, learning and assessment."

Brooks-Harris and Stock-Ward (1999: 8) refer to the need for a paradigm shift for teachers and facilitators, notably "a shift in the perception of their own role as educators." In *Higher Education by Design* (Mackh, 2018: xi), comments that "higher education as a whole has changed little since the mid-20th century."

28 Design Basics

Knowles uses learner-centred language to outline six key areas for curriculum design: helping learners to diagnose their needs; planning, with learners, a sequence of learning experiences to answer their needs; creating conditions conducive to learning; using appropriate methods; providing resources; and helping learners measure their outcomes (taken from Jarvis, 2004: 273). The active involvement of learners, and other stakeholders, leads to an inclusive and collaborative approach to design. One expanding area of research in this area is *Participatory Design* (see DiSalvo et al., 2017). Laurillard, in *Teaching as a Design Science*, notes that learning design is not an exact science, and she notes that "when the teacher gets the design right the situation 'co-produces' the knowledge through the learner's activity" (2012: 75). Laurillard presents six key features of learning experience design in both physical and digital formats: *acquisition, inquiry, practice, discussion, collaboration,* and *production. Production* can include a performance, an essay, video, blogs, models, or an animation for example.

There is always an important interplay between macro and micro design, that is, the big picture and the fine detail. Micro and macro design ideas are exposed in the following definition of experiential education:

> a holistic philosophy, where carefully chosen experiences supported by reflection, critical analysis, and synthesis, are structured to require the learner to take initiative, make decisions, and be accountable for the results, through actively posing questions, investigating, experimenting, being curious, solving problems, assuming responsibility, being creative, constructing meaning, and integrating previously developed knowledge.
>
> *(Itin, 1999: 93)*

A learning experience can be real, or simulated, or virtual, or both, and design considers the use of tools, technological aids, objects, animations, touching and selective pointing for example. The design of visual cues can also enhance learning about difficult concepts (see Lin & Atkinson, 2011, on design and scientific concepts).

Designing the Navigation of the Learning Journey

Consider the following quotation about transformative learning:

> Although the notion of transformative learning points to a desirable destination for educational endeavours, the difficulty in the journey is often neglected. Our intention is to map the experiential micro-processes involved in transformative learning. . . . We employ the notions of liminality, comfort zone, and edge emotions to elucidate the transformative process.
>
> *(Malkki & Green, 2014: 5)*

Design Basics **29**

In this extract learning is portrayed as a *journey*, towards a *destination*, using a *map* as a *navigational* tool to help to get *there*. When coming across *difficulties*, the tendency is to return to our *comfort* zone even though obstacles create potentially transformative emotions by experiencing being at the *edge* (of a cliff or precipice). Journeying involves *difficult terrain*, and sometimes people get *lost along the way*. In this chapter these journey metaphors are integrated with architectural metaphors, such as drawing boards, structures, frameworks, plans, navigation, maps, and schema. The term *experiencescape* (see Pizam & Tasci, 2019) is a useful overarching concept for learning design.

A journey through the experiencescape might have a zone structure, involving multiple experiences such as prior *anticipation*, the *beginning*, the *middle*, the *ending*, and *follow up*. The broad notion of *experiencescape* design necessitates paying attention to the use of resources, supporting technology, artefacts, activity, involvement, touchpoints, people interactions, the sensory and physical environment interactions with, for example, lighting, colour, ambience, mood, rules and procedures, smells, symbols, layout of the furniture, cleanliness, food, drinks, the natural elements, welcoming culture, the sense of belonging, power relations, valuing people, and so forth. The whole experience landscape is more than the sum of the parts. Design can be a daunting task, and so these basic elements of design will be introduced in this and other chapters.

Some experienced facilitators have the skill and expertise to design very little in advance and simply work with the capacities and capabilities brought to an event by the people present, including themselves. All participants are the resource start point, and a programme can be created in an inclusive way when everyone arrives. A spectrum exists from little or no planning, to very detailed planning. The same spectrum applies to equipment and resources.

Starting Out at the Drawing Board with Basic Structures

Design sketches typically start with a large blank canvas for the plan, or drawing. A very large roll of paper offers part-whole design perspectives, whereas digital screens are often limited in size. Design is made visible by the sketch which invites the sharing of ideas about the look, feel, and flow. Here are a few starter ideas about design drawings:

1　Start with a big table, and a big sheet of paper!
2　Draw a line down the middle of the canvas and divide it into ZONES: (1) Before (anticipation/preparation); (2) Beginnings (e.g., belonging/icebreakers); (3) Middle; (4) Ending; and (5) Follow up.
3　Begin with the end in mind, then work backwards to deconstruct the end point, breaking the *whole* into its component *parts* (*deconstruction*). Learning involves the *reconstruction* of the *parts* from beginning to end (the opposite direction).

30 Design Basics

4 Ask: What is the end? The desired outcome/aims/objectives (e.g., *content*) and assessments for learning, or change or transformation? Who will decide the objectives, and what is the problem that needs to be solved, and/or the solution to be found?

5 Create information boxes/circles for the sequence of "activities" (experiences) along the central line like "stations," so that the sketch is like a route/direction/journey map on MTR/underground train maps.

6 If you have traditionally designed using "content," this is fine to start with. Shift the focus from content and "teaching" into the design of learner *experiences* (that will engage and involve). This can be done using two layers at each station: one for content and a second layer for the details of the experience.

7 Work in small design teams and be creative – the more brains working on the design the better.

8 Look at the overall variety of *experiences* in terms of the sequence, flow, and rhythm. Where are the high and low energy experiences? Look at the flow of *active* and *passive* experiences.

9 Use the seven-dimensional model to highlight experiential touchpoints, such as an emotional touchpoint. Annotations and icons can help (see later).

10 List and note the resources needed. As the learner-centred experiences build there is a realisation that the resource bank required will be extensive. Can the learners create these resources?

11 Consider: *who are the learners and what do they bring?* What are their needs? How much of the learning design will be determined by the learners (see Chapter 7 on power and authority and voice)?

12 What was traditionally "taught," change all or part to engaging active, hands-on *discovery* experiences for learners.

13 Consider the overall shape and form, part-whole sequence of experiences.

14 Consider artistic and creative approaches to choreography.

15 Decide when to do facilitation inputs along the route. Significant inputs, or light touch?

16 Where, when, and with whom will the learning take place (space/place/timings)?

Diagnosis: Aims/Objectives and Experiential Descriptors

There are relatively few models that generate the creative, artistic, and choreographic elements of experiential learning design. When working with a limited "brief" of the requirements of a learning experience, the creation of aims and objectives can be helpful to clarify outcomes, or end points; however, balance is required between content and process design.

> In an age preoccupied by outcomes, the processes of experiential learning are often seen to be of subsidiary interest. As a result, a theory of experiential

Design Basics **31**

learning, which focuses principally on processes rather than outcomes, runs against the current tide of fascination for competence, performance, and anything that can be tightly linked to the products of learning.

(Stein, 2004: 19)

For adult learners involvement in the creation and ownership of outcomes and the overall design enhances engagement. In Europe in the 1960s the term *andragogy* was created as a label for a growing body of knowledge on adult learning based on the following five assumptions: learning is self-directing because adults want to take responsibility for their own lives, including planning, implementing, and evaluating learning activities; adult learners bring with them a great deal of experience on which to build their own understanding and to share with others; adults want to learn things that they feel have significance to their lives, such as filling a need, or presenting opportunities for self-actualisation; external factors such as pressure from authority figures, salary increases, and so on are less significant (adapted from Knowles et al., 2015: 278).

Starting with the end point and working backwards is one design approach. Breaking up outcomes into smaller parts, and then aligning experiences to match forms a basic start-point design framework. Different objectives (know, do, feel, sense, etc.) can be written for different levels (course, programme, module, or activity). There are many books on the market concerning the writing of learning objectives, and the revised Blooms taxonomy is a well-known source of material (Bloom, 1956).

Objectives are typically written in the style of statements, and they have traditionally involved a skill, knowledge, attitude, or behaviour. They can focus on a destination, or an end product. The design statement might be as follows depending on who is determining the design:

1   Participants/we/I will be able to **list, know, remember** . . . x, y, z.
2   Participants/we/I will be able to **critically evaluate** the seven . . . by. . . .
3   Participants/we/I will be able to **change their/our approach** to . . . having practised the . . . **skills** to generate new **behaviours** and to **act** differently in the future.
4   Participants/we/I will develop their/our **relationship management** skills, enhancing the sense of **belonging** by. . . .
5   Participants/we/I will have **opportunities** to **generate** new ideas, to solve problems or generate products that. . . .

Jonassen (2011: 18) notes that problem solving designs often have "vaguely defined or unclear goals with unstated constraints. They possess multiple solutions, with multiple paths." In design terms, learning experiences often fall into the category of "ill-structured problem solving" as several of the key elements that help with design are only partially known or unknown. If the learning objectives involve *problems* to be solved, then a problem can also be viewed in less negative

32 Design Basics

terms, as an opportunity, a challenge, or even an adventure. Learning experience design is always an iterative process: preliminary designs are followed by detailed designs, and post-delivery feedback allows designs to be revised. Outline designs create the programme outline given to learners. Detailed annotated designs can be used by facilitators to track and to constantly modify the planned journey.

Objectives are sometimes referred to as General Intended Learning Objectives (GLOs) in recognition that there will be other unexpected end points. A range of initial design frameworks taken from several different perspectives (all can be variably combined) is as follows:

1   *Content* linked designs, using outcomes and objectives, for knowledge and skills and so on – by the end of this session participants will be able to . . . for example, how do we get young people to develop resilience?
2   *Assessment*/evidence linked designs: the objectives usually have links to the desired achievements. Verbs and the object of the verb such as produce a digital presentation, calibrate, interpret, and so on.
3   *Process* designs (learning how to learn, metacognition, group relations work, etc.) – for example, what experience designs enhance the ability to ask deep questions, to develop enquiry, experimentation, reflection, and reflexivity?
4   *Resource* linked designs – for example, we have 25 participants, two days, 25 canoes, and 50 bicycles and a forest to use to develop the. . . .
5   *Problem-based* designs – identifying and solving problems, particularly good at building on existing knowledge, creating curiosity, and developing skills of enquiry.
6   *Activity-based* designs – a design focus on for example abseiling, debating, adventure expeditions.
7   Guide/*Facilitator-centred* design (*supported or provided by who*) resource design – we will have two semi-retired educators, one retired member of staff from the Zoo, and one Forest Schools officer for the second half of the day . . . (so how can we best use their expertise to enhance the learning programme for Outward Bound Instructors?).
8   *Place & Space* linked designs – (1) a tall ship will be available for leadership development work on day two; (2) the community hall will be available during the early stages of the service learning.
9   *Holistic Experience Design* (*complex whole – all of above*) – example, a focus on the broader aspects of the design of *experiences*, involving learning from *doing*, learning from *sensing*, learning though *feelings*, learning how to *think and know*, learning to *belong*, to *become* and to *be* in the world.

Designs *for* and *of* Learning

Design requires an understanding of the interactional dynamics between the external world and the internal world of the learner, though design has more influence on external interactions: the internal world is mostly private. Then there is the

Design Basics **33**

experience design *for* learning, where the focus might be on a topic, for example, and the design *of* learning, that is, how people learn. Both are equally important, though these twin aspects of design are integrated or separated to varying degrees.

The experience *for* learning might have low levels of reality in serving as a vehicle for learning. An example would be the experience of chocolate making, including the design of packaging, and marketing to learn the intricacies of managerial teamwork. The experience *of* learning relates the understanding of the learning processes, that is, how people will come to learn about teamwork from taking part in this chocolate making experience.

Drawing Up Outline Plans: Macro- and Micro-Structure and Sequencing

Tversky (2016: 79) notes that *"depictions, such as maps, that portray visible things are ancient, whereas graphics, such as charts and diagrams, that portray things that are inherently not visible, are relatively modern inventions."* Design structures include grids and maps, to make design explicit and visible. The designer can see and craft the beginning (B), middle (M), and end (E). In Design Illustration 2, in the next section, standard design frameworks are presented in *portrait* and *landscape* view. Eight time slots are typical for a two-day programme and each slot has a connection to the other slots.

For a two-day introduction to management course, the first four blocks might focus on managing the self, whereas day two might focus on managing others. For the beginning phase it is important to allow sufficient time for people to get settled and established as a group. This period offers opportunities to talk about and experience power relations, engagement, and ground rules: these social dynamics affect individual and group *belonging* (Beaumeister & Leary, 1995) (issues covered in more detail in Chapter 7). Each of the eight blocks present design opportunities. Breaks, such as tea and coffee breaks, present opportunities for informal learning, and networking, and they can be part of the design of informal-formal dynamics that affect the shape and flow of the whole experience. A technique known as "coffee and papers" (see Chapter 7), is essentially a quiet solo reading experience that can be undertaken as an experience integrated into a tea or coffee break: suitable refreshments in such a *reading experience* can have a positive impact. In this experience a solo reading session is followed up with a collaborative analysis.

The level of *challenge* and *support* (see Dainty & Lucas, 1992) can be suitably altered across the eight slots, and participant choice can be designed into the experience. These slots could also be empty, left for the participants to design or co-design with the facilitator.

The Drawing Board: First Structures

The way that information is presented affects the efficacy of use. Consider which of the following might be best for a programme layout.

34 Design Basics

DESIGN ILLUSTRATION 2 THE SIGNIFICANCE OF LAYOUT.

Design Structures

Try this simple experiment.
    Your secret six-digit bank account code number is: 982 651.
    First memorise the number by saying it several times.
    Now, without looking at the six digits above, fill in the requested numbers with design 1:
    Put Your Secret Code in here.

Put the 3rd number here

Put the 5th number here.

Put the 6th number here.

Now do the same for this second layout. Put Your Secret Code only in the boxes marked with a x.

    Q: Which way was easier for you? Was it design 2? Why was this?
    The way a programme is presented affects the "look" and the *readability*. One example following shows information from top to bottom, and the other shows information that is read from left to right. Which one do you prefer?

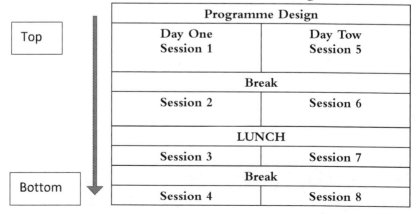

Top to bottom is different from the left to right orientation following.

Landscape Design

An Introduction to Management	BEGINNING	MIDDLE		END
DAY 1 Managing yourself	Session 1	Session 2	Session 3	Session 4
DAY 2 Managing others	Session 5	Session 6	Session 7	Session 8

Liberating Structures

What happens if the boundary lines are removed in the landscape design shown previously? The importance of representational structures should not be underestimated (see Lipmanowicz & McCandless, *The Surprising Power of Liberating Structures*, 2013). Structures influence thought and action: they can liberate or constrain. The programme outlines shown previously use a traditional grid, yet more exciting options can be created, such as the use of journey maps, *menus* with options, using QR codes, or interactive touch screen apps. Time, space, and contents of the learning journey can be made explicit as illustrated later. User control is significant to the way these designs are used: co-creation and stakeholder engagement creates design input from a user perspective. Creative, non-linear structures, rather like spider diagrams or mind-maps, are used for art and design work in studios. A design structure like a spider's web branches out in an organic way from the centre with different routes creating choices and flexibility. Structures create the potential to liberate learning.

Navigating Routes: The London Underground Map

Cartographic maps are selective: what is shown or not shown is important. In the 20th century maps and schematic depictions became abundant in communication systems: one highly successful modern expression is that of Harry Beck's schematic representation known as the London Underground Map. Originally designed in 1931, transport maps across the globe have appropriated this simplified, colour-coded map; it is "acknowledged as a seminal work in both the history of graphic design and cartography" (Hadlaw, 2003: 26). Throughout the world this style of map, with its deliberate simplification, helps people to *navigate* their way around the complex reality of built-up cities. As Hadlaw (2003: 12) remarks "what set Beck's map apart from the underground maps that preceded it was that it bore no relationship whatsoever to the geography of the area it represented." As Kalbach (2016: 20) remarks "it is sparing in what it includes: tube lines, stops, exchanges, and the River Thames – nothing more." It is rather interesting that in the United Kingdom it has taken nearly 80 years for buses to adopt a similar public navigation system akin to Harry Beck's underground map: it was assumed the passengers knew where they were going! It is taking longer to realise how these cartographic principles can help people to navigate their learning. Shapes, lines, colour, arrows, codes, indexes, and the simplification of reality are just some of the key components in the design of navigational learning maps.

> **DESIGN ILLUSTRATION 3 DESIGNING CREATIVE STRUCTURES: DIGITAL LEARNING JOURNEY MAPS AS "ROUTES."**

The Left to Right Learning Journey Design: Titles, Stations, Annotations, and Icons

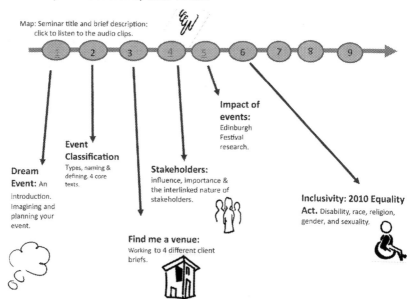

Design Basics   **37**

My new idea for University students - helping them to navigate
Smartphone connected interactive learning journey

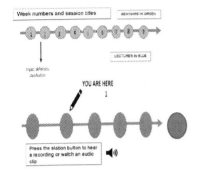

Elements of time and space are made visible in the pilot navigational designs in Design Illustration 3. A blue line can be used, for example, for lectures, a green line for seminars, and assessments are represented by a red *square*. A moving arrow or "you are here" sign denotes the current location. Time and space relations are clearly depicted, with the circles (stations) containing week numbers. Haptic (touch) interaction (see Skulmowski et al., 2016) can increase engagement: the act of touching stations can release a video or sound bite. Students can hear about a present, future, or past session.

These maps make the journey visible so learner/s can easily *navigate* the route. The *destination* is made visible. The part-whole journey is easily seen and there is a sense of *progression*, a movement towards arrival at *stations*. The *tracks* are important and should not be neglected. Journeying along the tracks can be just as important as the arrival at stations. *Switching/splitting* tracks provides *choice*, which can be important for learner control. Multiple platforms, and *arrival-departure links* such as things to do whilst *waiting*, are all design options for the learner experience. These *infographics* become design *storyboards*.

If you are a tourist on holiday travelling on a train, the *journeying* is just as exciting as *arriving* at the stations. Sometimes people are so busy looking at the stations and checking where they are on the overhead map that they miss opportunities to see what's going on outside. In design terms the lines between stations on the learning journey maps represent important opportunities for learning: what happens before an activity (station) or after an activity can significantly affect the *experiencescape*. The lines could involve linking experiences, such as the preparation for arrival at the next station. The lines could represent an informal walk with reflective or reflexive conversation on the way to the next activity, or to the lunch break. The lines might represent a specific job to do, or where learners pick up a brief for the next session or to collect two papers to read for a *Coffee*

38 Design Basics

and Papers experience (a Design Illustration, Chapter 7). In residential outdoor activities participants wake up together, and the making of beds together, and the collective washing-up of the pots, presents opportunities to choreograph the *experiencescape*: these opportunities are often underestimated.

Interactive Touchscreens

The late 20th century saw the emergence of the *experience economy* (Pine et al., 1999), which has contributed new ideas about consumer experience design. The Anne Frank and Van Gough Museums in Amsterdam use hand-held devices with audio enhancement to improve engagement through educational content. These devices enhance the navigation of the museum experience using a *learning journey app*. These hand-held touch screen devices release educational content under the control of the consumer and so enhance their personal experience. The journey concept shown previously has similarly undergone an experience makeover: the original format was on a presentation slide containing hyperlinks for auditory and video clips. From this prototype university computing students have converted this idea into a touchscreen interactive smartphone *app* that can be uploaded by students.

 DESIGN ILLUSTRATION 4 MAPPING EXPERIENCES, THE EXPERIENCE GAP, AND EXPERIENCE "TOUCHPOINTS."

A university undergraduate student conducted a small-scale piece of research into the experiences of several women from HSBC bank. They had volunteered to sleep out on the streets of a UK city for just one night. Their "experience" was designed by a charity as a project to increase awareness of the plight of rough sleepers and homeless people. The women had subjected themselves to a unique experience that had quite a powerful impact on them. Their guide for the night was a homeless man who had slept on the streets for over 20 years with his dog.

The information collected by this research related to the experiences of the volunteer participants and it was particularly interesting, but the student found the analysis of the interview data quite hard to interpret. The analysis and interpretation was more difficult because the data consisted of many pages of comments in the form of words. In this linear form data (sentences, several pages one after the other, etc.) it is difficult for any human brain to understand and analyse. Fortin et al. (2002) argue that any interpretation of a large corpus of data in textual form tends to place a heavy *relational* processing load on the hippocampus (the part of the brain responsible for relational-spatial understanding). What was required was an approach that would allow the student to understand and interpret this large body of data.

Design Basics **39**

The survey questions, however, were quite nicely ordered in terms of participants' experiences *before, during,* and *after* their sleep-out experience on the city streets. What I needed was a method for the student that would simply and quickly help to interpret this rich picture of the sleep-out experience. The design clue took the form of a *navigational* aid so that a schematic representation could be developed as a map on a long sheet of paper. To help the student to understand this data he was first asked to disaggregate the data into a number of modes of experience, by allocating specific data to each of the seven dimensions of the HELM model (presented in Chapter 3). He was asked to separate the data to explore the following aspects of their experience, that is, data relating to: (1) *knowing*; (2) *doing*; (3) *sensing*; (4) *feeling*; (5 & 6) *belonging* (people and more-than-human world); and (7) *being* (identity, values, etc.).

The subsequent creation of a map to show these modes of experiencing proved to be very helpful. The map was not dissimilar to the mapping processes that Harry Beck used to create the London Underground map (& MTR maps) that is now replicated around the world to depict transport system complexity. The student was also asked to show me the map on a large table, and significantly, he did this whilst *writing additional notes,* and *walking* along and *talking* through and *sharing* his ideas with me as his tutor. By exploring the data in this way specific issues become "visible": he *sketched, walked,* and *talked* through his data in terms of *time* and *experience modes.* The picture unfolded as he went along.

The participants' *sensory* experiences were significant in terms of the cold, the noise at the time when pubs and clubs shut, the noise of the Cathedral clock chiming, and the stars in the night sky, and so on. A sense of *belonging* emerged as a changing of the relationship with the homeless person and his dog, who acted as a guide for the night. Another particularly significant experience was visiting a specific place known as "cardboard city" by the city's rough sleepers. This was the area where the waste skips had a plentiful supply of dry cardboard for the beds for the night.

This approach to analysis was so successful in enhancing the student understanding that construction of such a schematic representation, or *experience map,* later underwent further trials by the tutor in a range of private and public organisations across the globe, notably the USA, Singapore, Prague, Hong Kong, Malaysia, India, and the UK. This process of *experience mapping* for research or design evolved into a collaborative endeavor, so that views of other people could be gained: they all interacted *textually* (writing data notes on sheets) and *conversationally* (oral) with *bodily* (corporeal-sensorial) *walking* along through the three chronology phases (*before, during,* and *after* the event). The process became known as Human Experience Mapping (HEM) and a paper outlining the procedures was published (see Beard & Russ, 2017).

Design: Sequence, Shape, and Flow

In architecture the shape of a structure is important. The whole design (part-whole) should *flow*. The example of a two-day Introduction to Management programme was mentioned earlier, where the structure could be based on the well-known sating that *you can't manage others until you can manage yourself*. The outline "structure" begins to take shape as *Managing Your Self* would form the basis of day one and *Managing Others* the basis of the design of day two. The smaller micro session design requires the whole to "fit" together, to create an experience *shape* that *flows*. Flow requires a balance of energetic and calm states: high energy states are not sustainable. Periods of reflection might involve quiet time. The notion of an energy wave can be utilised for design: combining the "adventure waves" of Mortlock (1987) with the "*flow*" learning of Cornell (1989) and the work of Dainty and Lucas (1992), a six-stage wave that builds interest, excitement, and energy can be created (Figure 2.1).

An energy wave can involve any of the following:

1. Create conditions for pre-contemplation – reading, thinking, imagining.
2. Awaken participant enthusiasm – belonging experiences, ice-breakers, and energizers.
3. Start to focus attention and concentration – sensory-focused approaches, medium-sized activities, narrow skills.
4. Direct and challenge the personal experience – larger, broader skills. Creative, critical, and conceptual thinking.
5. Encourage quiet personal reflection, review, and reflexive activities.

Waves are found elsewhere in learning design models, including a four stage: *nurturing, energizing, peak activity,* and *relaxing* (Southgate et al., 1980), and a six-stage programme design (Porter, 1999): *entry, pre-contemplation, preparation, action, maintenance,* and *integrated change* (or *relapse*). Big waves and little waves can be incorporated into a design sketch. Design waves can also incorporate the 7I's by Wood and Masterman (2006):

1. Involvement.
2. Interaction.
3. Immersion.
4. Intensity.
5. Individuality.
6. Innovation.
7. Integrity.

Design Basics **41**

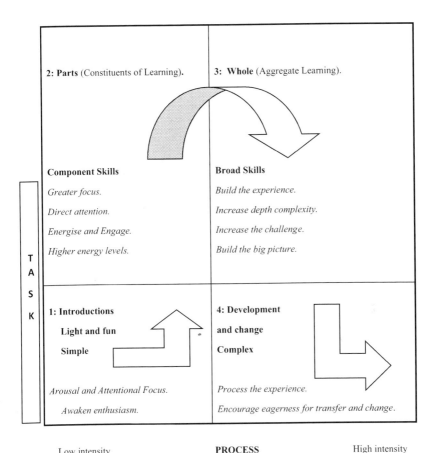

FIGURE 2.1 The experiential wave.

Creative Choreography: Drama and Stage Performance

Smit and Melissen (2018), in *Sustainable Customer Experience Design*, present waves as the "dramatic structure" to customer journey design. They refer to literature on *dramaturgy* as this approach they say offers valuable insights into the optimal design of the wave, like peaks and troughs.

> Dramaturgy means "the art of theatrical production" the main task of which is to examine the links between the world and the stage. The "dramatist" chooses themes from society and a place that reflects these themes. Pieces of work and music are then chosen to reflect these themes.
>
> *(Martin et al., 2004: 15)*

Martin et al. (2004) as leading authorities of the use of dramaturgy in outdoor experiential learning, present a series of interlocking social, physical, creative, and psychological *waves* that represent the theoretical underpinnings of programme design within dramaturgy. Whilst the programme structure and the waves are set at the beginning of the programme, the waves then evolve and change through the course experience. Programme design then becomes a co-productive process involving participants and facilitators. This choreographic approach draws on pioneering work by the Czechs and Slovaks on experiential dramaturgy which has high levels of design customisation using reactive feedback processes. There are five stages involved in the design of dramaturgy:

1 Development of the main course theme.
2 Development of the scenario (first part).
3 The practical dramaturgy (activity/game creation and selection).
4 The completion of the scenario.
5 The dramaturgy on the whole course.

As the term dramaturgy originates from the sphere of theatre, film, and TV; the drama principles of *script, production, performance, journey*, and *stage* are utilised to maximise the impact and outcome of the course. Dramaturgy is a method of selection: time taken, spaces used, and order of activities are all decided with the aim to maximise the pedagogical, educational, recreational, and other aims which the course seeks to reach. The design also integrates participant dynamics, taking account of their age, mental and physical maturity, and so on. In these programmes there is also a sense of fun, with the use of games and play.

> In Design Illustration 5 the structure is like two triangles on top of each other, rather like an egg-timer which is a glass container with sand in it, used for timing the boiling of an egg.
>
> **DESIGN ILLUSTRATION 5 DESIGN STRUCTURE, SHAPE, AND FLOW.**

Customer Service Recovery

The initial design structure took the form of two triangles coming together create a shape like an egg-timer (used for timing the boiling of an egg by allowing sand to *flow* from top to bottom). The diagram below shows the flow from practice to theory and back again to practice.

The structure can also be drawn sideways, in landscape mode (shown still later). This removes the "higher" "lower" dynamic and positions them both as

Design Basics 43

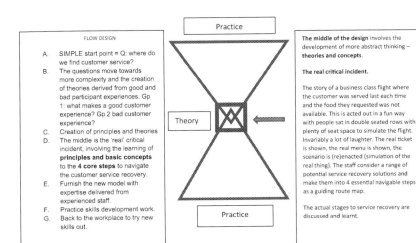

equal (for a more detailed account see Chapter 10). A critical incident is introduced in the middle part of the session design.

The more detailed choreography (design notes) evolved as follows:

To engage people at the start, the design commences with simple questions that everyone can relate to:

1. All participants are asked to gather into groups of three and answer the first simple question: *where do we find customer service?* After only a few minutes the groups discover that customer service is everywhere: the doctors surgery, the airport, shops, dentist, hotel, florist, delivery drivers, and so on.

2. The group is then divided into two halves. A greater depth of engagement, and a relaxed atmosphere are created by asking half the group to share their own negative customer service experiences, whilst the other half talk about their positive customer service experiences. It is interesting that the group talking about negative experiences often gets off to a faster and noisier start! (linked to the brain focussing on negatives for survival purposes). There can be a brief period of plenary sharing and reflecting on the levels of engagement that occurred when they were asked to talk about their own personal experiences.

3. The two groups then return to the stories that were shared to conduct a simple analysis. This establishes some of the core principles of customer service (from the perspective of being a customer) that may have emerged (analytical skills). Often the negative and positive principles are a mirror image of each other. This collaboration produces a list of customer service principles. The list can be quite extensive, and might include: (1) product knowledge;

44 Design Basics

(2) going the extra mile; (3) politeness and respect; (4) non-pestering; (5) not following them around a shop to tidy clothes up after they have looked at them; (6) not trying to oversell extras, and so on.

4   The group then engage with real experiences that are live, and unpredictable. This might include ringing several car showrooms to ask if a driving license is needed for a test drive or listening to out of office hours recorded messages. In both instances the quality of the customer service (voice and content) is compared and analysed. More principles of good customer service are added to the list in this way.

5   This is followed by a simulation of a "real" critical incident that occurred on a business class flight where a passenger (me) was served last on the first and second course and on both occasions the chosen meal was not available despite the cost of the flight being expensive, and the menu promising a luxury experience. This critical incident is the small square in the middle of the egg timer shape shown previously. In this critical incident the chief stewardess comes to talk to the passenger after service has ended, and she says "I understand you are not very happy about the meal service Mr. Beard?" (I didn't complain – but the steward that served me must have relayed the fact that I didn't want a main course as the only option available was fish–which I had to have for my first course). Participants are asked to set out the room like a business class section of a plane (i.e., plenty of leg room and space between customers. I play the stewardess and give scripts to those carefully chosen to act as me as a customer on the plane. I act out the scenario and improvise using a chair as the service trolley. I drape over the chair the business class wash bag, and I show the real ticket, the price and the rather nice menu that had Taj Hotel, Mumbai, the chefs that cooked the food, and the wine taster (the sommelier). The session experience is playful and often generates a great deal of fun and laughter (see Whitton & Moseley, 2019), and it is often noticeable that people relax even more during and after this part of the session, and I feel that my relationship (see theories of *relational learning*) with participants has become closer.

6   The simulation comes to an end at the point where the chief stewardess makes the makes the comment to the passenger. Participants are asked to go away and discuss how they would deal with this passenger service recovery scenario from the senior stewardess comment onwards. The groups are asked to discuss what they would do and how they would recover the situation. Only after substantial discussions do they collaboratively devise a series of *four to five steps* as a generic navigational map for dealing with such a customer service issue.

7   When they are ready each group is asked to place their cards on the floor alongside four large laminated numbers 1–5. They explain their customer service recovery approach by walking their 4/5 steps (thus making visible their thinking). Usually there is a reasonably high level of understanding

Design Basics **45**

amongst the groups. Most groups understand the need to deal with the emotional dynamic, as well as the need to find a solution to the problem.

8   At this stage of the session design the whole group is introduced to a comprehensive textbook four stage approach to customer service recovery. The steps are: (1) deal with the emotions first; (2) establish the facts from the customer perspective; (3) move towards a solution; and (4) follow up (on two aspects – the customer follow up – *can I get you another glass of champagne?* and the organisational follow up with an in-flight report so that the organisation can learn from the experience (recommendation that stewards should change service direction for different courses). This use of a real critical incident creates the theoretical part of the programme and this is the point at which the egg timer design broadens back out towards the details of practice as each of the four or five steps of the customer service recovery process requires specific skills in order to deal with the customer.

9   At this point of design experienced staff can be brought in to support the learning and development of more detailed skills associated with the four steps (for example, to know the limits and boundaries to the solutions that can be offered).

These notes created nine potential experiences. This thinking is then transferred to the structural design in landscape form, as shown in the following image:

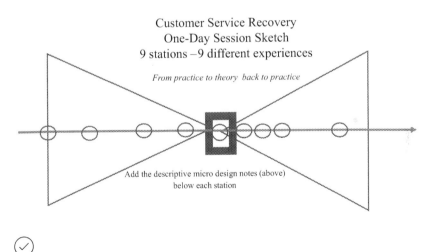

Metaphors as Design Clues

A metaphor is a *figure of speech* that, for rhetorical effect, directly refers to one thing by mentioning another. Metaphors act as natural models, leveraging the understanding of familiar things to explain for example an abstract concept. In this way a metaphor can provide clarity or identify hidden similarities between

46 Design Basics

two ideas. Becoming conscious of the way metaphors are used in speech generates design clues, and navigational tools. In *Philosophy in the Flesh* Lakoff and Johnson (1999) provide a list of primary conceptual metaphors developed early in life. They are present across many cultures. An example of this is the understanding of *quantity as directionality* (up is more), or the understanding of *time in terms of money* (spending time). When a young child sees water being poured into different glass containers the conceptual idea that *up is more* is made visible.

Here are a few more examples: affection is *warmth*, important is *big*, knowing is *seeing*, understanding is *grasping* (school reports or university feedback suggests a student has a good *grasp* of the subject), seeing is *touching*, happy is *up* (*upbeat mood, feeling down*, looking *down* is what we do when we are sad), difficulties are *burdens*, more is *up*, categories are *containers*, similarity is *closeness* (*that is close but not quite the same colour*), linear scales are *paths*, organization is *physical structure* (organisational charts), help is *support*, time is *motion*, change is *motion*, actions are self-propelled motions, purposes are *destinations*, purposes are *desired objects*, causes are *physical forces*, relationships are *enclosures* (she is *in* a relationship), good is up (*high-quality* work). Time is not only *motion* (going forward), we *spend* time.

Showing a credit card whilst explaining time management principles can visually enhance the metaphor: the notion that we all have roughly the same amount of time *to spend*: the same 24 hours in a day, seven days per week. We need to *spend our time wisely*. These conceptual, linguistic, and visual metaphors present design ideas about ways to scaffold learning by making concepts *visible*.

Micro Design and Navigational Tools

We keep a significant amount of information in our heads, in the form of mental maps. They help us to understand the complex world. External *representations* make ideas and concepts visible, and in doing so they enhance communication and understanding. External schematic representations depict and transmit complex ideas in physical and/or digital form to "conceptualise, visualise, or materialise an entity into another format or mode" (Wu & Puntambekar, 2012: 755). External representations are both *descriptive* (describe, e.g., text/equations) and *depictive* (show/spatial/visual/photos/drawings). External representations help with the formation of internal (mental) maps. At this stage of the chapter colour, symbols, equations, icons, graphs, steps, touching, pointing, movement, models, and *production* will be briefly explored.

Congruence in Representations

The notion of *congruence* is important in design: the idea, the text, the image, and the metaphor should be aligned. When writing a literature review it is important that students are taught to identify *categories* and *themes* that emerge. If the metaphor of a *"container"* is used to depict "categories," students can be shown coloured waste bins that visually depict the idea of themes. Visually it can be shown that themes are placed together in waste bins that *contain* similar ideas. Different coloured bins represent different themes, and additional text and animation can add to aid understanding of this concept. With animation, illustrative themes can be *moved* into appropriate containers (like recycling bins): in this way depictions, descriptions, and animation are *congruent* in supporting understanding (see Design Illustration 20).

Use of Colour

Colour has already been mentioned several times in this chapter: for example, identification, coding, separation, to highlight, and to create categories. Harry Beck got his cartographic idea underpinning the London Underground map from the simple *colour coding* of electrical wiring. The learning routes explored earlier use colour to differentiate lectures and seminars. Colour can also be used to identify different types of experiences or activities in a programme. Colour consistency is important. It is confusing when material uses colour for one explanation, and then a slightly different colour or shade elsewhere: lack of correspondence causes confusion.

Different colours should be used carefully. For example, to portray a mixture of sugar and water particles as red and blue is better than white and blue. If visual explanations are supported with text, then the key words should be highlighted in equivalent, corresponding colours to enhance understanding (see Richter et al., 2016 *Journal of Educational Research Review*). The use of "slideware" enables colour, and other forms of *signalling*, to be used quite flexibly, including the design of movement (e.g., moving arrows) rather than static text. Tangen et al. (2011) suggest that good slideware capacities can resemble a cinematic experience.

Semiotics, Signs, and Symbols

> Nothing distinguishes more sharply between humans and nonhuman primates then our extraordinarily flexible and creative use of symbols.
> *(Deloache & Pickard, 2010: 487)*

Signs and symbols are created as ways to represent other things: a symbol stands for something other than itself, and semiotics is the study of symbols and signs. Written language is a series of symbols as words that "*mediate, shape, inform and solidify experience*" (Richhart et al., 2011: 243). Language communicates with others. It is also spoken inside our head. Spoken language is complex, and it has evolved to enhance communication and understanding, but at times language is problematic in its linearity. Spoken words come out of the mouth one word at a time like a piece of string: because of this, language struggles at times to explain

48 Design Basics

non-linear things. Language helps the brain to navigate and understand, and it does so through the abundant use of spatial words. A simple example would be the use of the word *higher* education. *Higher* is a spatial term, and height is *more*.

Spatial metaphors are also used to understand time (temporal reasoning). Time is often explained in our language in relation to our own bodies. We say things like: you need to put those worries *behind you*, I am really *looking forward* to that day, *forward planning* is essential. Bodily metaphors are also in common usage: I feel *burdened* by the pressure of work, mathematics is usually a matter of understanding the *step-by-step logic*, the law was *rushed through* by parliament. Thus, we can "see" or derive spatial and/or temporal meanings from these words. These types of words present sensorimotor or spatial clues to enhance abstract reasoning. Awareness of how language is used in this way, of this linguistic form, is important for good communication for learning. In Design Illustration 19 for example depictions are used to *represent* the phrase *"points of view"* which can support the development of writing and thinking skills in *higher* education.

Drawings and maps are a form of *language* older than writing (Tversky, 2016). Maps represent a *spatial language*. Almost all languages have original *graphic primitives*: for example, 0–9, and operations such as +, −, and =, in mathematics. Printed music also contains *graphic* notations (Hyerle & Alper, 2011). Numbers and letters are said to have originally been in *graphical* form, to *depict* something. In Figure 2.2, count the angles in the numbers 1 2 3 4 5 6 7 that are shown in the Roman graphic primitive to highlight how numbers may have evolved from lines and angles. The English alphabetic system contains 27 letters (a form of image) plus punctuation. The alphabet was derived from many sources, but in essence it involved one *sign* (graphic) to represent one *sound*. The letter Q is derived from a picto*graphic* representation of a monkey. This is significant as it shows that the written text (*descriptive* form) you are now reading originates from pictures (a *depictive* form). Let me explain. The Phoenician scribes (now Lebanon, Syria, and Israel) transformed spoken language into common *sounds*, such as the sounds we now call vowels and consonants. They developed the *aleph-beth*, that was then developed in Greece to become the alphabet. They used the Hebrew word *quoph*, meaning monkey for the consonant sound of Q. The Hebrew for water, *mem*, became the M, thus letters became this "icon form" because they *represented* different sounds made with the breath (see Abram, 1997). Etymology, the study of the meaning of words, and the way their meaning has changed throughout history, is rarely explained within formal education. Knowing the historical origins of signs and symbols can enhance understanding. In Figure 2.2 see if you can *represent* the numbers 8 and 9 with straight lines and 8 and 9 *angles*.

It should not be assumed that *terms, concepts, labels, letters, and numbers* used by certain groups of people are universally understood. In botanical language some plants are referred to as *hirsute umbellifers*, which simply means hairy and umbrella-like: unless you were a botanist you probably wouldn't know this. Similarly, the understanding of a division sign as a symbol of *sharing* (one sweet above the line,

Design Basics   49

FIGURE 2.2   Graphical primitives: letters and numbers.
Source: Drawing by Raymond Ong, Singapore.

one sweet below the line as described in the very first chapter) is another example where understanding can be enhanced by careful and considered explanations.

Graphics, Annotations, Notes, Highlighters, and Sticky Notes

Simple symbols like icons are increasingly being adopted for quick and easy forms of communication, partly because they convey messages across a range of cultures and language barriers. The iconic sign for disability is very familiar. In 2016 Microsoft Office introduced a suite of several hundred icons, as well as a feature called "Design Ideas" for slideware presentations. Objects can also be used to visualise a concept: a whole new research area of object-based learning has emerged (Chatterjee & Hannan, 2016). In mathematics symbols are fundamental and taken for granted, yet a wide range of other symbol types can support learners in areas other than mathematics. Signs and symbols can show relationships between elements and develop abstract thinking and reasoning. Animations can similarly be used to enhance speech and text (see Richter et al., 2016), and multi-media theories suggest that text and visuals enhance learning more than text alone. *Cues* and *signals* (see Skulmowski et al., 2016) can also enhance understanding as shown in Design Illustration 6 (for a comprehensive overview of multi-media theories see Mayer, 2014).

> **DESIGN ILLUSTRATION 6 VISUAL CUEING— COMMUNICATION USING EQUATIONS, ICONS, SIGNS, SIGNALS, AND SYMBOLS.**

The division symbol in Design Illustration 6 suggests dividing: one above the line and one below. The arrow in box 2, when placed between two objects, focuses on the *relationship* between the objects. In this way the arrow supports the creation of abstract thinking, that is, the *relations* suggested. Box 3 makes emotions visible, whilst Box 4 can make thoughts visible by adding text. More ideas are presented in later chapters.

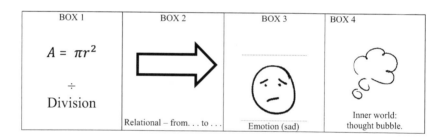

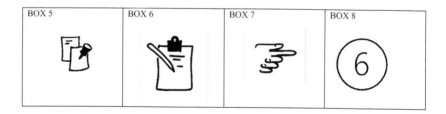

Picture Words: "Widgets"

Words can be written in a concise or long-winded form. Here is an example: "As soon as the workshop starts it is important for the facilitator to focus on the role of assessing engagement of the people participating." A more concise form becomes: "Once the workshop begins the facilitator can focus on engagement levels.". A depictive form (picture or icon) can be even more precise than the descriptive form (text).

Design Basics **51**

> **DESIGN ILLUSTRATION 7 TEXT, ICONS, AND "WIDGETS."**

Symbols and icons are increasingly being used to enhance learning. One company, Widget.com, is offering a bank of over 18,000 images that they are calling Widgets. Their software automatically adds widgets as the words are typed. This use of both *text* and *pictographic* formats can be used to enhance understanding, communication, and memory. The following illustration is an example showing the company promotional storyboard.

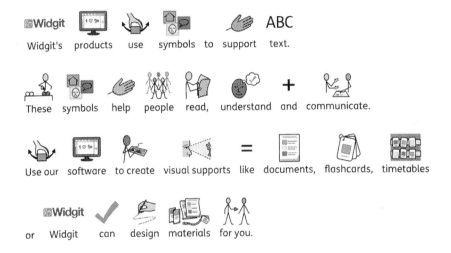

Reproduced with kind permission of Widget Software (www.widgit.com).

Bodily Learning, Movement, and Gestures

The body interacts with the outside world. It receives information about the world (*reception*) which is processed (*perception*) to form the building blocks of understanding and meaning making (*conception*). Movement is particularly important in human learning; indeed, movement is said to be the origin of thinking (Sheets-Johnstone, 1990), because all living creatures move towards or away from something (such as light, food, or predators).

Major sensory organs related to movement are located on and in the body. One significant sense is the natural "GPS system," used for spatial awareness, indeed Baddeley (1986) suggests that there is a working memory devoted to this

52 Design Basics

visual-spatial dynamic. This is particularly important for learning design: frequent movement in spaces (altered GPS reading) affects the neural areas responsible for spatial understanding. London taxi drivers with extensive navigational experience are found to have a significantly larger posterior area of the hippocampus (Maguire et al., 2000), a part of the brain that plays an important integrative role in *associative*, *relational*, and *sequential* memory (see Dolins & Mitchell, 2010). More on this later.

Movement attracts attention, changes our perception, and physical bodily movement energises the brain. For example, if information is moved into different positions, it can be understood in a different way: sticky post-it labels are popular because information can be so easily moved and thus *reconfigured* in spatial terms. Emotions as said to *move* us, and emotions are played out in the *theatre of the body*. Ground-breaking research by Nina Bull in the 1950s explored body–emotion–brain connections. Through hypnosis she confirmed that a "postural attitude" of the body (moving into a specific body state) is necessary to feel the *corresponding* emotional state in the mind (see Sheets-Johnstone, 2009: 200). Experiences of the body shape the mind, and the mind shapes the body (see Gallagher, 2005).

It is important to remember that writing and speaking are bodily actions: speech involves movement of the tongue and lips and exhaling breath. Gestures are bodily movements whose origins are pre-linguistic (also referred to as *post-kinetic*, Sheets-Johnstone, 2009). Gestures are fundamental to communication and social interaction: they direct attention, send messages, and so enhance cognitive processing (see Gallagher, 2005). Goldin-Meadow et al. (2009) have shown how children's vocabulary can be predicted by the degree to which they used gestures at 14 months of age, and this in turn is dependent on how much their parents use gestures with their babies: these findings remain relatively unknown. Gestures are also the basis of sign language that uses hand shape, movement, and space to create visual representations. Italian gestures for example can be found in separate dictionaries and gestures are considered complementary to spoken language. Hands thus help us to learn through the use of gestures: whether one-handed or two-handed, gestures reveal our thinking, but they also play a part in creating new ways of thinking (see Goldin-Meadow, 2003). To ignore hand movements such as gestures is to ignore an important communicative element of learning.

The hand can touch and manipulate things, and we speak of experiencing *first-hand*. The importance of the hand is clear from the moment we get up out of bed. The act of cleaning teeth, shaving, washing, and applying make-up, making breakfast, and making a coffee, the hands are involved in the many intricate movements of pouring, squeezing, brushing, manipulating, holding, opening and closing containers. As Wilson comments this is "nothing short of a virtuoso display of highly choreographed manual skill" (Wilson, 1998: 3). The involvement of the hands in experiential learning should not be underestimated.

Design Basics 53

The stimulation of the sense of touch through movement is referred to as haptics, and this is important in both physical and digital learning. Design Illustration 8 shows a *"Behavioural Analysis Touch Card."* The card can be touched, physically or digitally. Alternatively, small-coloured discs can be placed on the squares to create graph-like piles showing the frequency of use of behaviours. This design can be applied in group discussions. Pointing to specific behaviours increases engagement and self-awareness: sensitising an individual to their behaviours used, and their frequency of use, encourages the use of a wider repertoire of skills.

 DESIGN ILLUSTRATION 8 BEHAVIOURAL SENSITISATION USING PHYSICAL OR DIGITAL TOUCH CARDS.

The body-brain interaction is facilitated by this example of a touch screen which can be designed in physical or digital formats. The following example is for *behavioural awareness* in social interactions (e.g., meetings/group work).

Self-Awareness Sensitisation Cards			
PUSHING APART		*PULLING TOGETHER*	
Telling/giving information.	*Blocking*/shutting out.	*Deep Listening*	*Merging* others' *ideas/pulling strands together.*
Disagreeing	*Arguing* a specific point.	*Clarifying & Seeking Information*	*Building* on alternatives.
Countering Opposite views	*Pushing* out your own view.	*Agreeing*	*Paraphrasing*

✓

Computers and smartphones utilise an extensive range of *gesture-based technologies* (GBT) that employ a range of body movements, such as hand gestures that point, swipe, slide, and expand. As larger touch screens become available more parts of the body will engage in these movements, and the natural synergy between body and brain will be restored: they have evolved together in partnership for thousands of years.

Research on math teaching shows that spatial awareness using body-brain interactions can create high levels of understanding (see Lakoff & Nunez, 2000). Figure 2.3 shows some of the recommended sequences for quality primary teaching (see, e.g., White Rose website, a math teaching website for primary teachers). Children are asked to move things around with their hands first, to enable them

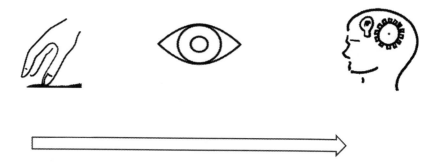

FIGURE 2.3 Primary schools three-step math teaching sequence: hands, eyes, head.

to see the core spatial conceptual underpinning. Eventually they learn to see these spatial-visual movements solely in a cognitive way, that is, in the "head." The sequence used is hands (doing/sensing), eyes (seeing/sensing), and head (thinking/cognitive processing/understanding), and the example given in Chapter 1 shows the dividing of sweets, to see sharing, which then becomes division, which becomes a symbol. Hands are important to this sensorial-kinaesthetic experience.

Walking to Learn

Many actors pace up and down when rehearsing their lines. Some of the great philosophers from the East and West walked whilst questioning as a way of helping people to learn: Socrates often walked whilst asking his subjects difficult questions. Darwin, who developed the theory of evolution, marked out a three-quarter mile *thinking path* known as the "sand-walk" (Desmond & Moore, 2000) in the grounds around his house, which he regularly walked round at mid-day to get away from his desk: the sand-walk is said to have helped his big picture thinking, the routine walking first emptying his mind, to then allow a focussed synthesis of the information he was trying to deal with when developing his thoughts about the encounters with many species and habitats across the globe. Mundane, rhythmic activity like walking or swimming is known to clear the mind and make way for new thinking (Daudelin, 1996).

The principles of thinking (aloud) whilst walking (through a route), observing, and sharing, can also be used to enhance the learning of highly complex material. A Design Illustration called "Walk the Talk," presented in detail in Chapter 10, was developed as a learning experience design for students studying the evolution of the environmental movement. The history is difficult to learn as it involves a complex number of events, numerous laws, and the involvement of many voluntary organisations, key individuals, political lobbying, the designation of special sites, and the setting up of government departments. In this example the

Design Basics **55**

"steps" that are walked though are not linear in form; there are hundreds of steps and numerous routes and the resulting map, created by learners, is like an exceptionally complex version of the London Underground Map. In the example of "Walk the Talk" the landscape of complex spatial-relational "data" is understood and navigated through a complex ecology of walking (motor/corporeal), oration (linguistic social interaction), visual schematics (spatial-relational), and abstract reasoning (higher cognition).

Thinking Aloud

Outer world experiences can be observed whereas inner world experiences are private. One way to externalise and foreground elements of private thoughts and feelings is to ask people if they are happy to share and describe what they can *see*, or what they are *thinking*, or what they are *feeling*, or what *they think is happening* in a social dynamic, for example. This externalisation of thoughts tends to start with basic descriptions, and with encouragement and further reflection these thoughts can shift towards propositional-conceptual thinking (see for example *Making Thinking Visible*, by Ritchhart et al., 2011). This process can also generate a greater awareness of the experience *of* learning, i.e. how we learn. An example of such a conversation is described next:

If an arrow is placed between an old metal key and a plastic hotel swipe card a tutor can ask questions such as "Describe to me what you can see," "tell me what you are thinking," "what makes you think that?" . . . The learners might respond by saying:

> I can see an old key, and a plastic swipe card. . . . The key is metal. The key is heavy, whereas the plastic card is light. The card can be reprogrammed and used for a lot of functions. . . . The card is recyclable . . . it could become multi-functional, including unlocking doors, for financial transactions such as buying things, and located on a smartphone? . . . If the metal key is lost, then it is more difficult to replace . . . plastic keys are more frequently used these days for hotel room keys, for secure access to work, for identification, . . . and this could maybe be seen as an environmental benefit to the use of plastic?

Description often leads to analysis and conceptualisation. When learners get *stuck* it is quite remarkable what happens when they are asked to *describe* what they can *see*, or *feel*, and/or what they are *thinking*. This same process is used with clients in experiential therapies (see Elliott et al., 2004), where a therapist acts as an *experiential guide*, asking for example: *tell me what you are experiencing right now*.

Speech recognition is useful to work with learners to co-create something live, for example, a handout or to develop writing skills. I use speech recognition to expose and *make visible* the structure and content of a literature review using

56 Design Basics

highlighted key words which can be separated and positioned at the side of the main text. I then help *make visible* the real time *crafting* of, say, a conclusion, by joining together these key words to create a succinct narrative.

Stories, Sound Bites, and Film

We live our lives through stories, and they can be very engaging: they often have *elements*, and essential *structures*. Props used in theatre, such as objects and scenery, contribute to the sense of reality of the storyline. In *The Story Teller's Secret*, Gallo (2016), a communication coach for several leading corporate organisations, suggests that the brain is hardwired for storytelling, and that many inspirational leaders turn their passion into a performance, through their ability to tell brilliant, persuasive stories that win hearts and minds. Gallo's advice is to have a *hero* in the story, that overcomes a *challenge or struggle*, and to divide the story into three chunks: a beginning, middle, and end. *Images, videos, photographs, metaphors*, and *analogies* improve the impact. This advice is essentially a mixture of *navigational* tools for thinking, along with *emotional* threads within the storyline to create underlying feelings.

Sound and film bites can be used in many ways to simulate the experience of learning. Speech, like texts and drawings, is used to create thoughts and ideas in the minds of others. Words are *processed*, and we make sense of them. Words create several dimensions of thought, and this is reflected in the words we use as highlighted earlier. When designing an audio, *pace* and *emphasis* are important in speech. Speaking too fast reduces processing time: rail station announcements use overemphasised pauses, allowing greater processing time. Read these words to yourself with a brief half second pause before moving to the next line: The next train (pause), to arrive (pause), at platform 3 (pause), will be the 7.35 (pause), from Liverpool Lime Street (pause), calling at (pause), Birmingham New Street (pause), Cheltenham Spa (pause), and Gloucester central . . . (pause). This prevents passenger confusion. A good storyteller, or news reader, has good pace and emphasis.

Codes, Steps, Equations, and Jigsaws

To remember complex information, *steps* or *stages* are important: examples include *four steps* to assertiveness, and *Seven Habits of Highly Effective People* (Covey, 1989). A simple and easy to remember equation is L > or = C, developed by Reg Revans in his work on Action Learning, meaning learning should always be greater than or equal to change. Seven items is significant for memory load, though later in the book the spatial and temporal memory strategies used by world memory champions are explained (see *Moonwalking with Einstein: The Art and Science of Remembering Everything*, 2011, Joshua Foer).

The following example highlights the use of a code to help groups to go through a series of steps that shift thinking from *descriptive thinking* through to *conceptual, abstract* thinking when designing object-based learning. Based on observations, people tended to pick objects up and *handle* them (H), then *discuss* (D), then objects are *organised* and moved in some way, to spatially highlight relationships with other objects and this process can be encouraged, for example, the use of arrows (O), patterns and relations are then *analysed* (A), finally *conceptualising* their findings (C) can emerge. The code H.D.O.A.C. helps memorise the steps.

Jigsaws are about fitting the *pieces* together in the correct place to form the *whole picture*. The jigsaw allows us to see the relationship between the many *parts* and the *whole* picture. We locate missing pieces and put them in their correct place. *Jigsaw* designs are often used in design, along the lines of *deconstruction* and *reconstruction* described earlier. This is also what is meant by starting the design process with the end in mind: it is designed to be broken down into smaller *parts*, to be built up as a complete jigsaw as the *end* goal.

Conclusion

Laurillard (2012: ix) argues that the teacher who prefers to be entirely spontaneous would have no use for learning design. In my experience, if they are competent, they carry many designs in their heads, orchestrating a range of options as they proceed. Similarly, the London Underground map is not required by people who have lived in London for many years. Experienced teachers or facilitators do not necessarily need design maps: their internal mental maps come into play as needed.

Experience designs *for* learning have to take into account the experience *of* learning, that is, how people learn. These design skills are important in *experience-based* approaches where the *learning experiences* take centre stage. Learning and development specialists, such as facilitators, teachers, and university lecturers are increasingly spending more time designing learning experiences. This chapter was a short introduction to a range of design issues. There is much to learn and so many of the design issues covered in this chapter will now be explored in much more detail in subsequent chapters.

3

THE HOLISTIC EXPERIENTIAL LEARNING DESIGN MODEL (HELM)

A Complex Web of Interactions

This chapter creates a new holistic experiential learning design model consisting of seven *foundational modes of experiencing* that form the basis of the experience design approach taken in this book. The way the model has evolved and developed, and the thinking that underpins the selection of what to include and what to exclude will be explained in this chapter.

The model transcends traditional disciplinary boundaries so that it is integrative, and holistic, representing the complex interactional flux of the many modes of experiencing. Learning design models should ideally attempt to be comprehensive to reflect the inherent complexity that is involved in the human experience of learning. The search involved working towards something that was simple whilst at the same time being more comprehensive. The solution had to possess an *elegant simplicity*.

The way that learning is "experienced" involves more than the *doing, reflecting, testing,* and *application*. Cyclical models of learning, founded on the "*scientific method*" of enquiry, were extensively developed in the 19th century. They usually consisted of four steps, or stages, despite being round. The circle is the basis of the reflective enquiry approach that Kurt Lewin uses when working with groups. His stages were later adopted by David Kolb and his colleagues in the late 1970s.

The visual *representation* of Kolb's experiential learning theory as a learning *cycle* accounts for both its success and extensive criticism. Criticisms relate to the simplistic, mechanistic, and formulaic approaches to learning (see Rowland, 2000; Moon, 2004) that prioritise, separate, and sequence four modes. The foundational roots derive from the "scientific method" of discovery that Dewey advocated for schooling. The stages also mimic the systematic management planning and training cycles of *plan, do, evaluate, learn,* such as the Systematic Training Cycle, presented in a monograph on experiential learning by Boydell in 1976.

DOI: 10.4324/9781003030867-3

Holistic Experiential Learning Design   **59**

These circular models reached a peak of popularity in the 1970s, but began to lose their status by the early 1990s as can be seen in the following satirical comment:

> They first began to appear about 25 years ago. Neatly laid-out circles in the pages of training textbooks, journals and Industrial Training Board publications. They quickly came to seize the imagination of a growing band of training professionals. They must have been created by a superior intelligence, being so neat and logical and all. . . . Within a few short years the "systematic training model" [or "training cycle" to some] became the orthodoxy of the training profession.
>
> *(Taylor, 1991: 258)*

Kolb refers to these four "learning modes" as four different individual *abilities* (Kolb 1976: 28) involving the learner being actively involved in an experience, reflecting, using analytical skills, being able to conceptualise, and generate solutions to solve problems through experimentation. Kolb (1984: 38) states that "learning is a process whereby knowledge is created through the transformation of experience." This reference to and focus on "knowledge" locates his ideas within the cognitive psychology tradition. The term *concrete experience* is also problematic in that *experience* is not added to the other terms in the circular model. Thinking is not presented as a "thinking experience," and reflection is not presented as *reflective experience*. Reflection can be a *concrete experience*, when it is regarded as another *layer* of active experience to explore the future, the past, or the present. In 2017 Kolb and Kolb made adjustments, declaring that "James's radical empiricism helps us to understand that all modes of the learning cycle are experiences" (40). This is a significant point for the approach taken within this book, notably that human *experiences* of learning involve much more than concrete, reflective, abstract, and experimenting experiences. His theory has certainly provided learning designers with a basic structure to follow. He suggests that there is "considerable heuristic value in the learning cycle as a guide to the design of learning experiences and curricula" (Kolb & Kolb, 2017: 38). The term heuristic refers to its *investigative* potential.

Whilst Kolb has played a major role in the global spread of experiential learning and his ideas continue to influence many practitioners, criticisms include the focus on an individual (Holman et al., 1997), and on cognitive (mental) processes that divorce learning from the social, historical, and cultural aspects of self, thinking, and action. The focus on cognitive processing raises questions about where the mind and body begin and end. Is the mind confined within the skull, or does the neural network spread into the body: if it does, then what is its role in learning? His representations see the learner as cognitively (mentally/mind) reflecting on concrete events as an isolated individual, as an "intellectual Robinson Crusoe" whereby the experiential interactions with the world "out there"

60 Holistic Experiential Learning Design

somehow does not exist, and that "knowledge is extracted and abstracted from experience by the processing mind" (Fenwick, 2003: 21). Such a view, Fenwick argues, treats learning as some-*thing* that is concrete and knowable, rather than existing in a fluid state. She too argues that knowledge, understanding, and meaning making occurs within social, cultural, emotional, and psychological structures. These structures should ideally be included in any new modelling of experiential learning design.

The learning cycle neglects other aspects of *experiencing*, such as the *sensorial, emotional*, and *bodily interactions*, which leads to other problematic questions such as: can the brain think without the body, does the world influence the mind or does our mind influence the way we see the world? Does the body remember, and do the hands inform the brain, or does the brain inform the hands? Many of these issues are explored in this book. However, the development of a new and more comprehensive model is the immediate concern.

Experiential learning has evolved over a long period of time with *learning* and *experience* now understood as being far more complex than previously perceived. Dewey long ago argued for a sound *philosophy of experience*: any philosophy of experience, he suggested, should investigate the complexity of life as humans *experience* it. According to Crosby (1995: 11), Dewey maintained that as humans "We find ourselves in continual transaction with the physical, psychological, mental, spiritual world, and philosophy should be a systematic investigation into the nature of this experience." The investigation of these transactions creates some of the foundations on which to build new theories of experiential learning design.

The 21st Century: Accepting *Learning* and *Experience* as Complex Concepts

Central to the creation of a new model is the notion that the inner self interacts with the outer world environment. To construct an integrative and holistic experiential learning design model that differentiates and integrates parts and whole is always going to be a difficult task. Lao Tzu notes that human experiences consist of many elements that are all connected. He comments on the way that *thinking* is connected to *becoming* and *being* in the world. Lao Tzu suggests we are careful about our *thoughts* which can be turned into *words*, and our *words* into *actions*, and our *actions* into *habits*. Our *habits* in turn embed themselves within our *character*, contributing towards our *being*, and our destiny.

A brief examination of the recent changes in what was known about the way humans learn is useful before progressing with developing a new model. The shifts in focus proceed from the behavioural and cognitive focus towards a humanistic and social focus. What is particularly significant is the continuing movement towards ecological complexity, denoted as "E" in Figure 3.1.

Holistic Experiential Learning Design **61**

Time Periods		1900-1940s	1950s	1960s	1970s	1980s	1990s	2000
HUMAN LEARNING THEORIES B.C.H.S.E.	**B**	**BEHAVIOURISM. Design implications**: ethology, original research on animals, stimulus-response. Environmental stimulus and responding behavior. Early roots of *transmission* approaches to education. Programmed instruction. Conditioning. **OBSERVABLE BEHAVIOUR. EXTERNAL FOCUS.**						
	C	**COGNITIVISM. Design implications**: focus on *thinking* processes. (Computational focus on the understanding of the functioning of the brain. Cognition). **THINKING PROCESSOR. INTERNAL FOCUS.**						
		H	**HUMANISM. Design implications**: Focus on empathetic/nurturing, esteem, love & belonging, the recognition of the affective, attitudes and values. Rooted in counselling psychology. Early roots of student-centred, transactional approaches. **FEELING/SENSING. INTERNAL FOCUS.**					
				S	**SOCIAL CONSTRUCTIONISM Design implications**: social collaboration, social communication, constructing knowledge together, active and interactive. **BELONGING/INTERACTING/CONSTRUCTING KNOWLEDGE. INTERNAL & EXERNAL FOCUS.**			
					E INTERNAL AND EXTERNAL FOCUS. CONSTANT EXPERIENTIAL FLUX. MULTI-DISCIPLINARY AND HOLISTIC e.g. Biological, physiological, cognitive, social, humanist, and behavioral, flux. **BELONGING and BEING through SENSING, DOING, KNOWING, AND FEELING** **Design implications**: embracing rather than rejecting preceding theories of learning. Multi-disciplinary. Also influenced by new cognitive neuroscience and other recent findings about human learning.			**ECOLOGICAL COMPLEXITY** SYSTEMS THEORIES and embracing a range of other notions including DISTRIBUTED COGNITION. BIOLOGICAL INTERDEPENDENCE. ACTOR NETWORK THEORIES ETC. Transformational approach. 'Revisionary postmodernism'.

FIGURE 3.1   A simplified history of dominant theories of how humans learn.

The Need for New Models That Reflect the Complexity of Learning

The calls for more complex modelling are substantial. Peter Jarvis conducted a research experiment with nine different groups of adults. He asked them to consider a learning incident from their own lives. They shared these with others in the group and then they were given a copy of the experiential learning cycle by Kolb. They were then asked to consider this model and reconstruct it, if necessary, based on their chosen learning incident. The result was that participants did indeed undertake a major redesign. The new modelling was much more complex, and not surprisingly, many were similar to a *spider's web*. Their new modelling emphasised the learner as a whole person, and recognised that learning is a complex, interactional process. Jarvis also acknowledges, as mentioned earlier, that in much of his work on human learning he also did not "*manage to capture its complexity*" (2006: 12).

62 Holistic Experiential Learning Design

Knud Illeris (2002), the Danish educator and professor of lifelong learning, suggests three important dimensions of learning: *cognition, emotion,* and *society.* These three aspects of experiencing are, in my view, also insufficient. In *Nurturing the Whole Student* (Mayes & Williams) the subtitle is *Five Dimensions of Teaching and Learning* (2003). This book argues that these five dimensions are the foundations of holistic learning and education. The five chapters explore these five dimensions: the *organic, psychodynamic, affiliative, procedural,* and *existential* dimensions of the holistic experience of the experience of learning. *Embodied* approaches to learning involve *sensing and doing,* and the *psychodynamic* involves *emotions* and *feelings.* The *affiliative,* that is, the recognition that we have a deep human need to *belong* in the world, becomes *belonging,* as two dimensions. Belonging in the human world (HW) and the more-than-human world (MTHW). Their fourth dimension is *procedural,* which Mayes and Williams refer to as *cognitive apprentice,* which becomes thinking/knowing. Finally, their fifth dimension is *existential,* about existence: the existential *self.* I refer to this as our *being,* though in fact we spend much of our lives *becoming.*

From Forest School programmes to sustainable development education, and early years development frameworks to new thinking in the "experience economy," there are many calls for a broader understanding of learning. In Forest Schools young people are said to develop their *physical, social, cognitive, linguistic, emotional, social,* and *spiritual* aspects. The early years educational learning framework in Australia describes childhood as a time of *belonging, being,* and *becoming.* Belonging is portrayed as the basis for living a fulfilling life: children feel they *belong* because of the relationships they have with their family, community, their culture, and their sense of place. *Being* is about living here and now. Childhood, it is argued, is a special time in life and children need time to just "be" – time to play, try new things, and have fun. Becoming is about the learning and development that young children experience. Children start to form their sense of identity from an early age, which shapes the type of adult they will become. In *Sustainable Education* Sterling notes that "in 1996 an international commission report to UNESCO proposed four pillars as the foundations of education. These are in sum: *learning to live together, learning to know, learning to do, and learning to be*" (Sterling, 2001: 75). Few models embrace these aspects of learning.

Writing from the perspective of an occupational therapist, Wilcock (1999), considers the dynamic between *doing, becoming,* and *being,* arguing that the dynamic between doing and being is central to healthy living and wellness. She suggests that an occupation should be seen as a synthesis of *doing, being,* and *becoming.* Purposeful action, in her view, is important for self-actualisation (see Maslow, 1968), that is, the idea of *becoming* someone. What people do with their lives shapes not only the self, but also communities, and whole societies.

Within *Experiential Education* Warren et al. comment that "we find ourselves in continual transaction with the physical, psychological, mental, spiritual world,

Holistic Experiential Learning Design **63**

and philosophy should be a systematic investigation into the nature of this experience" (1995: 11). Caine and Caine (1994: 116) in *Making Connections: Teaching and the Human Brain*, recommend making connections between the core elements of experience, suggesting that in designing immersive learning experiences "educators need to identify and appreciate the various elements of experience and need to know how to bring them together effectively." Whilst calls for a more holistic approach to experiential learning modelling are extensive, space will not allow fuller coverage here. Chapter 8 offers more information, though a more comprehensive account of the historical trajectory towards complexity and multidisciplinary approaches to experiential learning can be found in Beard (2016).

It is also important to remember that experience is "highly personal, subjectively perceived, intangible, ever fleeting and continuously on-going . . . [and] located in the minds of individuals" (O'Dell, 2005: 15), and any model is only an external representation to "conceptualise, visualise, or materialise an entity into another format or mode" (Wu & Puntambekar, 2012: 755). Models can, however, "aid cognition, give structure, and facilitate memory, communication and reasoning" (Gattis, 2001: 2), and external representations in turn enhance the construction of internal (mental) models: "from the point of view of instructional design, the process of internalisation is where we can influence the construction of mental models by providing well-designed external re-representations of phenomena to be explained" (Ifenthaler, 2010: 83).

The Holistic Experiential Learning Model (HELM)

At this stage it is useful to return to the simple models that have endured over time. Their simplicity appears to have influenced the extent of their popularity. One such model is created by Borton (1970). Drawing on his experience of running workshops in the 1960s, he recognised three important functions of the processing mind: *sensing* (as experience), *transforming* (as sense making) and *acting* (as engagement in the world). From this he created a useful, practical design model which asks three colloquial questions that best connected with and represented these three functions: *What? So what?* and *Now what?*

Another simple approach that has remained popular, and which also considers three dimensions, is the 3*H* model, of *head, hands,* and *heart,* as a holistic approach to education. There is controversy as to who first developed this notion. The heart represents the *affective* domain, the head represents the *cognitive* domain, and the hands represent the *psychomotor* domain.

However, both these models have limitations in that they consider only three modes. In the three H model the *hands* are often interpreted as *representing* the psychomotor capacities involved in learning. As will be shown in the next few chapters the capacities of the hands, and the whole body, have many other important functions, including sensory, spatial, and communicative capacities.

64 Holistic Experiential Learning Design

There is clearly a need for both simplicity and complexity. This is the challenge. What is required is a model that is *elegantly simple* yet at the same time quite complex in coverage. To do this I have chosen to expand and develop the popular *3H* model to create a more complex *H* model that is more holistic. Five *Hs* will be used to represent *Head*, *Hands*, *Heart*, *Home*, and *Human*.

However, two of these *Hs* represent twin experiencing modes, and so this leads to the model encompassing seven modes of experiencing. To go beyond seven may make the model too complex as a representation. A useful shorthand code, that can act as a remembering trigger for the model is: 5H-7M (five Hs that point to seven Modes of experiencing). To further enhance the memory of this modelling I have developed the chart in Figure 3.2 to illustrate the 5Hs using additional visual depictions in the form of icons.

The *5H* model is a useful stepping-stone to the use of seven modes for the purpose of design. The origins of these seven modes are the result of many years of research and practical enquiry, including an examination of an extensive body

Icon	5H's	Representing
	*H*ands	Representing DOING & SENSING. As a symbol of the important role of the body for learning the hands are an ideal symbol.
	*H*eart	Representing FEELINGS. This represents the part played by emotions in learning.
	*H*ead	Representing THINKING. The thinking mode includes many capacities such as reflecting, abstract thought, memory etc.
	*H*ome and/or *H*abitat	Representing BELONGING. We live, reside, dwell, and belong, with 'others', in space, and place. In the (1) social (human) world,  & (2) More-than-human world. 
	*H*uman	Representing The *H*uman - BEING. This concerns the levels of self-awareness, and our sense of identity, beliefs, values etc.

FIGURE 3.2   The five Hs: foundations of the Holistic Experiential Learning Model.

Holistic Experiential Learning Design **65**

of literature to identify the modes of experiencing that are more commonly included with reference to the way we humans learn.

Moving to seven modes partially addresses the critiques concerning overly simplistic approaches. The seven modes of experiencing are explored in detail in Chapters 4 to 9, and in Chapter 10 a particularly complex design illustrates the level of complexity that can be developed.

Feeling and thinking, sensing and thinking, body and mind, culture and politics, individual and group, and aspects of nature and nurture, are all areas of experiencing that overlap, interact, and *bind* together (~). The interactions underpin learning; they do not occur through seven separate modes of experiencing. As Davis and Sumara suggest, "*The focus of enquiry is not so much on the components (modes) of experience but, rather, on the relations that bind these elements together in action*" (1997: 108). Because of this each of the Chapters four 4 to 9 that follow examine more than one mode of experiencing. Many smaller *elements* of the seven experiencing modes are surfaced within the chapters: *sensing*, for example, incorporates the sub-level modes of *visual, haptic, auditory, kinaesthetic, olfactory, spatial awareness, and so on*.

Davis and Sumara ask a particularly poignant question about what might happen if we think about learning in a different way:

> If we were to reject the self-evident axiom that cognition is located within cognitive agents who are cast as isolated from one another and distinct from the world, and insist instead that all cognition exists in the interstices of a complex ecology of organismic relationality?
>
> *(Davis & Sumara, 1997: 110)*

Multiple Representations

It may be of interest to see my early thinking that underpinned this new modelling that was developed during a doctoral study many years ago. A schematic representation is shown in Figure 3.3. The previous quotation by Davis and Sumara highlights that the boundary lines are artificial.

A visual representation containing some explanatory graphic detail is also shown in Figure 3.4.

A simplified version with the seven modes of experiencing with icons and numbers is shown in Figure 3.5. The icons are useful to use as depictive, shorthand symbols in the sketching and mapping processes of experience design.

Finally, a more mechanistic representation, known as the *Learning Combination Lock*, is also shown in Figure 3.6. It can be created in physical form with paper cups that slide into each other and rotate. The cups can also be written on.

The preferred choice of representation will differ widely among readers, and it is worth repeating here that a model is only an external representation to "conceptualise, visualise, or materialise an entity into another format or mode" (Wu & Puntambekar, 2012: 755). At this stage the model will be furnished with

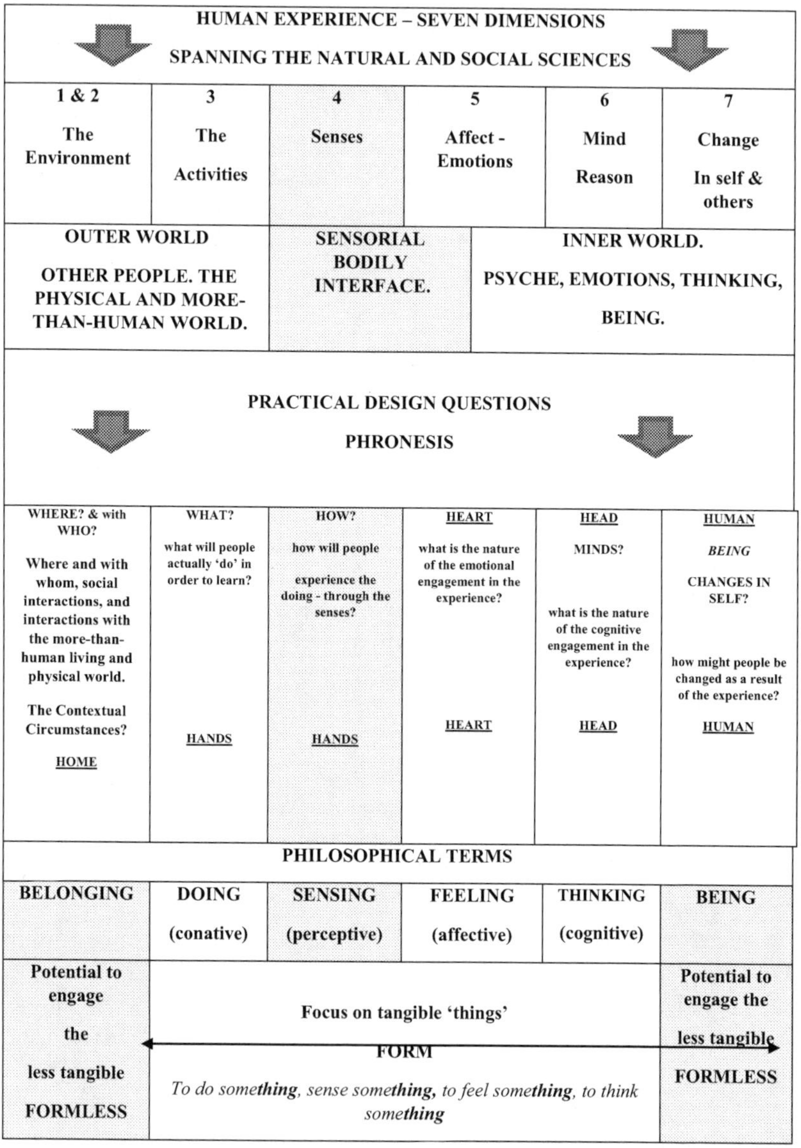

66 Holistic Experiential Learning Design

HUMAN EXPERIENCE – SEVEN DIMENSIONS SPANNING THE NATURAL AND SOCIAL SCIENCES					
1 & 2	**3**	**4**	**5**	**6**	**7**
The Environment	The Activities	Senses	Affect - Emotions	Mind Reason	Change In self & others
OUTER WORLD OTHER PEOPLE. THE PHYSICAL AND MORE-THAN-HUMAN WORLD.		**SENSORIAL BODILY INTERFACE.**	**INNER WORLD. PSYCHE, EMOTIONS, THINKING, BEING.**		

PRACTICAL DESIGN QUESTIONS

PHRONESIS

WHERE? & with WHO?	WHAT?	HOW?	HEART	HEAD	HUMAN
Where and with whom, social interactions, and interactions with the more-than-human living and physical world. The Contextual Circumstances? HOME	what will people actually 'do' in order to learn? HANDS	how will people experience the doing - through the senses? HANDS	what is the nature of the emotional engagement in the experience? HEART	MINDS? what is the nature of the cognitive engagement in the experience? HEAD	BEING CHANGES IN SELF? how might people be changed as a result of the experience? HUMAN

PHILOSOPHICAL TERMS					
BELONGING	DOING (conative)	SENSING (perceptive)	FEELING (affective)	THINKING (cognitive)	BEING
Potential to engage the less tangible FORMLESS	Focus on tangible 'things' FORM *To do some**thing**, sense some**thing**, to feel some**thing**, to think some**thing***				Potential to engage the less tangible FORMLESS

FIGURE 3.3 The origins of the Holistic Experiential Learning Model (HELM).

Holistic Experiential Learning Design 67

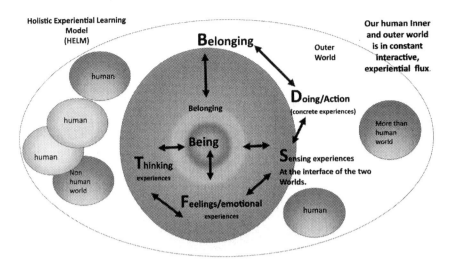

FIGURE 3.4   The Holistic Experiential Learning Model (HELM).

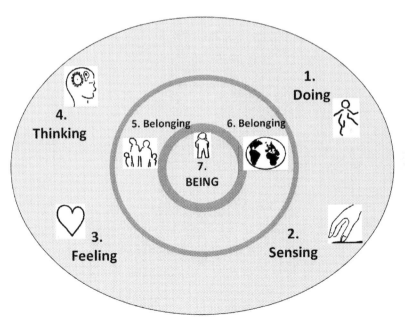

Doing, Sensing, Feeling, Knowing, Belonging (social), Belonging (MTH), Being.

FIGURE 3.5   A simplified version of the Holistic Experiential Learning Model for use in design.

68 Holistic Experiential Learning Design

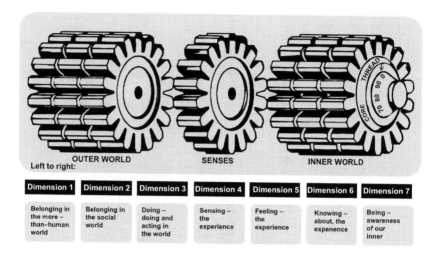

FIGURE 3.6 Other *representational formats* of the seven modes of experiencing: the learning combination lock.

theoretical and practical detail. The next chapter starts the detailed exploration of the seven core modes of experiencing, starting with learning involving experiences of *doing* and *sensing*.

4

EXPERIENCE DESIGN

Doing~Sensing

A Focus on Hands-On Experiences

Experiential learning is regarded as a learner-centred approach that is less about "instruction" and "teaching" and more about the broad *experience* of learning by becoming *acquainted with* rather than just *knowing about*. In this chapter the question of *doing what?* is explored in detail. *Doing*, and *sensing*, is represented in the 7H-model by the H for Hands, and this chapter focuses on *active, hands-on* experiences, involving many sensory experiences. Significantly, the sensing and doing capacities of the hands play a remarkably important role in experiential learning. In this chapter the notion of experience as *doing* will also be exposed as overly simplistic: there is much more to *doing* than might be expected, and so it is time to unpack this idea. The implications for design are significant.

Rote learning was the dominant experience of learning in education in the early 20th century (see Curtis, 1963). Dictionary definitions, however, regard *experience* as *something that you do*; something that happens *to you*; something important that *affects you*; *knowledge* and *feelings* of past events, that make up *life* or *character*. This broad definition of experience includes *doing*, though, as outlined in the modelling in Chapter 3, active *doing* is just one of the several core modes of experiencing.

In the learning cycle Kolb (1984) refers to the important role of doing as a "concrete experience," implying an *interaction* or *encounter* with something material, physical, or living, as sensed, or felt. The other three stages or modes of experiencing in his model do not have the word *experience* attached to them, which has led to misunderstandings of *doing* as synonymous with experiencing. The mantra *let the learners "do" the learning* is not just about physical activity. Worst still if people are too busy *doing* there may be little time devoted to *critically questioning, thinking*, or reading, thus diminishing the capacity to learn. This is

DOI: 10.4324/9781003030867-4

70 Experience Design: Doing~Sensing

the "activity trap" when learning is dominated by physical activities. Balance is required between active and less active experiences (active~passive).

Reading and quiet reflection are perceived as passive activities, but they don't have to be. Similarly, when reflection is designed as an active rather than a passive experience it can be more effective. Roger Greenaway, for example, recommends reviewing *activities* be designed in creative ways, to share experiences before, during, and after other activities. Reflection, he suggests, can be an experience of *thinking through action*, rather than something done after a "concrete experience," thus separating *thinking* from *doing* as in Kolb's (1984) learning cycle (see Roger Greenaway's website: reviewing.co.uk). It is also not helpful to regard the "experiencing body" as *doing*, and the brain as *thinking*: separating the body as merely "material" and "physical" undervalues its role in learning. The neural systems do not end at the skull (head), and the body and the hands play a particularly important role in *thinking*. *Doing* is a notion that requires further critical examination.

Embodied cognition is a theory proposing that the body is involved in the creation of conceptual knowledge, especially the perceptual (sensory) and motor (action/ movement) systems (body~mind). *Situated cognition* proposes that learning is situated in social, cultural, and physical settings. The brain and the body evolved in partnership together, and as Daniel Siegel in *The Developing Mind* notes, mental processes emerge "from neural functions throughout the whole body (not only the brain in the skull) and from relational processes (not only from one bodily self or nervous system)" (Siegel, 2012: 5, brackets in original). The *extended mind hypothesis* proposes that "material thoughts" are spatially distributed over brain, body, and the environment, that is, beyond the skull and skin. Gallagher and Zaham (2008) point out that if a visually impaired person uses a stick to navigate, then the stick becomes more than just an object: it becomes an *extension* of the arm and body.

Doing something is not the simple act we might imagine. Many processes occur at once. In her doctoral thesis Palmer (2020) superbly illustrates the intimate complexity of the body-brain partnership in the act of *throwing* clay during pottery making. The supposedly simple act of picking up a cup of coffee is outlined by Rizzolatti and Sinigaglia (2008: 2):

> intertwining of sensations (visual, tactile, olfactory, proprioceptive), motivational connections, body arrangements, and motor performance, not to speak of postural adjustments – which anticipate the execution of each of these movements and their consequences and guarantee the required control over the body's dynamic balance – and the role played by the learning process and the know-how we have acquired in identifying, localising, reaching for, grasping objects in general. All these factors interact more or less harmonically with each other and with the objects which populate our world.

The experience of *doing* involves several capacities: (1) *solo or social activity, agency, and action*, (2) involvement of the *experiencing body*, especially the *hands* which can "read" and communicate, (3) bodily *movement* in *time* and *space*, (4) and *sensory-body* engagement with *concrete* things such as *objects*. These important capacities occur because we are "mobile active beings; replete with limbs/effectors; richly endowed with sensory systems; with vast swathes of neural tissue devoted to the detection (interoception) of our own bodily states" (Clark, 2013: 265).

Design options for *doing* and *sensing* learning experiences are wide-ranging. When we consider what learners might *do*, it is the *active* verbs that generate ideas about a range of activities, including for example: *producing* a document, podcast, video, or radio program, *choreographing* a dance, *designing* a webinar, *filling in* missing words, *completing* a quiz or anagram, *solving* a puzzle or problem, *drawing* a cartoon strip, *practicing* a skill on a simulation, *baking* a cake, *bandaging* a volunteer, *diagnosing* something, *undertaking* an adventurous *journey* or *expedition*, *operating* machinery under safe conditions, *analysing and exploring* case studies, or *sorting* and *categorising* things or information. *Action*-based *experiential* verbs often involve the body, particularly the hands.

The three a's of *actors*, *action*, and *artefacts*, all play a part in *doing*. Doing activities can be intense, or simply for fun: the leisure and hospitality industry, for example, design fun team building events, where the activities can be quite complex though the depth of learning can be relatively low.

Doing as Moving?

Doing is not so simple as it first appears, and there is more unpacking to do. Even opening a book and reading the words on this page is an act of *doing* something: we move our eyes across the page, scanning all the symbols to create an internal, imagined storyline that we "speak" with the inner voice. The degree of physical movement varies.

In evolutionary terms movement has been, and still is, important to the experience of learning. The origins of thinking are said to lie in movement: Sheets-Johnstone (2009: 5) argues that "movement is the mother tongue of all animate forms." Even the most primitive single celled animals from three plus billion years ago *moved* either *towards* food or *away* from prey, and it is significant that animals that *moved* in more complex ways, in the predator-prey relationship, developed larger brains. Relatively smaller brains are found, for example, in basking sharks feeding on krill compared to the larger brains of sharks that feed on fast swimming creatures that are harder to catch. The same is true for apes: those feeding on plant leaves, such as gorillas, have relatively smaller brains compared to apes that search for and catch food. It seems that active *doing* influences brain development.

Doing often involves movement, and when our bodies are physically doing things, we become energised through *serotonin* production: running produces more serotonin than walking or moving about in a classroom. Serotonin is an ancient *regulator* of neural and muscle networks, as a source of positive feelings of well-being and happiness. Found in all living systems, including plants, serotonin has many functions. It is different from the morphine-like *endorphins* that diminish pain and trigger positive energising feelings produced after active exercise.

72 Experience Design: Doing~Sensing

Understanding sensory-motor capacities, and the part they play in cognitive (mental) processing is especially important for the development of experiential learning design. We continually scan the environment by moving our bodies, and we respond rapidly to, and quickly focus on movement, particularly in novel environments. Looking out of the window as I write, my attention is immediately drawn to the moving clouds, leaves, and birds flying. Movement certainly captures attention. In *Making Connections: Teaching and the Human Brain*, a story is told of a young teacher trying, but failing, to teach punctuation to young children. Several times the teacher explained the purpose of commas, full stops, and exclamation marks, yet the pupils could not *grasp* the ideas. In frustration the teacher took the children outside and had them walk around in a big circle as she read out of a book. She told them that when she said the word "comma" they should slow down, when she said "full stop" they should instantly stop moving, and for an *exclamation mark* they should jump in the air. This learning method worked rather well! (Caine & Caine, 1994: 116). Books for young children have changed to include a greater variety of sensory stimulation, including movement: *pop-up* books, books that *unfold* and open out, and even books with a train set inside. There are books that use *scanimation* so a young child can see an animal moving across the page at the same time their parents read out "the chicken struts across the farmyard." Movement is synchronised with the story.

To get the children to appreciate books, some schools are sending young children home with full homework bags: but they are not full of books. They contain one book, and the rest of the bag is filled with props made by parents. Parents and children have fun playing out the drama of the book. If there is a teddy bear in the story, there is a teddy bear in the bag. If the teddy bear jumps, the children jump. This fun, acting out, encourages a playful physical, bodily expression of the story that also engages the senses, emotions, and of course, their brains. Furthermore, *pleasure* is associated with reading and bedtime in their bedroom space: the bedtime story becomes a very different *experience*. It is remembered because the storyline comes alive: the habit of reading and the sensory experience, and the affective pleasure of being cuddled by loving, caring parents at bedtime should not be underestimated.

Corbett (2006) in *Storytelling into Writing* recommends that teachers use movements in the form of gestures, as well as icons and route maps to create and tell children stories and expose the essential structures of writing so that they are understood by the children. Corbet produced an *Action Bank* of gestures at the rear of his book to complement the stories: *Once upon a time* uses the opening of hands as if opening a book; *early one morning* is a gesture whereby the hands are placed together to one side of the head with action to pretend to wake up from sleep. The hands speak. Corbett uses story maps to create a sense of a *journey*, and icons show the main features. The mind-body connection is and always has been an important and integral part of any learning experience, and the brain craves these multiple sensory inputs.

Experience Design: Doing~Sensing **73**

Early in life the infant activity of bodily movement is important to understand the world around them. They learn their bodies, and their bodies learn to move. The following explanations highlight the role of the moving body in learning. Young children learn to climb steps, and at the same time they learn to count by *actively reciting* the numbers with adults. The greater the number of steps climbed, the *higher* the flight of steps. When children pour and measure water *contained* in a glass tube, they actively learn a concept that *higher* means *more*. They also learn that categories *contain* (hold) certain *types* of things: *categories as containing types* is best remembered by *putting* things *into* containers. Later children learn to add, subtract, and divide also by doing something physical ("concrete" experience referred to as mathematics manipulatives). Primary children *grasp* the idea of division by "sharing" sweets (relevant objects in the world of children!). *Sharing* thus becomes *dividing*. "Taking away" sweets, becomes *subtraction* (-), and putting the sweets together becomes *addition* (+). The hands are not used solely for manual skills: the hands play a central role in thinking (cognition). Later these concepts can be referred to in purely mathematical *symbolic form*: division becomes ÷. This highlights the shift from the physical, concrete, *bodily* experience to that of *symbolic*, abstract cognitive (purely mental) processing. In these examples the bridge between the kinetic, aural, visual, and conceptual becomes established. These design principles are also significant in adult learning. My wife, a primary school teacher, explains to young children that the symbol divide (÷) is a line with a sweet above the line and a sweet below the line. This visually re-*presents* dividing as *sharing*. This is a wonderful spatial explanation that helps children *embed* their understanding of symbolic representation. In this way there is congruence and continuity between the *spatial*, the *linguistic*, *symbolic*, and *conceptual* explanations that enhance understanding (more on this later).

I have long held the view that many children get *left behind* because learning activities involving the active body are cut short too early. The transfer from seeing, touching, and moving (hands) to a purely cognitive and symbolic form takes time. I wonder if this is why many families send their children for extra mathematics tuition: wherever I have travelled in the world extra maths tuition is on offer in shopping malls. Jeanne Ormrod (2018: 346) in her eighth edition book *Human Learning*, notes that "of all the subjects taught in schools, none seems to elicit as much anxiety for as many students as mathematics." One possible reason Ormrod suggests, is that schools introduce abstract concepts before pupils are cognitively ready to receive them.

"The first mathematical experiences that children have are with concrete objects." This quotation was taken from *Children's Mathematics: Lost and Found in Space* (Bryant & Squire, in Gattis, 2016: 175). The title clearly indicates the importance of spatial dynamics in mathematics teaching. More advanced details can be found in *Where Mathematics Comes From* (Lakoff & Nunez, 2000). Counting is likely to have originated through seeing two as more than one, and this has developed further using fingers and toes, and bodily gestures. Thus, it is not unreasonable to assume that our

74 Experience Design: Doing~Sensing

digits gave rise to the binary system (two hands, two feet, two ears, two nostrils, etc.) and the decimal system (ten fingers, and ten toes). Success or failure in maths can, to an extent, be explained in terms of the way spatial attention cues are presented, or not presented. The manipulation of physical objects, multi-sensory applications, and the movement using hands and objects are all important for learning mathematics. The manipulation of objects in space involves children *doing* some*thing* in order to learn and importantly this leads to the learning of basic concepts. Children are expected to acquire these concepts through what we call *conceptual metaphors*, as was explained earlier for the symbol of division (÷). This use of spatial, sensory cues makes sense, as humans have long used spatial knowledge to navigate and remember space, to find food, and more generally to survive. For many thousands of years humans have carefully observed locations, orientation, and movement of objects, of people, and plants and animals. Lakoff and Nunez (2000) note that "most of the brain is devoted to vision, motion, spatial understanding, interpersonal interaction, coordination, emotions, language, and everyday reasoning." It makes sense that these highly evolved capacities should be utilised for learning.

> For a long time now psychologists have recognised the possibility of connection between the way children think about space and their understanding of mathematics, but they have done so in a negative way. Space, for them, is part of the problem in mathematics, not part of the solution.
>
> *(Bryant & Squire, in Gattis, 2016: 175)*

Design Illustration 9 and Figure 4.1 are simple examples.

DESIGN ILLUSTRATION 9 *DOING* MATHS: "LOST AND FOUND IN SPACE."

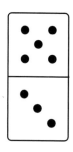

Add up the numbers on the domino on the right and think about how easily you did it!

The visual patterns possess a familiar spatial structure. Imagine what would happen if these dots were arranged in a messy, random way. Maybe then the numbers would not so easily be added together. We can learn to remember the spatial representation or layout, and so can quickly complete the task. Dominoes are objects that present visual layouts for easy understanding: they are *spatially designed dots* presented in a way that makes counting easier. My wife, a primary school teacher, puts spots on Ladybird insect wings (Figure 4.2).

FIGURE 4.1 Spatial layout and memory on a domino.

Experience Design: Doing-Sensing **75**

Numicon is a business that has adapted the style and format of dominos to generate excellent visual touchable educational tools, so that each domino style block can be moved, joined to others, in single or multiple layers (side by side or on top of each other) in ways that enhances mathematics development in children. (www.youtube.com/watch?v=yYgwM5Z1tMo).

FIGURE 4.2 Numbers presented on ladybird wings.

Solid objects are also commonly used in elementary school mathematics instruction, especially with topics that cause learners to struggle in such tasks as multiplication. They are frequently used in the classroom by teachers to *represent* concepts: the physical manipulation of objects is important in experiential approaches to learning mathematic principles. Try the simple mathematical examples in Figure 4.3 that promote the use of space, movement, and objects.

37 − 12

Each single number is represented by one piece ▬

Ten is a rod ▬▬▬

||| ⁝⁝⁝ − |⁝ = ?

3 rods = 30. 'Take away' one rod, leaves two rods = 20

7 discs 'take away' 2 leaves 5 discs.

Take 12 away..... leaves

          Originally 3 rods (30). 'Take away' one rod, leaves two rods = 20

Originally 7 discs (7), 'take away' 2 leaves 5 discs (5).

THE ANSWER = 25.

FIGURE 4.3 Using mathematics manipulatives to subtract.

In this example children can use *sweets*, or *rods and bricks* (concrete objects) and then move on to use *symbols*.

This illustration explores the utilisation of specific human capacities used to learn. Whilst the example is about children *doing* mathematics, the same highly evolved human capacities need to be utilised in adult learning.

For additional reading see: Laski, E., Jor'dan, J., Daoust, C. and Murray, A, (2015). What makes mathematics manipulatives effective? Lessons from cognitive science and Montessori education. *SAGE Open, 5*(2): 2158244015589588.

The experiential approaches used in the previous examples show how teaching and learning methods have developed to become more experiential. An advanced experiential learning design for adults is outlined at the end of this chapter – *Industrial Ecology or Circular Economy).*

Spatial understanding is explained In *Learning to Learn from Experience* (1984: 62) by Edward Cell:

> When we interpret, we see connections between things, pulling them together into a meaningful pattern, and we assess their value and disvalue for us. We record our ways of seeing such things in terms of spatial and temporal relations, what things cause other things to happen, the kinds of purposes that give shape and meaning to our human life and the means available to pursue those purposes.

Doing: The Design of Movement in Time and Space

As mentioned earlier taxi drivers have remarkable navigation abilities and spatial awareness, and brain scanning research has found that taxi drivers have larger hippocampus areas associated with processing spatial memories (Maguire et al., 2000; Foer, 2011). Movement is their generative source of spatial perception and spatial cognition.

Movement and manipulation of objects is also central to abstract conceptual learning, from an early age and on to adult learning. Learning is made easier when learning involves *doing*, with *things*, in *space*, using *bodily sensory* capacities. It is important in experiential learning design to understand in more detail how space is used in the development of abstract thinking. The vestibular system, and the mechano-receptors and proprioceptors, collectively act like a human spatial sensing system, like a GPS, tracking, and interpreting positioning in space: this bodily-kinaesthetic spatial awareness is very important in learning. This system is sometimes referred to as the *seventh sense* (the sixth sense being *intuition*), activated when we move our bodies to gain different perspectives in *relation* to (egocentric) or without reference to (allocentric) our body position. Movement is "the basis of our concept of space, time, and force and is the primary mode of sense-making, basic even to the world of written languages"

Experience Design: Doing-Sensing 77

(Sheets-Johnstone, 2009: 361) (e.g., "*moving forward,*" "*let's push on*"). The experience of movement, in multiple forms, provides continual stimulation that the brain craves, and movement is important in experiential learning design: "thinking and movement are not separate happenings" (Sheets-Johnstone, 2009: 5).

The unusual symbols that form words are written across a page, and children move their heads and eyes to read them:

> As a child learns to read, the visual forms it sees awaken a lingual-kinetic dynamics, the kinetic dynamics of the sound making that is speech. In the process, otherwise strange and alien visual shapes that have been artificially matched to living body realities – to the fluences of a spoken word – become meaningful. Learning to read is from this experiential perspective a process of bringing the unknown into the world of the known by way of movement.
>
> *(Sheets-Johnstone, 2009: 360)*

The way we see things in space has developed over a long period of time: about one and a half million years ago humans developed advanced spatial capabilities, derived not only from hunter-gatherer work, but more specifically from the creation of tools (Wynn, 2010). The striking of flint and other materials to *hand*-craft three-dimensional axe heads played a significant role in the development of the cerebral cortex in terms of its ability to co-ordinate several regions of the brain concerned with sensory data. Indeed, Baddeley (1986) argues that the development of human skills in tool making are said to have involved the evolutionary foundations of a complex visual spatial memory system (VSMS) that allowed humans to develop a unique capacity beyond that of ape-grade spatial cognition. Like Gallese and Lakoff (2005), Gattis, in *Spatial Schemas and Abstract Thought* (2016) similarly suggests that humans have recruited old parts for new uses. The ancient sensory-motor neural structures have now been put to use in the creation of abstract meaning whilst retaining their original spatial functions. Representations make visible that which is less discernible. It is argued (Lakoff & Johnson, 1999; Lakoff & Nunez, 2000; Gattis, 2001) that humans use a combination of *spatial* and *verbal cues* to create physical (external) and mental (internal) maps or schema to enhance abstract thinking. This spatial-verbal dynamic is embedded within everyday language that offers design cues: *further away, more dense, parallel* to, *higher than, in line with,* and so on. The three modes of experiencing of *doing, sensing,* and *perceiving* don't occur in isolation in the process of learning.

Baddeley suggests that the sensory processing areas of the brain play an important role in memory. He proposes two short-term memory systems: (1) the *visuospatial* sketchpad (responsible for processing *visual* and *spatial* information) and (2) the *phonological* memory system (verbal – *sound* and *speech*). The verbal includes reading, as we "speak" inside our head when reading. In 2000 Baddeley added a third system called the *"episodic buffer"* as an integrating role and a bridge to long-term memory. There is also evidence suggesting motor information may be an additional processing area responsible for working memory system (Sepp et al., 2019).

78 Experience Design: Doing~Sensing

The design of sensory activities that involve the manipulation of objects in space create an important interactional dynamic involving sensory-perceptual experiences linked to abstract cognitive processing. An example of the *integrative* role of the senses, movement, and spatial processing in advanced online environments includes the use of virtual reality (VR) and 3-D gesture-based-technologies (GBT), to create simulation experiences for medical students to apply movement to explore, rotate, and extract various human body parts including organs, muscles, nerves, arteries, and veins.

Research suggests that we create *representations* (also known as schema), both externally and internally. *External schemas* include graphs, models, maps, and drawings. External schema designs are important for experiential learning design as they appear to support the formation of *internal schema*, as the mental (cognitive) equivalent.

Detecting movement is one of our most complex sensory capacities. It is central to learning because movement is a generative source of spatial perception and spatial cognition. We move ourselves to gain different perspectives, we move data, and objects, and furniture to change room layouts in ways that change the environment for learning: *form* in space is connected to *function*. Bodily movement is an "ever-present modality whether an infant or adult: we cannot switch it off like we can close our eyes or clasp our hands over our ears, and kinaesthesia and tactility are the first sensory systems to develop" (Sheets-Johnstone, 2010: 331).

> Throughout the ages philosophers, and educators have believed in the importance of giving students first-hand experiences in learning. Plato, Pestallozi, John Dewey, and other greats have promoted the importance of designing learning activities that engage students' senses and involve them physically in mastering new skills and understanding abstract concepts.
>
> *(Mayes & Williams, 2013: 10)*

In *Relational Being: Beyond Self and Community* psychologist Kenneth Gergen considers movement from an ontological perspective: "in being, we are in motion, carrying with us a past as we move through the present into a becoming" (2009: xxvi). Movement is also used in language to denote the changing self, our *becoming* and *being* someone. We also speak of having *your whole life in front of you* and so language reflects life as movement in time and space (see Chapter 9).

"Hands-on": Doing and Sensing

One of the reasons why the body plays an important role in learning is because it is richly endowed with both internal and external sensing capacities. Those located on the exterior of the body (exteroceptors) connect the outer and inner world experiences and include sight, smell, taste, hearing, and touch, though this "list" doesn't do justice to the considerable sensory capacities. This list implies the hands play an important sensory role because of touch, yet the hands are capable of so much more. Our haptic (touch) senses "interact with vision and other sensory

Experience Design: Doing-Sensing **79**

modalities and so we can look at an object and imagine what it would be like to touch it" (Prinz, 2013: x). The capacities of the hand include a range of functions under the broad categories of perception, action, extended cognition, social interaction, and communication. Prinz argues that the dominance of a visual culture "has cast a shadow on an equally important organ: the hand" (Prinz, 2013: ix). The hand, he says, is *several sense organs* in one, detecting for example heat, cold, touch, pressure, curvature, soft or hard, smooth or rough, wet or dry, and the positioning of the fingers and wrists; that is, they tell us a great deal. Prinz points out that the hands are so important that they are rarely restricted by clothing.

The importance of hands is also embedded in language, with numerous metaphors relating to the importance of using hands to interact with the world. We speak of *first-hand* experiences, *hands-on* experiences, winning *hands down*, *handwriting*, *hand-made, hand-crafted*, and a *hand full*. In experiential learning the importance of integrating the hands within holistic modelling (*hands, heart, head, home,* and *human*) reflects their importance. Homunculus Man is a symbolic figure depicting the size of body parts in proportion to the processing area represented in the brain: interestingly, the hands are enormous. A large area of the brain (left frontal cortex) is involved in the organisation of hand movements, as well as speech and sign language. Hands have a remarkable capability to carry out many different skills or tasks.

Hands become experienced, and along with the brain are capable of amassing considerable amounts of sensory data. Data continuously flows back and forth between hand and brain, as a vital process when engaging in "concrete" tasks. This intimate hand-brain partnership is important in design, and it makes sense to take advantage of the considerable capacities of the hands when designing experiential learning.

The hand has undergone considerable evolutionary transformation to enable it to carry out its many new functions. Bipedalism freed the human hands from supporting the body, enabling them to be used to hunt, catch prey, eat a variety of foods, manipulate objects, and craft tools. Thus, the hand has moved from a *locomotor* function to a finely tuned organ that has the dexterity to explore, manipulate, and craft objects in complex ways. The evolutionary elongation of the human thumb has been important in the development of the considerable dexterity of the hand: "the hand without a thumb is at worst nothing but an animated fish slice" (Wilson, 1998: 128). The thumb evolved to become extended to allow each of the fingertips to interact with the thumb so that the fingers are ideally placed to make fine adjustments using its many tactile receptors. Hands, especially the fingertips, are exquisitely sensitive, containing more tactile receptors than any other part of the body. The hands not only act as receptors obtaining important sensory information, but acting as extensions of the body located at the extremity of the upper arm, sharing nerve endings, blood supply, and muscles (Wilson, 1998). These receptors are termed mechanoreceptors, sited in the dermal layers, the epidermis, the dermis, and the subcutaneous layers. They detect tactile sensations and finger muscle indentations. Mechanoreceptors give

80 Experience Design: Doing~Sensing

instantaneous feedback to the brain, and the brain in turn responds to the signals, so that necessary adjustments can be made to tendons and muscles.

It is important to consider how "hands-on" experiences enhance learning: the hands are capable of extended reach, to feel, point, pinch, and detect changes in movement, texture, and shape of objects. But collectively these capacities extend the role of the hand as an extension of the brain.

Research on the capacities of hands is extensive, and the following titles are worth reading as they illustrate the importance of the hands for learning: *From Hand to Mouth: The Origins of Language* (Corballis, 2002) describes how hand gestures were important to language development. *The Hand: How Its Use Shapes the Brain, Language, and Human Capacities* (Wilson, 1998: 7), highlights how the hand had enhanced our human capacities, proclaiming that "no serious account of human life can ignore the central importance of the human hand." In *The Hand and the Brain: From Lucy's Thumb to the Thought-Controlled Robotic Hand*, Lundborg (2014) notes that the hand has been referred to as an *outer brain,* a *reflection of the mind,* and an *extension of the brain.*

Doing: Touching and Manipulating Objects

The hands interact with objects and materials, and this capacity is particularly important in the design of a concrete experience. Haptics is the study of the perception of objects by touch, or proprioception (proprioception is the ability of the body to perceive its own position in space). Chapter 2 discussed the use of touch screens, gesture-based movements, and pointing (of fingers). We attend to, and integrate sensory information about shape, colour, distance, relations, patterns, similarities, difference, and movement; we hold, rotate, construct, and draw objects, and they can be used to *represent* something other than what they are.

Sociologists refer to objects as offering *affordance,* that is, what an object offers to an agent (person) as they interact with it, in a particular setting. The holding of objects can stimulate curiosity or project our thoughts. Objects can be used as a "talking stick." where only the person holding the object can speak, whilst others listen. Objects can include artefacts, 3-D models, specimens, and art works: all can be used to evoke and provoke engagement in learning, and a significant body of literature has recently emerged about the way objects can be used to scaffold and facilitate learning. Known as Object-Based Learning (OBL) (for more on this topic see Chatterjee & Hannan, 2016), this approach involves multi-sensory interrogation of real, related, and/or artificial objects, either alone or with others. The use of objects was briefly explored in Chapters 1 and 2 in relation to their use in museums and art galleries. Much of the literature on OBL relates to museum and art gallery collections within the context of *handling, interpreting,* and *reading* objects. This method of thinking through object manipulation can really engage learners, and object-based learning can be used to support learners who struggle with speech-dominant or text-dominant explanations.

The hands actively manipulate external objects, stimulating imagination. Objects support the construction of internal meaning through physical-sensory-emotional-cognitive interactions. The active manipulation of objects can also generate a questioning or investigative approach: the hands stimulate investigative processes to support the formulation of abstract ideas. Objects allow for differences, similarities, and defects to be identified. Objects such as artefacts found in archaeological sites can create an understanding of historic events and generate a sense of wonder. An emotional response can occur when ancient objects used long ago by our ancestors are handled.

Woodall (2016: 133) explores the idea of *rummaging* when using museum collections as a strategy for creative thinking and imaginative engagement, thus "allowing for the unknown, the serendipitous and the unexpected to take place." In chainsaw training I have seen several chains being passed around to identify defective parts that had serious implications for safety. Zoologists are taught through the manipulation and examination of specimens: establishing what the legs and body shape indicate about locomotion, what the mouth and teeth suggest about diet, and so forth. Zoologists learn to *read* specimens, as material texts.

Talking whilst handling material aids the learning process by thinking aloud. In a practical environmental charity that I worked for, the experience design for a session called "An Introduction to Practical Tools" was based on seeing tools as valuable like antiques, with a design based on a TV programme called *The Antiques Road Show*. Tools were placed on the floor and people were asked to select a tool, and see if they could work out from observation of their design what they were used for, and what they cost to buy. Correct answers were then offered with discussion.

In a Training the Trainer session I have seen a participant demonstrate tree felling by bringing objects indoors: a *real* tree stump, with a ready-made wedge and felling cuts, and they used masking tape on the floor to highlight safety and danger zones. Their session proved to be highly engaging. Objects were variously used for simulation, imagination, and to develop awareness of important safety issues.

And More: Hands That "Read" and "Talk"

The hand also communicates inwards in its role in the body-brain partnership. The hand also communicates outwards, playing an important role in social life. "We use hands to greet, to console, to caress, and to fight. A hand on the shoulder can bring comfort, and a handshake can promote trust." (Prinz, Foreword: Hand Manifesto, in Radman, 2013: xiv). "Touch precedes, informs and overwhelms language" (Classen, 2005: 13). Linguistically the use of the word *touch* has different meanings. We shake hands as a form of greeting, or to seal a deal. We talk of *being out of touch*, *touching* on issues, or being *touched* by a

82 Experience Design: Doing~Sensing

gesture of kindness. In the Hindu caste system, the term *"untouchables"* infers low status. Many sensory words associated with thinking are tactile based, such as a person being regarded as being *sharp*, that they *grasped* the meaning (visual sensory metaphors are also located within language: they are *brilliant, so bright*). Books have traditionally been regarded as *tactile* objects, and this, to an extent, is still the case as touch is required to read and turn over the pages or open a dictionary in a digital book.

> The pen was destined to become my life. And so it did, as I slowly worked my way toward a professorship in psychology. I loved to ponder and to write; the sound of the pen on paper, the flowing of the ink, the mounting columns of "my thoughts" – all produced a special thrill.
>
> *(Gergen, 1999: 1)*

The keyboard may be replacing the sensory experience of the pen on paper, but we refer to the digital *touchpad*, and *touchscreen*. When we touch something, it also touches us, and this is the notion of reciprocity introduced in the first chapter which demonstrates how we more fully feel our own fingertips when we touch something or someone. Often the experience of touching is taken for granted, and so touch is often neglected as an experiential mode for learning.

In non-verbal communication the face is important, especially for the communication of emotions. The face communicates through numerous facial expressions. In fact, 42 of the 600 muscles of the body are located around the mouth and face. The movement and spatial orientation of the hands is the basis of a gesture. Sign language involves the extensive use of hand gestures. The use of braille for those with considerable visual impairment allows the "fingertips to delicately stroke meaning out of the surface textures" (Classen, 2005: 13). It is also interesting that the congenitally blind who have never seen purposive gestures use their hands when they talk. Those born without limbs also report that their minds gesture, and their bodies attempt to carry out these movements. Important in non-verbal communication, a gesture is an intentional hand movement directly tied to speech, and gestures are important in terms of their relationship to language and thought. Susan Goldin-Meadow spent many years studying this: her mentors included Piaget, and she learnt how important it is to "watch" children as they learn: "I chose to watch their hands" (2003: x) she remarks. Her book, *Hearing Gesture: How Our Hands Help Us Think* (Goldin-Meadow, 2003), outlines how the significance of gesture became more apparent whilst watching tapes of children in Piagetian conversation tasks, first with the sound only, and then without sound. What she discovered was that children could not keep their hands still, and when she watched the tapes with no sound their gestures frequently conveyed the same information that they had articulated in speech. The second breakthrough was the significance of gesture-speech mismatches that revealed *unspoken thoughts*, that sometimes indicated that children were receptive to new

Experience Design: Doing-Sensing **83**

learning. The title of Goldin-Meadow's book points to the fact that hands not only speak, they help people to think.

Gestures are said to reduce cognitive load (see also Meyer & Roxana, 2003). The way gestures are categorised indicates the importance of concepts of space, movement, pictures, objects, metaphors, and concepts in reducing cognitive load in learning. *Kinetographic gestures* depict bodily action, *spatial gestures* depict a spatial movement, *pictographic gestures* depict a drawing in the air, *metaphoric gestures* depict abstract ideas rather than a concrete object, and *dietic gestures* are used to indicate people, objects, or locations that exist in the real world. These gesture categories reflect the main topics covered in this chapter, and collectively they highlight the complex role played by the moving body in our ability to learn. We talk and think in gesture, and *"the message that moves between speaker and hearer includes not only what comes out of the mouth and goes into the ear but also what comes out of the hands and goes into the eyes"* (Goldin-Meadow, 2003: 241). To ignore gestures, Goldin-Meadow suggests, is to ignore a significant part of the conversation.

Recent neuroimaging research on semantic memory by Binder and Desai (2011) shows how specific parts of the brain, notably *sensory, motor,* and *emotion* systems, all *participate* in the understanding of language. In other regions of the brain multiple perceptual streams converge enabling higher level abstract processing, such as object recognition, language comprehension, the storage and access of information about people, and the ability to remember the past and imagine the future.

Doing the "Real" Thing

A design question to consider is whether it is better to design an activity that is perceived as real? The "Tell, Show, Do" Cone of Instructional Techniques (Dale, 1969) implies that we learn more from doing it for *real*, the *real* thing, rather than just watching, or simply being told about something. This idea requires closer examination as it is unclear as to what constitutes *"real."* Much depends on learner *perceptions* of reality, and elements of realness can be subtly influenced by careful design. The opposite of *real* might be a simulation, a virtual reality, a digital enhanced animation, or the use of an artificial environment. The notion of *mixed* reality or *alternative reality* (e.g., an avatar) are all worth considering in design. *Lowering reality* can create a perception of lower consequential risks.

In technologically supported learning online the sense of "reality" is limited by the two-dimensional nature of a screen experience. *Virtual reality* appears three-dimensional, and it is increasingly used for medical teaching on a virtual human body: this use of a digital reality has distinct advantages and disadvantages. Human bodies, that is, the real thing, are traditionally used, but VR simulations present different opportunities for learning about and manipulating body parts such as organs, bones, muscles, and nerves with gestural hand movements. Body parts can be taken out and put back, they can be rotated as digital objects in these three-dimensional formats. Students can understand spatial *positioning* of body parts in relationship to other parts. Simulations require careful design in terms of the interactional dynamics and the functional potential of the technology to maximise learning opportunities. Note the earlier mention of the Titanic Museum where an old sepia photograph is projected onto a screen and made more engaging by digitally superimposing *real* people, dressed in Victorian outfits, walking across the picture.

Shifts in assessment practices are resulting in movement away from traditional essays and exams, towards more *realistic* and *authentic* assessments. A typical example would be to move away from a standard series of exam questions to the use of "real life" scenarios and case material taken from professional practice, or from newspaper reporting of real events, for example. *Production* might be in a variety of formats: viva, report, schedule, or plan of action to take, relating the case to the situation regarding the law, design of an infographic, step-by-step guide for a specific group or community, a guidance leaflet (e.g., healthy eating), design of a workflow cart, conducting research, writing a reflective log. Here it is useful to re-consider the active verbs presented in Chapter 1: *produce* a (real) video, radio or television program, podcast; *choreograph* a dance; *invite learners to teach* a webinar, play, blog, *design* a slide presentation . . . to/for others; *fill in* the blanks, jigsaws, quizzes, crosswords, anagrams, *solve* puzzles . . . *draw* up a set of ideas, draw a cartoon strip, an image to represent . . . *practice* on dummies, bake cakes, fill cookies, make buttons, embroider information, bandage a volunteer, operate machinery under safe conditions . . . *analyse and explore* case studies, real-life scenarios; *sort and categorise* information; *devise* questions to ask another team . . . *create–build* models, a replica, body sculpture; *create* a digital game that. . . .

 DESIGN ILLUSTRATION 10 AUTHENTIC, EXPERIENTIAL ASSESSMENT OF LEARNING.

Traditional Exam or Essay Question

Outline the principal physiological changes that a subject deprived of water in a hot climate would experience, describing the effect of dehydration on the body, and how the homeostatic mechanisms of the body would try to retain water and regulate body temperature in a hot climate.

Authentic Assessment Example

Context

June (55-years-old) went missing for 2 weeks in the Australian Outback near Alice Springs. She and her friends in their 40s were on an afternoon four-wheel drive across the outback near Alice Springs, in Australia. It was on this journey that their car got bogged down and stuck in the mud. Jane stayed with the car whilst the others walked to get help. Left alone with the car in the isolated outback, Jane dug a hole underneath the car to provide shelter during the scorching daytime temperature of 40°C and slept in the vehicle at night when the temperature dropped to 25°C. Jane had limited food and drink. Initially, she drank 2 litres of bottled water left in the car, but when she ran out, she drank dirty water collected from puddles, which she purified by boiling and filtering it through a T-shirt. The only food she had was two packs of biscuits and some dry noodles. After 10 days when supplies had run out, Jane left the car and set out to find shelter and water, leaving a note in the vehicle. After wandering for several days in the outback she eventually stumbled across a drinking hole for cattle. It was here that she was later found by police and airlifted to hospital suffering the effects of dehydration, heat exhaustion, and starvation. Her two friends were not found. (All names are fictionalised, although this has been based on a real case).

Experiential Task

- *Prepare a literature review* including a list of at least three websites, two journal articles, and one other data source you would use to inform yourself about this kind of context.
- *Provide a short audio commentary* (200 words) in which you explain how you accessed and prioritised the reference sources to which you have referred.
- Evaluate the information that has been provided in this scenario *in the form of a note for your files*, explaining the physiological changes that Jane would have experienced during her ordeal, the effect of dehydration on the body, and how the homeostatic mechanisms of the body would try to retain water and the regulation of body temperature in a hot climate such as that found in the outback, and what happens in heat exhaustion (up to 1,500 words).
- Using what you have learned in this exercise, *draft an advice leaflet for travellers* setting out on such a journey, containing advice on staying safe and what they should ensure they have in the way of equipment and supplies before setting off.
- This example is adapted and reproduced from original material developed as an assessment question by Nikki Jordan-Mahy, Sheffield Hallam University. It is adapted and reproduced with her kind permission. Further examples can be found on the website https://sally-brown.net/kay-sambell-and-sally-brown-covid-19-assessment-collection/.

Doing as Playing

Through *Play for Peace*, children, youth, adults, and organizations around the world have a platform to come together and create powerful, meaningful interactions. These individuals are transformed into architects and leaders who design experiences to promote and enhance peace across the world. These experiences can move whole communities and societies towards a more peaceful world.

In the design of learning experiences, the role of fun, play, and enjoyment in the desire to learn and the enjoyment of learning should not be underestimated. Play and playfulness is important to everyone, not just children: play brings out our creativity and sense of fun, offering a wide range of social, emotional, physical, and mental benefits. The website *Play for Peace: From Conflict to Compassion*, highlights how this concept of play can be used as a platform for children, youth, adults, and organisations around the world to come together to create more meaningful and powerful social interactions, as architects and leaders of peace.

Starting from a young age we are often reminded that there are more "important" things to do than play: for adults "play deficit" is common. Moseley and Whitton (2019: 4) describe playfulness as "a state of mind or an attitude; a willingness to accept and embrace the constraints of . . . any activity, to try something new, to attempt something difficult where success is not guaranteed." Their book, *Playful Learning: Events and Activities to Engage Adults* (Whitton & Moseley, 2019) contains many creative design ideas (for more fun ideas see Chapter 10 on customer service training).

Gamification theory in education suggests that learners learn best when they are having fun. Gamification applies many of the core features of operant conditioning such as using rewards to change behaviour in a game. Gamification encompasses many theoretical areas taken from cognitive psychology, technology, design, and strategy, and is based on nudging people to change their behaviours through play. Gamification involves using "game"-based elements such as competition between peers, scoring points, teamwork, and league tables, and these are said to drive engagement and help learners assimilate new information and test their knowledge. The game play environment must be comfortable, enjoyable, and experimental and players can test, explore, practice, and, importantly, fail safely. Gamification is big news in the learning world at the moment and is heavily focused on computer-based gaming technologies, but gamification can be done with a pencil and paper.

The use of digital games to enhance teaching and learning at all educational levels has increased in recent years. Whitton (2014) explores the research and theory of four aspects of games that use the digital medium: games as *active learning* environments, games as *motivational tools*, games as *play*grounds, and games as *learning technologies*. Her definitions of gaming as (1) a challenging activity; (2) structured with rules, goals, progression, and rewards; (3) separate from the *real* world; (4) undertaken in the spirit of *play*; and (5) often played against or with other people offers a design structure (see also *Digital Games and Learning: Research and Theory*, Whitton, 2014; *Digital Games and Learning*, de Freitas & Maharg, 2011; *Instructional Design for E-Learning*, Arshavskiy, 2017).

In gaming, high-fidelity simulation graphics create a compelling impression of reality, of *visual realism*, though this is less important when there is little need for accurate representations of reality such as that of a basic flight simulator. A full pilot training flight simulator is an example where the requirement for many elements of the experience to be real are high, including the gadgets, sounds effects, movements of the plane, hand movements, switches, and the overall look and ambience, despite it not being real. The consequences of mistakes when flying on real planes is high. A different reality principle arises in experiential management development or team building activities using the outdoors. Raft building has long been a popular activity in outdoor learning. The building of the raft, and the paddling of it, becomes an experience used *for* learning: to facilitate the exploration of real group dynamic processes that can occur in relation to leadership issues, or communication processes. Abseiling down a cliff is not perceived as a "real" experience for managers exploring group dynamics, yet understanding and overcoming fear, or the development of self-confidence, self-esteem, or strategies for developing resilience in the face of adversity, might be the reason for the design of these learning experiences. These *activities* are not perceived as real but the mental *processing* they provoke are often very real.

Doing as a Simulated Experience: Sports Coaching

Sports coaching has advanced considerably in the design and use of *simulations* that mimic *real* conditions. Sports coaching involves *breaking down* skills and skill errors, including the conditions under which the errors occurred. Practising rugby passes after dipping the balls in buckets of water to simulate rainy conditions, wearing headphones that recreate the loud crowd noises of booing and hooters just before kicking a penalty, running with heavy weights, swimming with buckets attached, or swimming with clenched fists, are all simple examples used in sports coaching. The trampoline coach teaches back somersaults in the early stages by allowing the novice to experience the movement by dropping onto one side of the bed of the trampoline in a tightly bundled body form so that the feet and bottom simultaneously land on the bed and flip the body over backwards in a safe way (the vulnerable head is tightly tucked up). In this way the basic bodily sensations of performing the backward somersault are experienced first.

Thus, different layers or elements of reality can be manipulated: real products, real people, or real emotions can be adjusted in simulated experience designs. Design Illustration 11 explores these layers with respect to the design of negotiation skills training.

> **DESIGN ILLUSTRATION 11 DOING IT FOR REAL.**

If learners are learning to negotiate, then design negotiating experiences. If they are going to learn to design and deliver an event, then let the learners design, deliver, and evaluate a real event to a real audience. They can charge real money to attend, to create profits for a charitable cause. Designs can flow from low levels of reality, low risk, and simplicity, to high reality, high risk, and high complexity. When learning to fly a plane or when attending to patients in an emergency crash situation, then it is important that there is some level of experience of the "real" thing. Flight simulators, crash simulations, and simulated negotiations all help with the journey of learning, moving towards being able to cope with complex situations, and develop the skills of accomplishing a difficult task in real life. The learning can be broken down (deconstructed) into its component parts or chunks, such as landing or take off. Simulation designs have many differing layers of reality.

In negotiating training, the experiential design might commence by including a simple paper-based exercise, for example, by drawing up and agreeing to a contract pricing for negotiation. Learners might move on to practice negotiating the purchase of a car, and the design might include trading in an old one. Although negotiating with a simulated car deal, real experienced negotiators (people), and real cars can be parked in the car park (real objects) to be physically examined. This experience provides the learners with access to real time information about the state of the car (tyres, engine, bodywork, book price) for the purposes of negotiation. The experience design might then create the types or contexts of negotiation that learners are required to become proficient in. Moving to full "reality" is thus a gradual process, and the levels of confidence and expertise develop gradually.

Construction and Reconstruction in Design

Learning can be enhanced when there is a perceived level of *relevance* and *reality* to the subject matter or the activity. The previous teaching examples highlight the need for care in design: deconstruction requires a sound, holistic knowledge of how people learn (and fail to learn). In experiential learning design it is recommended that good practice involves deciding the end point and working backwards: the end becomes a good starting place for *"deconstruction."* Questions to develop end point thinking might include: *what do we want learners to have learnt by the end?* (the HELM can be used as a diagnostic tool), though end points of any learning experience are not completely predictable. The process

Experience Design: Doing-Sensing **89**

of design by deconstruction involves simultaneously visualising the part-whole design.

The movement from simplicity to complexity requires a degree of *scaffolding* to support the learner in a staged approach, working between anxiety and boredom in the zone of "proximal development" (Vygotsky, 1978). Knowledge, concepts, ideas, emotions, attitudes, or skills can all be broken down into their basic components. The learner's experience is a reversal of the deconstruction from the end point: the learner's journey is one of *reconstruction* towards the end point.

Imagining Doing Something

Imagination is essentially a process of mental *simulation*. Recent findings from neuroscience show that *imagining* shares the same neural systems as used when we physically *do* something. Gallese and Lakoff (2005) suggest that if we read a sentence about someone picking up a glass, but can't imagine someone picking it up, then we can't understand the sentence. They argue that *imagining*, and *doing*, and *understanding* all share the same neural substrate. Language itself is infused with sensory, bodily, and spatial metaphors to help us to *imagine* and *understand*. We build internal mental working models from social interactions, bodily activity, spoken and written words, and from photographs and illustrations. Similarly, when we go to the theatre or watch a film we *imagine*, share, and *experience* the emotions performed by actors, because of what are called *mirror neurons* (see Rizzolatti & Sinigaglia, 2008). This demonstrates how our brains are profoundly shaped by social interactions.

When we read or listen, we imagine what the words on the page, or the speaker, are intimating: thinking involves *interpretation* and *imagination*. When we imagine moving, the same part of the brain is used as when we physically move. We think mostly through language, and language is infused with movement and body-spatial *metaphors*: to *grasp* (something) is a *bodily movement* representing understanding.

Large areas of the brain are devoted to movement, including the control of the muscles used in manipulating objects, eating food, and making facial gestures. In the design of learning it makes sense to create active *sensory-motor* (doing) experiences that help people not only to *imagine*, but to experience it *first-hand* and so create an *understanding* of, and *acquaintance* with, the actual physical act of *doing*. But different interpretive meanings occur when people imagine. People comment that having read the book, the film turned out to be not how they *imagined* it! When we teach by *telling* there are always going to be different *imaginal interpretations* or *errors of imagination*. In the transfer of thoughts from facilitator to learner when speaking or reading out, much interpretation is left to imagination.

In learning programmes for children on the web such as Lexialearning.com, many of the principles highlighted above are central to their successful design. Their online videos demonstrate that the use of movement (of numbers and words) using gestures on a *touch*pad or *mouse*, supports and reinforces learning. Touch screen computers are excellent to involve bodily engagement in learning, to identify and manipulate things, to enlarge, to move or drag words into categories (containers), to put words together after they have been broken down (deconstructed) into segments, and for joining syllables together (part-whole). *Gesture* based technologies continue to develop in ways that support the learning partnership of brain and body. Learners get immediate feedback, which is often a moving item, which focuses attention. Feedback takes the form of a "like" symbol with a thumbs up for a correct answer, or a specific sound such as a round of applause. Design Illustration 12 highlights a *movement*-based experience to understand the principles of classifying and categorising (e.g., for fauna and flora) using objects.

DESIGN ILLUSTRATION 12 SENSORY EXPERIENCES: TOUCHING, MOVING, OBSERVING, CATEGORISING, AND CREATING A CLASSIFICATION CHART.

Nails, Screws, Nuts, and Bolts

The design problem is concerned with the difficult task of learning about the topic of *classification*. This might include the classification of living things such as plants or animals, or the classification of events, for example. An important conceptual metaphor in classification is that each category *contains* similar things, as in a *container* (see the Design Illustration in chapter 6 on coloured containers (bins) for coding in research). Objects used in the following example *belong* to several groupings, and they need to be put in categories, and the rationale for the *categories* explored and explained, in order to form a *classification* or *typology*.

One small container is given to each group. The container *contains* many different *forms* of "fixtures and fittings," notably different *types* of nails, screws, plugs, and nuts and bolts. The contents are tipped out onto a large sheet of paper. Using careful observation, hand manipulation, and conversation (multiple senses), these items are classified into groupings or *types* which are then put in a classification *hierarchy* based on the core *features*. Features include *threads* and *no-threads*, the format of the head (screw shapes, smooth and flat heads, angled heads), the way they are used with tools as some are banged/hit, and some are twisted/turned; therefore some might be used with *hammers*, some with *screwdrivers*, and some with *spanners*. These *functional* differences are discussed. Some have related components, for example, *screws* go with wall *plugs*. This experiential design involves object manipulation, careful observation, and discussion of the objects, placing them on paper in a way that *represents* distinguishing features (similarity and difference). Each group then draws a classification "hierarchy" around the objects to make visible what they have discovered as a spatial-relational diagram. Colleagues have used stationary or sweets for this approach (often some sweets disappear).

A Classification Hierarchy Drawn to Make Observations Visible

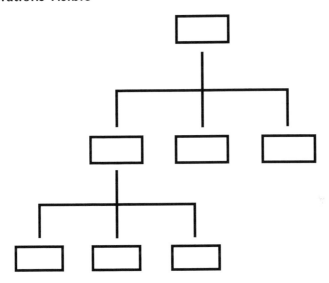

FIGURE 4.4 Classifying fixtures and fittings, sweets or stationary.

Doing as a Co-Creative Design Process

Doing can promote active engagement, participation, accomplishment, and achievement. *Doing* can also be about producing something and *doing* can include participants co-creating their experiential learning design. This is the case in Dramaturgy, for example, the activities are part of an unfolding *script, production, performance, journey*, and *stage*. Design structures are regularly revisited and monitored by facilitators and participants so as to co-create the evolving experiences. The underlying design principle is that of a series of *activity waves* that are carefully balanced: social, physical, reflective, and emotional waves all create experiences that require different energy levels. Martin et al. (2004) describe over 30 different *activities* under these headings. A 30-point activity design *typology*, based on my analysis of the designs of outdoor programmes, is presented at the end of this chapter. It includes setting a *target* or *goal*; creating a sense of a *journey*, a *destination*, and a *theme*; the design of physical, emotional, or social activities; the use of *fun* or *play*, *quiet time*, *collaborative* and/or *competitive* activities; the use of *rules*, *obstacles* or *restrictions*, and *time constraints*, and more.

The Multisensory Nature of Multimedia Learning

The term *media* typically refers to the use of a variety of artistic or communicative media. Multi-media refers to multi-sensory experiences, though in his introductory chapter Mayer argues that *meaningful learning* does not occur *per se* through mere engagement of the body and its senses: a cognitive engagement is also necessary. Multimedia is usually linked to the use of a computer to present and combine text, graphics, audio, and video with links and tools that let the user navigate, interact, create, and communicate. However, multi-media research concentrates on foundational principles about how people learn by building mental representations from *words* (spoken or printed text) and *pictures* (e.g., photos, maps, video, or animation), as included, for example, in textbooks, slide presentations, digital lessons, simulation, and gaming. The core multi-media theory is that of Dual Coding Theory (see Paivio, 1986; Sadoski & Pavio, 2013), which is concerned with two distinct cognitive processing channels: one for visual *imagery*, and one specialised for processing *words and text* (especially the sounds and symbols of language).

Multimedia learning theories have developed extensively over the last decade, and the findings have important design implications. The most comprehensive texts in Multimedia Learning, are the edited books by Mayer, and his second edition textbook (2014) presents 34 edited chapters with over 20 basic and advanced multimedia principles. All are concerned with experiences associated with processing words and pictures (see also DeSalle, 2018, particularly the chapter called "No Limits"). Mayer views learning as a "constructive process" whereby *meaningful learning* requires a depth of understanding, the creation of mental models, and the transfer of learning to novel situations, as opposed to rote learning where "information" is merely added to memory. Mayer asks what the best way is to promote meaningful learning. The answer, he suggests "rests in active learning – meaningful outcomes occur as a result of learner's activity during learning" (2014: 21).

Multi-sensory design is central to online learning and gaming environments, and many of the experiential learning pedagogic principles are applicable to digital learning designs (see Beard et al., 2007). In a chapter titled "Games as Multi-Sensory Experiences," Nicola Whitton discusses the range of multi-media principles that are concerned with core sensory experiences, particularly that of language (text-words) and graphics (visuals). Whitton points out the limitations of the dualistic examination of just text and visuals: "modern digital games employ an array of media types, including visual elements, animations, cut scenes and video, text, speech, sound effects and music" (Whitton, 2014: 169). Furthermore, the evolving haptic interface has also added gesture-touch and vibration capacities to enhance the online learning experience.

Experience Design: Doing-Sensing **93**

Activity Design: Sensory Dulling and Sensory Focus

The senses can focus attention on specific things: illustrated by the ability to tune into or out of a particular conversation in a gathering of people. Another classic example of sensory focusing is that of the commuter and the tourist. The same stimuli are available to both, yet often the senses of the tourist are excited and highly receptive, craving new stimuli, whilst the senses of the commuter are dulled by *habit*uation. Sensory variation applies to learning: the brain craves new or novel experiences, by changing the type, number, or frequency of sensory modalities in use. Attention and focus can also be enhanced by *guiding* awareness on specific experiences, as highlighted in the design of signalling-cueing multimedia principles in Design Illustration 13.

Visual presentations with too many slides, or speeches that last too long with little variation in terms of pace, or tone of voice, can quickly give rise to habituation, or sensory dulling. Abraham (1997) describes how a hurricane in the US destroyed many technologies that we can become dependent on. After the hurricane the whole community became much more *aware* of the natural sensory world all around them; hurricane damage refocussed their attention. Although the human brain craves stimulation, in design terms it is important to create changes in sensory experiences. Good design recognises and limits the phenomenon of habituation to reduce disinterest or boredom: the sensory modality and levels of stimulation should ideally be changed at intervals, sometimes as little as every 15–20 minutes. *Pod*casts, and video *clips* are popular because they are *bite* size sensory inputs.

Physical Intelligence

There are two important steps in the processing of information from the sensory organs. *Sensation* is traditionally regarded as referring to lower-level signals often operating below levels of consciousness, whereas *perception* is a higher level of processing, accessible to our consciousness and available to be communicated to others. In *Sensation: The New Science of Physical Intelligence* (Lobel, 2014), numerous research experiments are described where participants were influenced by their sensory experiences. Lobel explores the many subconscious influences of our sensory systems, describing how we might use such knowledge of these sensory processes to our advantage. The reference to physical intelligence in the title is interesting in that "behaviours appear to be influenced by physical sensations that are metaphorically linked to abstract concepts" (2014: 193). This reinforces the notion that there are multiple forms of intelligence, which was proposed by Howard Gardner in 1983.

The links between sensations, thinking, judgement, and language appear quite remarkable: *warm* temperatures make us temporarily friendly, and interestingly we also speak of someone showing *warmth*. Another linguistic metaphor is to shed *light* on the situation, and the symbol of a light bulb is often used as an icon to denote innovative thinking, sometimes referred to as a *lightbulb moment*. In a series of interesting experiments participants who were exposed to a lightbulb (rather than a fluorescent tube), performed better in an innovation experiment! Sensory intelligence, as the ability to focus on and stay with sensory experiences without over processing them (cognitively), is discussed in the next chapter (see also Beard & Wilson, 2018).

Doing: Tools and Technology

A digital learning *activity*, that is, digital *doing*, is defined as "*a specific interaction of learner(s) with other(s) using specific tools and resources, orientated towards specific outcomes*" (Beetham, 2020: 34). Architect Peter Broberg refers to humans as *Homo sapiens technicus*, and he created the term *technolution* to describe how technology has significantly influenced human evolution, particularly through the extension and improvement of the capacities of the human body and brain (Lundborg, 2014). Recent human evolution is inextricably linked to the story of technology: hunter-gatherer activities included the crafting and use of various tools and weapons and following this, extensive farming-agricultural technologies were developed. The printing press and the steam engine, for example, caused major changes in the way society organised itself. Now we are in a similar epoch: the age of digital technologies as tools. Whilst the digital screen experience limits the human capacities for learning due to size and flatness, as gesture-based and multi-dimensional technologies emerge, the capacities of the *brain-body dynamic* are being restored and continually enhanced. Digital technologies create a very different kind of relationship between learners and teachers and what is to be learnt, and user generated content is becoming an increasingly significant feature of the digital world. Whilst technology is driving the design of more personalised, self-directed, learning, ironically face-to-face learning in physical environments may well become an expensive luxury.

Attention involves arousal at three different processing levels: (1) to *alert*, (2) to *orientate*, and (3) to execute higher level *thinking and decision making* such as planning, danger avoidance, making decisions, detecting of errors, and other high-level cortex functioning (see Chapter 6). The following design illustration highlights the use of real physical objects with a design process that has high levels of attention (this can be adapted in a digital format).

 DESIGN ILLUSTRATION 13 USING THE HANDS TO EXPLORE COMPLEX CONCEPTS.

The Circular (Industrial) Economy (A "Living Systems" Approach)

The concept of an *industrial ecology* is described in the book *Perspectives on Industrial Ecology* (Bourg & Erkman, 2017). The following is an extract of the description of the concept on the rear cover of the book:

> Business as usual in terms of industrial and technological development – even if based on a growing fear of pollution and shortages of natural resources – will never deliver sustainable development. However, the growing interest in recent years in the new science of industrial ecology (IE), and the idea that industrial systems should mimic quasi-cyclical functions of natural ecosystems and "industrial food chain," holds promise in addressing not only short-term environmental problems but also the long-term holistic evolution of industrial systems. This possibility requires a number of key conditions to be met, not least the restructuring of our manufacturing and consumer society to reduce the effects of material and energy flows at the very point in history when globalisation is rapidly increasing them.

This is a difficult concept to fully "grasp," and so a useful learning design question is:

How can this difficult concept of industrial ecology be experienced so that it can be more fully understood through acquaintance with rather than merely knowledge of the concept?

One experiential approach presented next is merely an illustration. It is one format that uses movement, real products, object-based learning, spatial cognition, and navigational cues and codes, and group interactions. This learning experience has been extensively tried and tested (and continuously improved) across the globe.

Methods

The following is a well-known warm up activity for opening the mind to the process of discovery. The image below is given out to small groups to explore. There is a time limit of three minutes to answer the question: how many squares are in the picture.

With a plenary review the following thoughts can be surfaced and discussed.

(1) At first glance the answer is simple. (2) There is more to discover if the image is carefully explored. (3) Some individuals see things that others cannot see. (4) It is important to explore the detail (parts) and big picture (whole). (5) Be open and go beyond first impressions.

96 Experience Design: Doing~Sensing

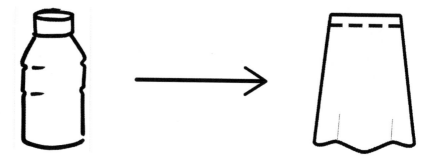

FIGURE 4.5 Plastic water bottle and a school skirt made from plastic bottles.

(For more short activities designs see *The Handbook of Experiential Learning*, Silberman, 2007.)

Then for the major session *real* commercial products, that in various ways demonstrate a reduced environmental impact, are placed in four bags. Each bag represents four areas for analysis: (1) Technology, (2) Materials, (3) Domestic products, and (4) Artistic products. The participants are divided into four groups and asked to empty out the contents of the bags onto a large table. They usually pick up these objects straight away, to explore them with their hands (a code is offered to remind people of the sequence – see Figure 4.5). Handling them initiates the skills of observation and enquiry. Closer examination of each of the objects also generates the questioning of their relationship to the other objects.

Next a simple relationship is exposed to demonstrate a simple analysis. The following example places a laminated signalling (arrow) to establish the *relationship* between these two objects: plastic bottles are used to manufacture clothing.

Other items, such as pencils and rucksacks, can also be made out of plastic bottles, and so a more complex radial analysis can be illustrated as shown in the conceptual representation in Figure 4.6.

To support further analytical processing, navigational tools are used to guide participants.

Navigational Tools

Cues

BLACK ARROWS are used to help learners make visible the patterns that they are able to detect and construct. Arrows made of card are supplied to support such relational thinking, for example, an arrow can be placed between a plastic bottle and clothing made from plastic bottles, or between a corn can and a carpet made from corn. Participants then proceed to a consideration of the abstract thinking that can be derived from the contents of all four bags.

Experience Design: Doing-Sensing **97**

Radial relational patterns that increase the value of recycled plastic due to increased demand

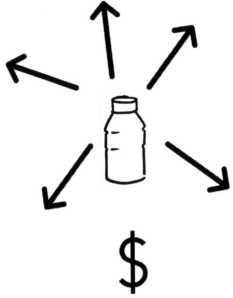

FIGURE 4.6 Radial relational patterns that show the increased value of recycled plastic due to increased demand.

Handling Sequence Code

H.D.O.A.C. = Handle-Discuss-Organise-Analyse-Conceptualise (designed from observations of participants over many years. *Looked at, handled, conversations, looking for patterns*, etc.). This simplistic format has similarities with Bloom's Hierarchical Taxonomy.

Using a Guiding Code for an Experiential Activity

Resource Suggestions (Objects)

Table 1 Technology Products: Examples might include a rucksack made from recycled plastic bottles with a built-in solar panel, windup radio, solar watch, solar calculator, solar phone charger, wind up phone charger with ordinary bulb and with LED bulbs, wind-up torch, toothbrush that lights up and flashes for 3 minutes, a plastic swipe card for access to a hotel room, a smartphone, a kinetic watch.

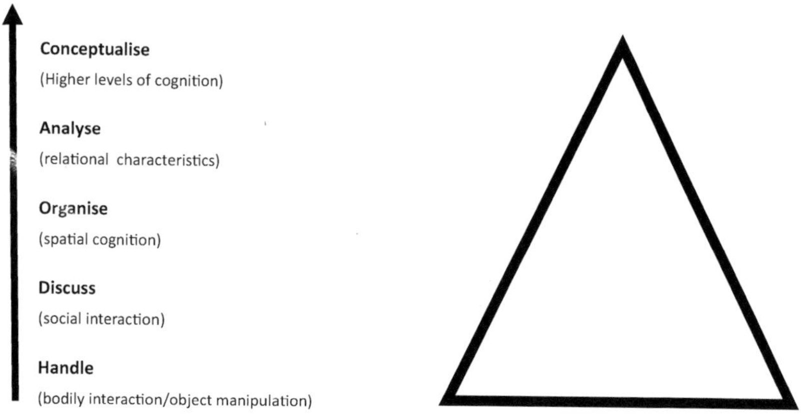

98 Experience Design: Doing~Sensing

Conceptualise
(Higher levels of cognition)

Analyse
(relational characteristics)

Organise
(spatial cognition)

Discuss
(social interaction)

Handle
(bodily interaction/object manipulation)

FIGURE 4.7 Using a guiding code (HDOAC) for an experiential activity.

Table 2 Domestic Products: Examples might include standard hotel toothbrushes, natural wood chewable toothbrush, chewable toothbrush in plastic ball, nail brush, eco washing disc to clean clothes in a washing machine, razorblades, various razors, washing up brushes with changeable heads.

Table 3 Artistic products: Examples might include a spoon redesigned as a coat hanger, a fork redesigned as a coat hanger, earrings made from bottle tops, necklace made from magazines, necklace made from electrical cable ties, belt made from old discarded climbing rope, belt made from old bicycle tyre, plastic drinking bottle made into a jewellery case, small sample from Finland of a knitted material door mat made from cut up plastic bags, ornamental ash tray made from a beer can, earrings made from bits of pink plastic, and a recycled plastic notebook cover, fridge magnets to hold paper up made from an old domino set.

Table 4 Materials Products: Examples might include a plastic bottle, plastic bag, Patagonia outdoor clothing material made from plastic bottles, pens made from recycled car parts, pen made from corn/maize, pen made from recycled paper, pens made from recycled car parts, notepad made from recycled CD cases, carpet flooring made from corn, pencils made from recycled CD cases, ruler made from packaging, pencil made from recycled newspapers, pencil case made from car tyre rubber, buttons made from natural seeds, pencils made from polystyrene vending machine cups, traditional highlighter pen and a highlighter crayon, roof slate made into a plant pot label, plastic swipe card for access to a room, sports bag made from tents left behind at Music Festival.

Some of the simple patterns that emerge are as follows:

There are linear and circular patterns to be detected. *Scores can be awarded* for demonstrating *simple* patterns (e.g., chronological developments) or more *complex patterns* (more points − e.g., radial/weblike).

Experience Design: Doing~Sensing **99**

Conceptual Exploration

There are several conceptual notions that can be explored such as:

1 *In the future there may be no such thing as "waste."* Waste could be considered as a process whereby materials are waiting to re-enter the industrial ecosystem. They are awaiting transformation into either the same or a different product. This requires the separation of waste streams, as reflected in the number of different "waste" bins available now in many locations, including waste disposal sites. The more recycled plastic is required to make rucksacks, pens, clothing, bricks, and other items, then the value of plastic will go up with demand. This means that even a plastic bottle will have increasing value placed upon it.

2 *Dematerialisation* is a simple concept so that, for example, with the breakthrough of LED lights a very, very small torch can be created with a very powerful light. Metal hotel keys are now replaced by swipe cards. The amount of material required in order to make some products can become very low. The smartphone is another example: the smartphone possesses, for example, a calculator, an alarm clock, a torch, and many other items thus reducing the need for these physical components to be possessed or manufactured.

Many of these ideas, along with others, suggest a transformation towards an *industrial ecology*, sometimes called the "circular economy." A radial pattern could be created for a smartphone in that many products have been incorporated into it: a calculator, maps, phone numbers, audio recording devices, camera, video capacity, word documents, PDF documents, torch light, and so on. In this way this product design is environmentally positive (*dematerialisation*).

The text shown at the start of this design illustration is then re-presented to the groups to see how their understanding has changed by using this experiential approach. The four groups are then merged and they collectively create an overview of their understanding so far, and, with real products, create a representation of the notion of an industrial ecology (see Figure 4.8).

The group might also be asked to generate creative ideas. This activity is useful to demonstrate how creative, critical, and conceptual (3 Cs) thinking can contribute towards a more sustainable society. In Figure 4.9 the kinetic watch generates its own energy through the movement of its wearer. This same energy is used to power the lights in the sole of the shoe (children's light up trainers are used). The third item is a sample of floor textile (carpet) made by Interface-Flor inc., which is one of the largest floor textile manufacturers in the world. The creative thinking here is that the same technology that has been built into the watches and shoes can be built into the flooring. Humans, just by walking on the flooring, can generate energy. Shopping malls and entrances especially are perfect locations (see also Beard, 2010).

The Web-like Industrial Ecology

The idea that industrial systems should mimic quasi-cyclical functions of natural ecosystems. Here eight products or materials in the industrial system flow in cyclical ways reducing the need to go to the earth for resources.

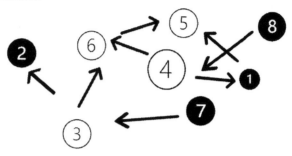

FIGURE 4.8 The web-like nature of the industrial ecology.

Signalling, sequencing, and relational connections.

1. Kinetic watch
2. shoe that lights up. . .
3. Floor textiles (Carpet) can be made from natural corn. . . .
Q: Can the carpet have the same technology inserted into it?

FIGURE 4.9 Signalling, sequencing, and relational connections.

This chapter has highlighted how the experiencing mode of *doing* is multifaceted and strongly linked to the *sensing* experiences. Many modes of experiencing overlap and so the relationship of *sensing* to *feeling* is the topic of the next chapter.

5

EXPERIENCE DESIGN

Sensing~Feeling

Introduction

The focus of this chapter is the two H's: *Hands* and *Heart*, because learning is an experience that involves the capacities of a fully embodied, sensual, and affective human. The previous chapter unpacked the notion of *doing* to expose its inherent complexity and unclear boundaries of meaning. *Doing*, as a concrete, active experience, involves many sensory capacities. This chapter continues the exploration of the important role played by the senses by examining sensory links with human emotions, particularly *arousal* and *engagement*.

What becomes clear from previous chapters is that an understanding of the processes which *foster* or *inhibit* the experience of learning is important in design. At the very beginning of the book the story about the Amazon rainforest illustrates several points about sensory and emotional arousal and the way they were utilised to capture, and recapture, the *attention* of the audience because "our senses respond only to change or contrast" (Rowe, 2001: 50). The complex nature of sensory systems, and the way they influence *attention* and *arousal* are further examined in this chapter. The profound role that emotions play in the processes of learning, and the relationship of feelings about what we *sense*, will continue to unfold.

Untapped Capacities

Each day our senses are operating in a continuous, complex state of flux. By scanning the internal and external environment, internal and external receptors impact on how we experience learning. Exteroceptors (external senses) located on the body surface, detect information from the outer world. Internal sensors

DOI: 10.4324/9781003030867-5

102 Experience Design: Sensing~Feeling

(interoceptors) check hunger, heart rate, and breathing, for example, and these are closely linked to bodily feelings. There are many more external senses than the five often quoted: the sensory capacities of the hand alone, as highlighted in previous chapters, are extensive. The influence of the senses on learning is often underestimated, and sensory capacities can be extensively developed. The palate of mayonnaise and wine tasters is much refined, as with the eyes of an artist, and the hearing of musicians. Because there are approximately a hundred touch receptors in each finger, people with limited or no visual capacities use their fingertips to read Braille by feeling the patterns of raised dots on paper. On average humans live about 23,000 days, and each day we intake about 23,000 breaths, each scanned by 10 million olfactory receptors in the nose receptors capable of detecting about 10,000 different smells. The auditory nerve carries messages from about 25,000 receptors in the ear, and 10,000 taste buds are present in the mouth. There are some 250 million photoreceptors gathering the information that enters the eyes, transferring information into approximately 8 million action potentials (electrical nerve pulses) per second. Amazingly, our eyes react in emergency situations generating improved sight: we see details we sometimes cannot see. It seems remiss not to understand and apply these capacities for experiential learning.

Sensory Arousal, Cravings, and Desires

Sensory receptors detect sensations that are integrated and interpreted in a process known as *perception*. We are often barely conscious of the raw sensations. In my Master Classes I often write a pretend blank cheque and give it to people, telling then to imagine buying something they really want. They are then blindfolded and asked to *imagine* and describe aloud (to externalise their thinking) the experience of the item purchased. What is intriguing is that they almost exclusively describe their sensory experiences: if an expensive car it is the smell of leather, the feeling of the solid door, the look of the dashboard, the sinking into the seat, the sound of the engine, and the power as it pulls away. This experience heightens awareness (consciousness) of the senses that give *pleasure* (emotion). We crave everyday *sensory pleasures*: fresh baked bread, chocolate, fresh coffee, fresh sea air, seeing the sunrise, the frosty morning, rainforest noises, or a material object. Sensory experiences create specific feelings that linger to facilitate memory retrieval (the Proust Effect, after Marcel Proust): visual and olfactory experiences are particularly powerful.

Companies focus on carefully designed "*sensory signatures*" that create sensory arousal, enhancing the experience. Singapore Airlines has for a long time led the way in sensory experience design (Lindstrom, 2005). The importance of sensory experiences in learning design, and the resulting memories, should not be underestimated. Remembering the names of the capitol of France, and several other capitols is relatively easy to learn by rote using *semantic* memory, a category of long-term memory that involves the recall of factual or conceptual knowledge.

Episodic memory involves remembering episodes and events. The former involves remembering *facts*, the latter involves remembering *experiences*. In experiential learning designs learners may require techniques to extract the required facts and figures from the experiential *episodes* for examinations that require mostly factual material. In *The Art of Making Memories* the CEO of The Happiness Research Institute notes how schools are increasingly using episodic or experience-based memories to enhance students' semantic or factual memories. The Institute also carried out a global survey on happy memories and discovered that over 62% of participant stories contained *multisensory* memories (Wiking, 2019); the next highest category was *emotional* content. Ringer (2002: 98) notes that narrative therapists work with *episodic memory* "during 'processing' or 'reviewing' experiential exercises. The experiential learning cycle is based in part on the assumption that verbalising 'episodes' will engender learning."

Getting Attention: Sensory Orientation, and Sensory Focus

Segal suggests that "the common distinction between cognition and emotion is artificial and potentially harmful to our understanding of mental processes" (2015: 148). Some researchers regard emotions as interwoven with the motivational drives that have evolved over millions of years. As noted earlier, Siegel (2012: 53) refers to the brain as "an 'anticipation machine', constantly scanning the environment and trying to determine what will come next", and that heightened brain activity signals are referred to as an "initial orienting response" (2012: 149). In fast-*moving* multi-sensory environments neural connections create arousal and alertness to develop interest and engagement. Arousal and attention are rooted in survival-based assessments and appraisals of whether something is good or bad, interesting or not interesting, to move towards or away from.

Constant sensory appraisal requires considerable information integration across a range of networks across many brain regions to prepare the body and brain for potential action: extreme arousal results in the emotion-linked, largely subconscious *fright, flight,* or *fight* response. Lower arousal levels are linked to *seeking* or *avoiding* behaviours. A difficult question about a contentious topic, the Amazon story in Chapter 1, or an emotional clip of a movie can act as an emotional "hook," creating arousal and attention. If you imagine sitting at the medical centre and the doctor calls out your name, attention and arousal is instant. Movement does the same because of sensory *change* and *contrast* (in colour, voice tone, and pace for example). Landscape designers understand how the senses are activated by contrasting stimuli:

> Landscape designers try to imitate, and improve on, nature's sensual wealth. Asian gardens are created with visual-tactile qualities in mind. A Chinese garden is composed of yin (soft) and yang (hard) elements – the softness

104 Experience Design: Sensing-Feeling

of water and of undulating perforated garden walls, the harness of craggy limestone rocks. An Islamic garden is a concordance of sight, sound, and scent, but it is also an oasis of thermal delight – its shades and coolness contrasting vividly with the glare and heat beyond its high walls.

(Tuan, 2005: 77)

The same sensory information can be experienced with differing states of arousal. The faces of city commuters traveling on a train often reflect the daily boredom of the experience. Their brains recognise the sensory information as familiar, and unimportant. The tourist on the same train, in contrast, is hypervigilant, in a state of heightened sensory alertness, paying attention to a considerable amount of novel sensory information.

During coronavirus virtual meetings many people seemed relatively disengaged: the flat screen meeting experience had low sensory novelty, contrast, or movement to arouse and alert. In contrast, the view outside through a window was full of moving things that resulted in heightened alertness: birds flying, washing billowing in the wind, chickens feeding on the grass, and clouds steadily moving. This sensory arousal *grabbed* my attention. Online presenters learn the importance of sensory stimulation: they move their bodies, stand up, show their hands, and use facial expressions in slightly exaggerated ways. Sensory experience designs have considerable potential to engage and develop interest.

Sensory Gating

We are exposed to considerable quantities of sensory data and so it is sorted, channelled, filtered, restricted, and *gated* to prevent overload. Buhner (2014: 29) invites his readers to intentionally look around the room they occupy:

There is an incredibly rich range of shapes, and functions, and relationships of objects to each other, and shadows, and light reflections off surfaces, and subtleties of colours and textures, in fact millions of bits of visual sensory inputs in just this one place alone.

Sensory "gating" involves regulating, by restricting or increasing, the substantial sensory flow. Typically, gating occurs instantly in the complex neural pathways of the brain: *interest, concern* or the gauging of *relevance* will open the gates more widely, allowing more inputs to reach conscious awareness. As discussed previously these are by "the *intensity* of the sensory inflow, its *novelty*, the degree of *contrast* between sensory stimulus and its sensory background, and its *rarity*" (Buhner, 2014: 35 italics added). These are just some of the design categories to consider for engagement, focus, and attention. Determining what is important to a task is not value free: relevance is determined and conditioned by past experiences, including, for example, schooling, parents, emotional and culture issues.

Sensory gating is influenced by practice: musicians, for example, possess high levels of sound receptivity so that they do not experience the usual sensory gating that reduces audio phenomena. They detect tiny changes in sound that others cannot hear. Some people (see the following example) have gating so open (and so see, hear, and feel the world very differently to others) that they are labelled as clinically "abnormal," having gating "deficits."

> Studies have found that one fourth of healthy individuals in every Western population report sensory inundation, difficulty in stimulus filtering (stimulus over inclusion), and the problem of orienting two inappropriate stimuli. It is much more common amongst artists (writers, musicians, painters, and so on), those who use psychoactive drugs, and the gifted. It is also common among people who have been exposed to severe environmental stressors such as war.
>
> *(Buhner, 2014: 44)*

Neurodiversity is a contrasting notion that acknowledges the complex spectrum of sensory capacities in humans (rather than normal-abnormal).

Sensory Thresholds

In *Sensory Intelligence: Why It Matters More Than IQ and EQ*, Annemarie Lombard, an occupational therapist, explains the gating phenomenon in terms of "sensory thresholds": her book contains a threshold questionnaire and analysis. Some people, she argues, merely have lower sensory thresholds, and for them, quietness and solitude is what they require lots of. In contrast, older people in retirement homes may find themselves close to the point of sensory deprivation: they don't move, touch, see, or hear as much as they used to. Lombard indicates how personal screensaver choice, or the degree of clutter in a room, offers clues as to sensory tolerance thresholds. Referring to older sensation seekers Lombard notes: "Your typical sensation seekers are the ones whose stories you read in the newspaper when they do bungee jumps and parachute jumps at the age of 70 and even 80" (Lombard, 2007: 30).

Lombard suggests that in people with low sensory thresholds their brains are potentially more in tune with the natural environment: they notice more things and go into sensory overload more rapidly. People with high sensory thresholds tend to be able to tune out information and sometimes notice less in their environment, taking longer to reach sensory overload. When designing experiences, very different sensory capacities and requirements need to be catered to. A balance of high and low sensory experiences can be variously applied to develop focus, attention, arousal, movement, social interaction, and quiet time. Attention and focus cannot be sustained for long: "*let's take a break*" can literally mean a *sensory break*.

106   Experience Design: Sensing~Feeling

> **DESIGN ILLUSTRATION 14 SENSORY DESIGN VIGNETTES.**

Sensory Desires, Sensory Stepping, and Creative Design: The Fleece, the Backpack, and the Solar Charger

The brain craves sensory stimulation, and in keynote speeches I often demonstrate the importance of sensory awareness using sensory *arousal* increases and sensory *stepping*. I do this first by telling the audience about the fact that many clothing items can be made from recycled plastic bottles. I note the level of (dis) interest! I then (2nd step) show an empty plastic bottle (a visual), and then I pick up material used to make outdoor fleece jackets made from plastic bottles by the company Patagonia. The level of interest rises – slightly. I then (3rd step) walk amongst the audience and ask someone to feel (*touch, handle*) the fleece and to comment on it. "*Hmmm, it is amazingly soft.*" I go to another person and do the same. Then, with a third person I see who wants to *touch* it; as they reach out I withdraw the fleece out of their reach. I move it back within reach, and as they reach out, I again withdraw it. The audience laughs. Finally, I let the person feel the fleece. Many people in the audience *want to experience feeling the fleece*. I create the *desire* for them to experience it with touch. These multiple sensory experiences utilise a staged trio sequence: (1) *hearing* (spoken), (2) *seeing* (plastic bottle and plastic material), and (3) *doing* (handling).

When introducing other environmental concepts, I use a backpack (rucksack) made from plastic bottles, with a built-in solar system in the rear of the backpack. I tell people about the rucksack: the initial level of interest is usually relatively low.

I then ask someone to hand me their smartphone. I charge it right in front of them, then ask them to confirm to the audience that it was charging. This creates much more arousal, and a desire to know more. I would then put the backpack on my back and then bend over and tell people the bright artificial light is charging the battery. I would then stimulate their imagination: if we all went into a brightly lit supermarket tonight, and we stole the electricity from the store! ("steal" is used for dramatic effect), and if 30 of us did this, would anyone notice that we had stolen 30 batteries worth of power? I would then say "are you thinking what I am thinking?" Intrigued faces as I ask where the electricity goes if we didn't take it? Then interesting discussions follow, about wasting the sun's energy, different forms of recycling, alternative energy sources, kinetic energy systems in entrances to shopping malls, and other ideas.

This illustration highlights the impact of sensory arousal experiences (*telling, showing, feeling, doing,* and *dramatic effect*). The desire to learn can be enhanced by imaginative sensory *experiencescape* design.

The Senses: Modes and Media

The term "multi-media" refers to learning materials that integrate two or more sensory media. Media refers to the medium used in production, such as print, graphics, photos, animation, video, audio, film, and so on. The experience of speech, for example, utilises specific sensory *modes*. The experience can be changed by utilising different *media*: an audio recording, lecturing, or a video. Mode and media are both important to the way we design materials for learning. Dual Coding Theory (Paivio, 1986), as foundational to multi-media research, proposes that we have two major processing systems: one visual, one auditory. This has led to creation of "instructional" design terms that classify learners as *verbalisers* or *visualisers* (Chen & Sun, 2012). To date this research, usually conducted in experimental conditions, has given rise to several design principles: the *Multiple Presentation Principle* for example suggests that people learn more deeply from words and pictures than from words alone. The *Modality Principle* suggests that learning is enhanced if design includes both *graphics* and *narration*, rather than *graphics* and *printed text*. There are many other principles (for a more comprehensive chart see Chapter 6). *The Signalling Principle* suggests that learning is enhanced if the design includes cues, pointers, and signposts, as this focuses learner *attention*.

Learning is an interactionally complex process, involving many *experiencing* modes, media, and materials: in design it is important to utilise a broad range of modes and media that arouse the senses in different ways. Dual coding theory focuses solely on *pictures* (predominantly involving the *eyes*), and *speech* (predominantly involving the *ears*). This can limit the understanding of the interactional complexity of experiential "interactions." Multi-media research has until recently tended to neglect the holistic experiential capacities of the body. Furthermore, the boundaries of speech and text are not clear cut: icons, for example, are simultaneously a *text* and *picture* format. As discussed earlier, the letters of the English alphabet that make up *text* are themselves derived from *pictorial* representations. Chinese text is just such a pictorial language.

Arousal occurs not only from sensory experiences: arousal is enhanced by emotional states (see Chung et al., 2015). A considerable body of research suggests that positive emotions influence and are almost indistinguishable from positive levels of motivation: both influence cognitive abilities. Early research on emotions in learning has tended to reduce emotion to *either* positive *or* negative experiences, neglecting the rich complexity of emotional experiences. Chen and Sun (2012) consider the effects of different multi-media materials on emotions and learning performance, for both *visualiser* and *verbaliser* styles of learning. In their research they consider a number of combinations of these two learning styles: static text, image-based, video-based, and interactive animations in learning. Their results are based on experiments with primary school children and out of the 160 participants 73 were considered *verbalisers* and 87 students were considered *visualisers*. More significantly, findings suggest that:

> visualisers learn best with visual instruction methods, whereas verbalisers learn best with verbal instruction methods. Moreover, this study demonstrates that video-based multimedia material generates the best learning performance, as it positively influenced the learning performance of both visualisers and verbalisers.
>
> *(Chen & Sun, 2012: 1283)*

In an article titled *Emotional multimedia learning: an investigation of the effects of valance and arousal and different modalities on instructional animation* (2015), Chung et al., conclude that merely pointing can create an emotional arousal state that has potential to enhance multi-media learning. Emotions are linked to arousal because continual processing of sensory information allows for judgement of positive or negative impact as an evolved survival strategy.

Describing Sensory Experiences

The link between the sensory experience and emotional experience is reflected by sensory language being used to communicate and express emotions. We refer to *feelings,* for example, a particular way: we speak of being *touched* by thoughtfulness, that *touch* of class, *coarse* language, of being emotionally *clumsy* (Linden, 2015; Classen, 2005). Sensory experiences are often difficult to fully describe. In a study of the language used in 85,000 wine reviews Paradis and Eeg-Olofsson note that, "with the exception of visual experiences, most people find it very hard to provide adequate and intelligible descriptions of sensory experience." This they argue is due to the difficulty of transforming the experience of sensory perceptions into spoken or written language. They also note that rather interestingly there is a "paucity of sensory vocabularies in world languages" (Paradis & Eeg-Olofsson, 2013: 23). They studied wine reviews because almost all the reviews provide descriptions, either individually or as a whole, of four sensory experiences, namely taste, smell, touch, and look. Their analysis adopts the view that the way we *perceive* the world is the way we *conceive* it: that concepts are *embodied* and grounded in *sensory perception*. Recent neurobiological research similarly indicates that our conceptual representations consist of multiple levels of abstraction from *sensory*, *motor*, and *affective* input (see Binder & Desai, 2011).

Experience Design: Sensing~Feeling **109**

Stay with the Senses: Resisting Feeling and Thinking

Our senses provide information about the outside world and judgements are made as to the nature of that information to respond. Judgements and feelings about the experience can be dramatic, and instant, occurring below the level of consciousness, whilst some responses are slow and carefully thought through. With practice, paying attention to, and staying with, the initial stream of sensory experiences can help suspend response and judgement. Robert Kull lived in a remote part of Argentinian Patagonia for a year so he could study the experience of solitude for his doctoral thesis. In *Solitude: Seeking Wisdom in Extremes*, Kull notes the power of sensory awareness:

> In conceptualising, organising, and thinking about these sensory impressions, the immediacy of experience can easily be lost. It requires patience and practice to soften this habitual activity by over and over letting go of thought and analysis to simply stay with the swirl of sound just as it is without trying to do anything with it.
>
> *(Kull, 2008: 279)*

Kull suggests that the act of "over-processing" raw sensory data, that is by thinking too much, can spoil the "immediacy" of the experience (more in Chapter 9). The design of less active experiences creates possibilities to learn by careful observation, being quiet, listening, reading, or meditating. Staying with the sensory experience, just watching, and observing, without evaluating or judging can be transformational. Sensing without judgement is the basis of compassionate communication (Gilbert, 2010). To interact directly with the immediate meanings of incoming sensory flows, to master this aspect of our experiences, results in *sensory intelligence*, similar to but antecedent to *emotional intelligence*. Being non-judgemental is very hard to achieve, and it takes much practice because perception naturally involves organising and integrating sensory information. This processing "generally refers to psychological processes whereby meaning, past experiences, memory and judgement are involved" (see Schiffman, 1990). These processes are the initial steps to meaning making, and it is hard to break the continuous integration of doing, sensing, feeling, and thinking.

A book introduced earlier, titled *Sensory Intelligence: Why It Matters More Than IQ and EQ*, suggests that sensory awareness is potentially more important than emotional awareness. Of course, what we sense and feel affects how and what we think, and vice versa. As Buhner notes, "the meanings in sensory flows always create an emotional response" (2014: 66). The pervasive nature of the emotional response to learning, in both classroom and online environments, in educational settings, is nicely illustrated by Artino (2012: 137), in their critical overview of nine articles on emotions in online learning environments. Students, they say, may:

enjoy the (classroom) discussion, worry about saying something offensive, or become frustrated when a discussion deteriorates into the shouting match. These emotions – enjoyment, worry, and frustration – likely influence her motivation, the effort she puts forth during the discussion, and even the study strategies she chooses to prepare for future classroom discussions . . . (and in the online experience) he may enjoy the activity, become confused because he has limited experience with online discussions, or feel embarrassed when the instructor critiques his argument, and writing, for the whole class to read. Once again, these emotions – enjoyment, confusion, and embarrassment – almost certainly affect how the student engages in the activity, his motivation to persist in the face of difficulties, and his desire to stay on task when the discussion is contentious (bracketed comments added).

Learning Design: Emotional Experiences

How often do learners get the chance to think about and express their pleasure derived from learning? Mortiboys (2002) notes the importance of creating a good emotional "space" or climate for feelings to be expressed. There are many ways to design experiences that help people pay attention to, surface, and improve their awareness and understanding of underlying emotions, and to promote discussion about the impact, on self and others. Learning is, by its very nature, an emotional process often difficult to describe.

Like sensory experiences, emotions can enhance or impair learning and memory retrieval.

> [T]he intrinsic reward of having found the solution, to getting a good grade, to avoiding punishment, to helping tutor a friend, to getting into a good college, to pleasing his or her parents or the teacher. All of these reasons have a powerful emotional component and relate to both pleasurable sensations and to survival within our culture.
>
> *(Immordino-Yang & Damasio, 2008: 184)*

Mortiboys recommends openly asking questions about the feelings associated with a favourite learning experience. The answers include " 'enthusiastic', 'fascination', 'happy and alive', 'being valued', 'confident', 'curious', 'excited'" (2005: 29). He suggests that this emotional climate is shaped by important elements such as the behaviour of the teachers and students, materials, and activities, and how they are engaged. The early establishment of the emotional climate is important. Rogers (1969) argues that realness and genuineness, prizing, acceptance and trust, and empathetic understanding are necessary for learning and development to occur.

Many programs start with what are called *icebreakers*, designed to settle people in and to create a positive *emotional climate* of trust, relaxation, and enjoyment. In *Playful Learning: Events and Activities to Engage Adults*, Cable (2019) explores the types of icebreakers, which are meant to break the ice at the very beginning of programmes as a participatory activity. Cable includes "energisers" and "group builders" in a category called "interludes," which can lead to a positive or negative effect. Energisers can take place after a lunch break or other interlude. Group builders are activities designed to help groups to form quickly. Interludes require careful design as some dread these experiences, resulting in a negative "cringe" factor (see the Design Illustration: Geometric Psychology, and "Different Beginnings" in Chapter six related to power and control). Learning is socio-emotional and so building quality relationships is the subject of a new body of literature on *relational pedagogy* (Bovill, 2020; Bingham & Sidorkin, 2004), a topic explored further in Chapter 6. The physical environment also influences the emotional climate. Many classrooms now have lightweight wheeled furniture for ease of movement enabling the layout to be quickly reconfigured. Mortiboys (2002) notes how long periods of sitting have a negative emotional impact: without movement, attention is hard to maintain.

DESIGN ILLUSTRATION 15 THE EMOTIONAL CLIMATE – FUN, FEAR, AND MAGIC.

High Ropes courses, extensively used across the globe to develop resilience, require people to actively participate in this climbing experience to overcome their fears. Interestingly, in the multi-million-dollar roller coaster industry fear is reframed and sold as pleasure. We talk of being emotionally *gripped* by fear, yet ironically the relatively restrained rollercoaster experience is not fearful enough for some people: they hold their arms up in the air to increase their sense of fear!

Some people fear heights, some fear presentations. This illustration offers a creative alternative on addressing a fear of presentations. The design involves reframing the underlying causes of the emotional state of fear of delivering presentations by lowering levels of fear. Participants are introduced to presenting by delivering a magic tricks party for peers, with an ambience of fun. By playing the part of a magician, using magic tricks collected from Xmas crackers over many years, a team of four or five presenters design and deliver a magic event. The session is fun to watch, and improvisations abound. The review session productively surfaces, and enables participants to talk about fears they had during the magic party, and in more formal presentation settings. People realised that the creation of a sense of fun, and the use of objects and demonstrations helped them understand what caused their fears in formal presentations. Formality was a common constituent part of the fear, as was the presence of people in higher authority, presenting to peers, audience focus on the presenter, that is, "you," and audience expectations. Following on from the magic party, practice in formal settings follows, using familiar objects and demonstrations that direct attention away from the self.

Understanding Emotional Responses

Why do we experience fear? The answer is because we "feel" a threat, though this may not be real. As information flows sweep through the brain, high alert states create *flight, fright, or fight* responses, or other coping mechanisms, and the parts of the brain that deal with this kind of response is referred to as the "threat brain" (Gilbert, 2010). Evolutionary psychology tells us a great deal about both the *threat* brain and the *pleasure* brain, and how they affect learning. Our brains direct attention and give priority to *potential* and *actual* threats more than pleasurable situations. An analysis of dictionaries reveals more negative than positive words (Beaumeister et al., 2001). Arousal and attention to threats creates conscious and subconscious feelings, such as anxiety or anger for self-protection: "nearly all psychotherapies focus to a greater or lesser degree on the complexities of the threat to self-protection" (Gilbert, 2010: 45). Gilbert (2010) suggests the positive emotions of drive/achievement give a pleasurable "high" (from dopamine), whereas affiliation has a positive effect that is calming (from our natural opiates/endorphins). Positive emotions serve to counterbalance negative emotions. The two positive systems are known as (1) the incentive, resource-seeking, drive-excitement system and (2) the soothing, calming, contentment system: together with the threat system, they make up the fundamental basis of the emotional rollercoaster of everyday experiences.

The Emotional Rollercoaster

The term *emotion* is difficult to define (Boler, 1999; Lee Do & Schallert, 2004): we use the term *emotion* to cover a range of moods and feelings that are often regarded as adaptive, oppositional states of experiencing. Russell and Barchard discuss the everyday shared language of emotions, noting how "most objects or events in the world are pleasant or unpleasant, upsetting or relaxing, exciting or depressing" (2002: 368), though the rollercoaster of emotions is more complex than these opposites. A substantive literature base exists on positive emotions, which are said to be important in developing resilience and coping strategies (Cooperrider & Whitney, 2005; Seligman, 2006: Gilbert, 2010). Biologists as well as social scientists have long been active in thinking about and researching emotions. Plutchik et al. (1980) concluded that there are endless possibilities of "emotional classes," which he argues can be determined to some extent by the socio-cultural context or situation. The four *primary* emotions are said to be fear, anger, sadness, and joy, though disgust and surprise are sometimes added to this.

Darwin produced *The Expression of Emotion in Man and Animals* (1872), in which he identified a comprehensive range of 30 emotions, which he classified into several categories, arguing that they were essentially adaptation and survival mechanisms. Seventeen emotions are used in the Academic Emotions Questionnaire which was developed from several qualitative studies (Pekrun et al., 2002). Early work by Wundt in 1897, one of the founders of scientific psychology, argued that emotions are experienced as combinations of three state dimensions: pleasantness/unpleasantness, calm/excitement, and relaxation/tension (Gross, 2001). Nearly a hundred years later, Thayer (1989) argued that the interaction of opposites of Energy-Tension and Calm-Tired lie at the heart of our mood states that affect learning and memory retrieval. Other proposed oppositional dimensions include the social: acceptance/rejection (Schlosberg, 1941 in Gross, 2001), and the psychological: sadness/depression versus elation/ebullience (Watson & Tellegan, 1985 in Russell & Barchard, 2002). Shame-pride emotions are said to influence academic success (Frijda & Mesquita, 1994; Kitayama & Markus, 1994), playing a key role in the establishment of identity and self-esteem (Scheff, 1997). Neurologist Damasio suggests that oppositional states characterise the struggle for human balance between *flourishing* and *distress* (Damasio, 2004). Ekman (1994) points out that certain facial expressions are universal in humans: six relate to facial expressions of anger, disgust, sadness, fear, surprise, and happiness. It is the amygdala that responds to four of these, that is, disgust, sadness, happiness, and fear.

Numerous attempts have been made to categorize complex emotions, including "master," "basic," "primary" and "secondary emotions." The latter are subtle variations of primary emotions such as euphoria, ecstasy, melancholy, and wistfulness. "Master emotions" such as *shame* frequently appear in the literature (see Frijda & Mesquita, 1994), as does the *shame-pride* dichotomy (see Kitayama & Markus, 1994). Significantly, pride and shame are related to *success* and *failure* within education, as they play a key role in the establishment and maintenance of identity, associated with a sense of belonging, differentiation, and self-esteem (Scheff, 1997). The notion of "master emotions" is problematic, however, because all emotions are intertwined. Plutchik (1980) cautions the use of simplistic classifications. Ingelton (1999), with reference to the work of sociologists Barbalet (1998) and Scheff (1997), has argued that the disposition to learn in the classroom is grounded in social relationships that play an important role in the construction of *identity* and *self-esteem* within the context of success/pride and failure/shame.

Emotions Play in the Theatre of the Body

Emotions are also called *feelings*, though to feel something is also a term relating to touch. We also say we are *moved* by something: a linguistic connection between motion and *emotion*. We process emotions in the brain, but these

114 Experience Design: Sensing~Feeling

emotions are also played out in the theatre of the body, as a physical experience. Immordino-Yang and Damasio contend that "the relationship between learning, emotion, and body state runs much deeper than many educators realise" (Immordino-Yang & Damasio, 2008: 184). Both physical and emotional states underpin every human experience. Emotional impact can, over many years, become engrained within the body: therapists refer to clients needing more *body work*. Below the surface structure of the cortex there are four structures, each with a twin in the opposite hemisphere: the amygdala, hypothalamus, thalamus, and hippocampus. These are connected to the limbic system, which is considered the main processing area for emotions, as well as with instincts, appetites, and drives. The amygdala (meaning almond shaped) is one area of the brain most active when we experience emotions: if the amygdala is damaged the capacity to feel fear is lacking. Research outlines how emotions are grounded in the body as a neuromuscular dynamic. Early work conducted by Nina Bull in the 1950s led to *The Attitude Theory of Emotion*. Psychiatrist Nina Bull showed that emotions are shaped by motor attitudes, and that a basic neuro*muscular* sequence is essential to the production of emotion. Her research strikingly demonstrates that there is a *generative* as well as an *expressive* relationship between movement and emotion (interestingly this proved to be an amplification of original work by Darwin).

Bull hypnotised her subjects, telling them that a word denoting a certain emotion would be spoken and they would then experience this emotion. They were asked afterwards to describe what happened, and the research explored how the emotions were manifested in their outward (bodily) behaviour in a natural manner. Six emotions were investigated: fear, anger, disgust, depression, joy, and triumph. With fear, for example, one subject reported that her jaws tightened, then her legs and feet, toes bunched up until they hurt, and the subject remarked how she felt afraid of something. In further experiments hypnotised subjects were read a particular description from one of their own experiential reports, the description beginning with phrases like "your jaws are tightening" (fear), or "you feel heavy all over" (depression). Following this initial descriptive reading, the subject was told they were locked in one of these physical conditions, and that there will be no changes in their body, no new bodily sensations until they were unlocked from hypnosis. The experimenter then told the subjects: "when I count to five, I shall utter a word denoting a certain emotion. When you hear the word, you will feel this emotion, feel it naturally, and will be able to tell us about it afterwards." The emotion named was antithetical (opposite) to the one coincident with the position in which the subject was locked. What the research showed was that the subjects were unable to have emotions other than the one they were locked in: they were unable to feel the designated contrasting emotion, and this was because such a change state would require a different *posture*, or *bodily attitude*. The subjects validated the thesis that a certain neuromuscular attitude is necessary to, and coincident with, specific emotions. We

Experience Design: Sensing-Feeling **115**

communicate many emotional states, whether consciously or subconsciously, in other ways. There are, for example, several thousand facial expressions, many of which are universal in humans.

The Pleasure of Learning: Positive Emotions

Research has tended to focus on negative emotions with less attention devoted to the "deliberate design and maintenance of positive learning environments" in higher education (Moore & Kuol, 2007: 88): the tendency is to "overlook and even ignore positive emotions" (Tugade & Fredrickson, 2002: 320), "placing more emphasis on the problem perspective" of emotions (Palmer et al., 2009: 39). Positive emotions are said to generate coping mechanisms, and produce more creative, resilient, socially integrated, and healthy individuals (Tugade & Fredrickson, 2002; Werner & Smith, 1992).

It is important to consider feelings in experiential learning design. Emotional space differs from, but is related to, physical space in terms of learning. The psycho-social space creates the learning *climate*, which is influenced by the physical space: careful design can facilitate expression, discussion, and acceptance of emotions in ways that contribute to positive learning experiences. In the early 21st century I became particularly intrigued as to why there was little research on the pleasures of learning. My own research led to a series of publications on positive emotions in higher education (Beard et al., 2007; Clayton et al., 2009; Humberstone et al., 2013; Beard et al., 2014). The research highlights the emotional *rollercoaster* affecting every aspect of what Ashworth (2003) calls the lifeworld of learners. Ashworth regards emotions as pervasive, influencing and interacting with many aspects of student life, including their:

- Personal Project: the ways their situation relates to their ability to carry out the activities which are central to their personal lives.
- Academic Project: the ways in which academic aspirations relate to the rest of their lives.
- Temporality: how their sense of time is affected by the situation.
- Spatiality: how the geography and the environment in which they live are affected by the situation.
- Sociality: their relationship with others and its impact on the university experience.
- Embodiment: the ways in which experiences are lived through the body and the concerns with the care of the body.
- Discourse: framed the whole, and students drew on the differing discourses of being a student to make sense of their experiences.

My research highlights the importance of emotions in social relationships, to changing emotions over time, and to student perceptions of academic studies

116 Experience Design: Sensing~Feeling

during life at university. The research argues for richer conceptions of learners as affective and embodied selves, and a clearer theorisation of the role of emotions in educational encounters. Positive emotions were found to enhance *retention* and *recall*, particularly when their experiences engender curiosity and intrigue. Positive emotions were enhanced by a sense of *realness*, and *relevance*, as well as the emotional *climate* created by teachers, particularly through the design of fun, humour, affiliation, autonomy, power, and control. The research suggests that experience design can be used to develop greater awareness of the pleasures of learning. Reviewing processes, for example, can help identify positive feelings that arise from learning experiences. Emotion charts (e.g., string to layout and depict the rollercoaster of learning experiences over time); or an image, icon, or object can be selected to depict thoughts and feelings. All these design examples present opportunities for discussion of emotional states during learning.

Blackie et al. (2010: 641) argue that all interactions with knowledge are "emotionally charged." Rowe (2013) explores how feedback and assessments arouse strong emotions (see also Crossman, 2007; Pavlovich, 2007; Varlander, 2008; Palmer et al., 2009). Emotionally satisfying experiences surface in descriptions of exceptional teaching (Moore & Kuol, 2007). Barnett notes that intense positive emotions, which he calls "enduring ecstasy," are experienced as joy and fulfilment such as when a student finally understands a difficult concept. These are potentially transformative experiences. 'Ephemeral ecstasy' or short-lived pleasure, for example, occurs when a student passes an examination or receives good feedback. Short-lived emotions, he suggests, do "not advance the student in her being," in a transformational sense (Barnett, 2007: 60).

My research with colleagues on student positive emotions reveals a pervasive though low level emotional state with little emotional awareness. Initially first year emotions appear anchored in the *anticipation* of working with new knowledge. Later this develops within the context of their wider academic project, taking the form of *action-achievement* orientated emotions (Pekrun et al., 2002; Gilbert, 2010). Our questions foregrounded specific positive emotions associated with a "high" or "buzz" related to *achievement/status*, and orientated toward functional acts of *getting*, *knowing* (knowledge), or *doing* pedagogic work, and suggest emotions have significant *utility* and *efficacy* in learning. Whilst ephemeral pleasure is pervasive, enduring pleasure was reported less frequently. Figure 5.1 highlights some of the findings.

This data creates awareness of positive emotional "touchpoints" within higher education degree studies. Such information can inform experience designs: happiness is said to be dictated by where we direct attention!

Experience Design: Sensing~Feeling **117**

Forms of Positive Emotions in Learning Experiences	Illustrative student comments
Anticipated pleasure and transition to university More than 24% of first year students expressed anticipated pleasure from gaining a degree, and the career consequences. Significantly the anticipated pleasure is linked to the possibility of new intellectual depths, grounded in the possibilities of a new identity.	*'I'm looking forward to (hopefully) realising that I am more academic than I believe, I look forward to opening my mind to new ideas.'* *'I am looking forward to getting a buzz from achieving something, improving my pool of knowledge, and hopefully getting good results. . . . Helping yourself is the best way to feel good and feel like you mean something; it's almost like winning, a feeling of euphoria.'*
Pedagogic activity: doing, getting, and knowing By year 2, ephemeral (short lived) pleasure included feelings of happiness, relief, pride, and achievement, brought about, for example, by finishing work, good grades, and praise and feedback in presentations and assignments. Positive emotions are associated with the top category of 'rewards and praise', e.g., gaining a good assignment grade. The qualitative data also reveal positive emotions associated with **'instant gratifications'** derived from 'relief' in completing or submitting an assignment. The sense of 'pride', or 'confidence' as emotional declarations are connected to 'achievement' in a piece of work. Emotional discourse (*feeling*) thus appears inextricably linked to be embedded within a social context (better than, the best, personal praise, etc.) and pedagogic tasks/activities (*doing*), which Cell (1984) refers to as 'referential objects'.	*'Getting back my first grades for my presentation, I got a very, very good mark and (got) a lot of positive feedback. It felt good. . . . Getting this spurred me on to strive for more and, with that, my confidence grew about being back in education.'* *'Good marks in assignments gave me a buzz. For example, getting a good mark in one made me try just as hard in the next, as I knew I could do it then.'*
Oppositional emotions *Surprised and overwhelmed.* *Nervous excitement.*	*'When I had an A in my first presentation, it gave me confidence for the rest of the year. I felt surprised and overwhelmed'.* *'I am looking forward to giving presentations, although I would be nervous, but I would get a buzz when I had done it.'*
By the second year many students refer to **pedagogic hardship as pleasurable**. These include '*challenge*', '*pressure*', '*working hard*', and '*being absorbed in work*'.	*'...the pressure of work and getting stuck into essays...'* *'That feeling [of] finally completing an assignment.'* *'...that feeling of finishing an essay at stupid o'clock in the morning...'*

FIGURE 5.1   The pervasive nature of emotions: the pleasure of learning at university.

118 Experience Design: Sensing~Feeling

	'...this year I want to change my feelings, I am doing some sport every day...I think I am getting better.... I hope I find some good friends this year and enjoy it more.'
Positive Emotions as a social dynamic **Emotions as Socially constructed**	'I found that working as part of a group in presentations gave me a positive attitude as it gave me the motivation to excel myself and it gave me a buzz when we got very good marks'
	'I felt working as part of the team was exciting, meeting new people of all ages and backgrounds and interacting with people from different parts of the country was exciting – people's different views and approaches to tasks were always different to mine and it made me look at challenges from different angles.'
Here comments relate to the pleasures of improvement, working with friends during presentations, different views, working with a diversity of people from different countries, of the pleasures of friendships in general, the buzz from getting good marks, the pleasure and reciprocal expectations of working with passionate lecturers.	'The lecturer is really passionate and makes it interesting – it doesn't matter what the subject is.'
The demotivating effect of experiencing lecturers who read out slides with information they have obtained from a book is also commented on.	'When the lecturers aren't working hard you get de-motivated. Now only 50 per cent go to that lecture because everyone's bored and there's no point – they can get slides off Blackboard and I can read the book. That's not an enjoyable module. It could be enjoyable but because the lecturers haven't put the effort in, we don't put the effort in.'
Periods of concentrated study were reported mostly by third year students: **'loss of time', loss of awareness of self, or 'flow'** (Csikszentmihalyi, 1990) quasi-meditative states. Other data point to the beginnings of ontological awareness.	'I had that last year, we had a module about adventure tourism, it intrigued me, and I went to the library and got a book out about Everest and just sat and read it. I missed my tea, Neighbours and everything!'

FIGURE 5.1 (Continued)

 DESIGN ILLUSTRATION 16 THE EVEREST EXPERIENCE.

In Design Illustration 16, the comments relate to the positive emotions and immersion that came from an experience design involving the reading of material relating to Everest (variations of this session have been used with

Experience Design: Sensing–Feeling **119**

Outdoor organisations to explore design issues). When this session was experienced by a group of Adventure Tourism students in higher education, the material inspired several of them to go and read important books, such as *The Death Zone, Into Thin Air, Climbing High,* and *Left for Dead.* This is the comment at the end of Figure 5.1 was made by one student after the experience of learning about Everest. Everest is the tallest mountain in the world. It is named after the British surveyor Sir George Everest, who did not want the highest mountain on earth to bear his name. Its real name is Chomolungma, meaning Goddess mother of the world. This experiential design involves me creating a timeline (shortened version following) of materials placed in chronological sequence along a desk to highlight some of the core issues about the history of Everest summits. First a few minutes of the trailer to the film "Everest" is shown to act as a *hook* to engage. The story evolving from the written material contains a lot of emotional content. The most significant books on Everest are picked up, and I talk through their significance, who wrote them, and why they were written.

The following issues are then briefly mentioned:

Early first attempts by explorers are noted; the mystery of whether Mallory and Irvine on the 1924 expedition died going up or coming down (a significant unsolved mystery), the search for and finding of the body of Mallory on Everest in 1999. The search for his camera to see if any film material might shed light on what happened. The body of Irvine has never been found. The first summit in 1953 by Edmund Hillary and Tenzing Norgay is briefly discussed, along with the question of who was the first of the two to summit. Issues of commercialisation are introduced, and the fees charged by climbing companies that provide climbing guides. The 1996 disaster is discussed where eight climbers died in a blizzard, and the person who was "left for dead" but walked into camp the next day with his outer limbs frozen. The amazing rescue helicopter pilot that flew "into thin air" to rescue him. Pictures of the long line of climbers waiting for up to two hours at the Hillary Step published in the press in May 2019 – a year when 200 people summited. By January 2021, 305 people had died attempting to climb Everest: the majority of the dead remain on the mountain. Extracts from one of the core texts is read out when one of the climbers sees the body of a woman who has been on the mountain for some time, sitting upright with long flowing hair.

When these basic facts have been introduced the groups then distribute the contents of a reading pack given to them containing extracts from a range of books, magazines, and other sources.

Some of the Core Texts that were used to explore The Story of Everest.

The real name of the mountain.	Early failed attempts to summit.	Story of Mallory and Irvine.	1953 Summit.	'Into Thin Air'.	'The Death Zone'.	'Climbing High'.	'Left for Dead'.	'Touching my Fathers Soul'.	Etc
	Nationally sponsored expeditions.		Edmond Hilary & Sherpa Tensing first to summit.	Eight climbers die in a blizzard in 1996 in this period of intense commercialization.				Speculation continues over who summited first.	

→

When the groups have read the extracts contained in their packs they then compile their own "storyboard" about the history of Everest. They walk through their storyboard and present to other groups.

One student, interviewed by an independent researcher, commented (shown in the final box of the previous chart): "I had that (experience) last year in the module on adventure tourism. It intrigued me and I went to the library and got a book out about Everest and just sat and read it. I missed my tea, Neighbours (a soap TV programme) and everything!".

Emotional Intelligence

The book *Sensory Intelligence* is subtitled *Why It Matters More Than IQ and EQ* (Lombard, 2007). The notion of a sensory intelligence adds to calls to reject the notion of a single intelligence. Lombard argues that we experience the sensory environment in our own unique ways, with some people thriving in an active environment with experiences that are stimulating by being brighter, louder, and faster, whilst others find this level of stimulation overwhelming. The latter escape high stimulation and seek out peace and tranquillity. Experiential learning design should ideally involve fast and slow energy waves.

Gardner (1983) creates a theory of multiple intelligences (plural), rejecting the idea of an "intelligence quotient" relating to a single intelligence (IQ). His work on multiple intelligences endorses the existence of an "emotional intelligence" (EQ), however Gardner prefers the term *emotional sensitivity* (Gardner, 2008: 123 in *The Brain and Learning*). However, it was Salovey and Mayer (1997), drawing on extensive psychological and cultural literature, who created the "first formal definition of emotional intelligence" (Barrett & Salovey, 2002: xiii) or EQ, that became popular due to Daniel Goleman's publication (1996). This term "quotient" is not helpful as it conceptually links it to the discredited idea of IQ, as

Experience Design: Sensing~Feeling **121**

something individuals "possess." Whilst emotions are often pitched against the rational/logical, Barbalet, a sociologist, offers two other positions: *critical* and *radical*. In the former, emotions support reason; in the latter, emotions and reason are "different ways of regarding the same thing" (1998: 30).

Mezirow (2009) suggests that educators seek further "clarification and emphasis on the role played by emotions" in learning and transformation (2009: 95). Mortiboys offers practical clarification in *The Emotionally Intelligent Lecturer* (2002), where he suggests that lecturers develop emotionally intelligent behaviours that improve the climate for teaching and learning. He argues that it would be disturbing if universities were emotion-free zones, yet, he says, "curiously, so much of the culture in higher education implies that they are" (2002: 7).

Attention, Habits, and Addictive Experiences

The inability of humans to recognise their own habits and addictive behaviours suggests that notions of agency require closer scrutiny. The chemistry underlying habit formation is complex. Neurotransmitters are generated by the nervous system, and hormones are released by glands in the body and distributed to the blood: both affect decision making. There are over 50 neurotransmitters operating within our bodies, some of which are *excitatory*, increasing the chance that specific neuronal clusters will fire, whilst others are *inhibitory*. Neurotransmitters tend to act very quickly and more directly compared to hormones. Hormonal impact is longer lasting, though that length of time can vary from a few seconds to several days.

Serotonin is a "feel good" neurotransmitter, which affects mood. High levels are associated with optimism (it is also important for sleep), whilst reduced levels are implicated in depression. Dopamine is an internal pleasure hormone, and it is addictive. Cocaine, which is highly addictive, taps into and stimulates the natural dopamine-based personal reward system, which controls levels of arousal in the brain. Despite the role of dopamine in addiction, it is also vital for *motivation*, released when we are curious: dopamine production is therefore important for learning. Endorphins are also hormones, sometimes referred to as natural opiates, because they modulate pain, reduce stress, and produce feelings of calm and relaxation: like dopamine they can become addictive. Dopamine results in pleasurable *high* excitement states (*Up*), whilst endorphins are calming (*down*).

Children and adults spend much time engaged in social media and other smartphone applications, that allow the digitally mediated expression of thoughts, feelings, relationships, and other interactions. Burnett and Merchant (2020: 12) explain the twin forces of *participation* and *exploitation* as "digital innocence." These are monitored and collated in a covert form of surveillance. Many platforms involve intentionally manipulating the brain's reward system through *conditioned experiences* that create habits, and sometimes addiction, yet there is little awareness of these influences. Extensive research on addictive behavioural design has been

122 Experience Design: Sensing-Feeling

carried out by Natasha Schull (2012). *Addiction by Design*, said to be one of the most important works of social science to appear in the last 30 years, outlines her research on the engineered reality of the gambling experience.

Quite apart from its interest, and the exposé it presents about emerging aspects of business behaviours, the book pieces together important insights about our cognitive architecture and affective drives. By digging deep into the experience of machine gambling, Schull illuminates the strange tensions that make such activity appealing. Crawford's book *The World Beyond Your Head: How to Flourish in an Age of Distraction* (2016) refers to Schull's research, noting that it's not uncommon for heavy users to stand at a gambling machine for 8 or even 12 hours at a stretch, developing blood clots and other medical conditions. The industry uses concepts such as the *frustration theory of persistence* and the related *theory of cognitive regret* in which players circumvent the regret of having *almost won* by immediately starting to play again. The gaming industry is well-informed about these psychological theories, utilising them to influence human behaviour, and increase profit. They provide small wins at optimal frequencies; this is the "reinforcement schedule" along the lines of the sort of behavioural conditioning that relies on random reinforcement. In experiments with rats, random reinforcement (in the form of a dose of cocaine) has been found to be the most powerful way to induce the animals to persistent behaviour (for example pressing a button with their snout), for which they are occasionally rewarded. There will persist so doggedly that they neglect to eat or drink, and so they die. Their instinct for self-preservation has been overridden by something more powerful. The survival instinct is deliberately overridden for the pursuit of pleasure derived from attempts to win money.

Human agency comes under question when so many minds can so easily be manipulated and controlled. Habits occur due to (1) the repeat of initial *Triggers* which create (2) the *Habit*, which is (3) *Rewarded* to sustain the habit, which can generate (4) *Addiction*. Exploring the details of triggers, and reward systems, can help raise awareness, which potentially allows individuals to gain greater control. Questions to create greater awareness include *where* (location); *when* (time); what *feelings* (emotional state); *people involved*; what occurs *immediately preceding action*; and the *memory* of the experience.

Understanding the chemical and other processes that lead to habits and addictions, often derived from coping with stress, is important. Alternative experiences can provide chemical production substitutes. Taking the form of alternative "natural highs" they have the potential to override debilitating behaviours, to create healthier lifestyles. These include experiencing sport, music, dance, wildlife, outdoor adventure, camping, hiking, and other ways of experiencing and learning new things. This is the underpinning reasoning that underlies the global spread of "Life Competences," to improve well-being and mental health, social competences, and resilience. Learning to learn is one of the three main areas in the Life Comps of the EU. The subject of the search for Life Competences is outlined in Chapter 10.

Segal highlights how "research suggests that emotion serves as a central organising process within the brain" (2012: 9). Starting early in life, emotions significantly influence the developing mind: ultimately emotions influence learning, and positive emotional attachments create healthy relationships with others. Information is continually appraised and evaluated, and, in simplistic terms, 'good' and 'bad' judgments are made. The links between feelings and thinking are emerging.

> Within perception and memory, the appraisal systems of the brain must label representations as significant or value laden. In this way, the appraisal and arousal processes – the central feature of emotion – are interwoven with the representational processes of "thinking."
>
> *(Siegel, 2015: 184)*

Siegel suggests that artificial boundaries between feeling and thinking *"obscures the experiential and neurobiological reality of their inseparable nature"* (Siegel, 2015: 184). The next chapter explores this inseparable dynamic that connects and integrates *sensing, feeling*, and *thinking*.

6

EXPERIENCE DESIGN

Feeling~Thinking

Introduction

This chapter focuses on understanding the design of experiences of the *Heart* and *Head*. I start by asking an apparently simple question: Do we know only what we sense, or do we sense only what we believe? The answer is: it depends. *Feeling, thinking, knowing, understanding*, and *remembering*, the focus of this chapter, are connected to other modes of experiencing, and all operate at *conscious, preconscious*, and *subconscious* levels. What we remember is strongly connected to who we are, and vice versa. "The meanings we chose to create arise from all the meanings we have created in the past. The old saying, 'if I hadn't seen it I wouldn't have believed it', might be correct in particular circumstances . . . but in general the saying should be 'if I hadn't believed it I wouldn't have seen it'" (Rowe, 2001: 50). Rowe also notes that "every meaning contains its opposite because, if the opposite did not exist, no meaning could be created" (51). They are *opposite* yet also *complementary* (~).

The brain has evolved to become bigger and very specialised, with an impressive capacity for processing experiences and storing them as memory. Our human biological and social histories help trace important developments in brain capacities, which have developed as a result of *warm bloodedness*; *myelin sheaths*; *changing sensory priorities*; *movement*; *upright posture*; *tool creation and use*; *searching, navigating, and foraging for food*; and *social grouping* giving rise to *emotions*, and *language*. The neural systems dealing with these capacities are both *localised* and *distributed*, within both brain and body. There are specialised, separate functions in some areas, and areas of specialised *integrative processing*.

Lakoff and Johnson comment that "the mind is inherently embodied. Thought is mostly unconscious. Abstract concepts are largely metaphorical" (1999: 3).

DOI: 10.4324/9781003030867-6

Whilst the brain helps to make sense of the world it has, until recently, known little about itself. Knowledge of the processing areas is improving due to sophisticated scanning, and many years of research on damaged brains. As knowledge of the major processing areas increases, so too does knowledge of how we learn. Some brain processing areas *specialise* and *segregate* distinct *modes* of experience. Other areas *connect*, *integrate*, and give *coherence*, and *continuity* to past, present, and future resulting in an "experiential whole" (metaphors of *river* or *movie* explored earlier). Indeed, it is said that "a defining condition of being human is our urgent need to understand and order the meaning of our experience, to integrate it with what we know to avoid the threat of chaos" (Mezirow & Associates, 2000: 3).

Thinking with the Heart

There are many ways of knowing and thinking, for example reason and logic; revisiting memories; using external representations; movement; sensory perception; emotions; imagination; language; through faith and spiritual meanings; mindfulness and meditation; and intuition. As noted in the previous chapter, there is almost always an emotional component attached to any experience: emotional responses are foundational to survival and appraisal-arousal systems. As Siegel notes "emotion and meaning are created by the same processes" (2015: 184).

Barbara McClintock had a brilliant scientific mind yet struggled under the institutional prejudice that occurs when someone doesn't think in the same way as the majority. McClintock was regarded as a maverick, yet she was eventually awarded the Nobel Prize when her work was finally given due recognition.

> As the historian of science Thomas Kuhn has shown, the scientist with a revolutionary, paradigm-shifting idea often meets with massive resistance because that scientist's colleagues are so emotionally, professionally, culturally, and sometimes even financially invested in the "truth" of a certain model of reality.
>
> *(Mayes & Williams, 2013: 13)*

In a moment of doubt about her abilities Barbara McClintock walked out one day into the fresh air with negative feelings about a problem she was trying to resolve in her work on plant genetics. She sat on a bench and found space to *think* things through. Within half an hour something happened, probably in the subconscious: "suddenly I jumped up, I couldn't wait to get back to the laboratory, I knew I was going to solve it – everything was going to be alright" (Keller, 1983: 115). It is a common phenomenon that ideas suddenly arrive from the subconscious.

McClintock absorbed herself in her work on corn genetics for hours on end, in a state of deep immersion, for many years. She often remarked that she had a "*feeling*" for her plants, and a biography on her is titled *A Feeling for the Organism*. Language connects the inside with the outside world: we use it to think in our heads and to externalise thinking. McClintock recognised the limits of verbal thinking and reasoning. She yearned for moments when her immersion would cause her sense of self to disappear. Artists and poets, lovers, and mystics, have long known and written about the particular "knowing" that comes from loss of self. These out of body, *immersive-feeling-thinking* states are experiences that occur when the mind is deeply focussed on the task. This *mind-body-emotion* fusion is sometimes referred to as "flow" (see Csikszentmihalyi, 1990). When "higher" order, transcendent modes of experiencing are at play, there is intense *focus*, *mindfulness*, *absorption*, and *deep engagement*, when sensory, emotional, and mental experiences merge. *Feeling* and *thinking* are clearly not distinct capacities.

Emotional Influences on Thinking

Immordino-Yang and Damasio caution that "when we educators fail to appreciate the importance of students' emotions, we fail to appreciate a critical force in students' learning. One could argue, in fact, that we fail to appreciate the very reason that students learn at all" (2008: 196). Emotions influence so many facets of life, including learning. Emotions influence the making of sound moral judgements, the sense of self, and social functioning within groups, communities, and wider society. Emotions influence thinking and thinking influences emotions. Words that we associate with positive learning experiences suggest the emotional dynamic: *curiosity*, *enquiring mind*, *resilience*, *creativity*, *awareness*, *focussed*, *engaged*, *making meaning*, *growth orientated*. *Embarrassment*, *envy*, *pride*, and *admiration* are clearly social dynamics: they are based in culture, and social comparison. What is emerging is that emotions are psychological, biological, and social constructions.

Many emotions act as gatekeepers to learning. They have an impact on the ability to think, to know, to understand, and to remember: "the appraisal of stimuli and the creation of meaning are central functions that occur with the arousal process of emotions" (Siegel, 2015: 164).

 DESIGN ILLUSTRATION 17 LIBERATING INTRODUCTIONS.

Design Illustration 17 concerns the establishment of an initial emotional climate, initiating group cohesion, and peer and tutor-participant interactions, as well as the ability to ask and craft questions. In Chapter 5 the idea of "interludes" was introduced, related to icebreakers, energisers, and group building activities. This illustration highlights a creative approach to beginnings. Introductions, of yourself as facilitator or teacher, present opportunities to influence power relations. Power can be *flipped* to positively influence the initial emotional climate. As a facilitator it is not always productive to spend time introducing yourself. Instead of starting as the expert with power and control, why not become a critical friend and co-learner right from the start?

Sit in a "hot seat" in the centre of the room, or at the centre back of the room. Ask participants to break into small groups (4/5) and ask each group to *craft* three or four interesting *questions* to ask you the facilitator. They get to know what they want to know. The group are asked to consider the *kind* of questions they create, and what the focus of interest is, and isn't. Advice can be offered, such as: (1) *interesting questions get interesting answers*; (2) *boring questions get boring answers*. The facilitator can refuse to answer inappropriate questions. The time for the design of the questions can vary (10 minutes). The time to answer the questions can vary (15 minutes).

Design Principles

- The session introduces a few core concepts that the group can discuss: a sense of belonging and togetherness, changing power relations, participant control, practicing the art of asking good questions, feeling comfortable with the tutor, setting the emotional climate, and settling in, taking responsibility, and motivation.
- Building good relationships is important to individuals and groups, and for learning: learning is a social process (see *No Education Without Relation* by Bingham & Sidorkin, 2004), and groups usually quickly develop their own *identity* (see Ringer, 2002).
- This activity presents opportunities for a facilitator to reveal elements of their *professional* and *personal self*.
- Learning is enhanced by our emotions, and this activity can begin to create a positive *emotional climate* or "space," where people can feel comfortable to express themselves.

FIGURE 6.1   The hot seat.

The "hot seat" is arranged somewhere among participants, ideally not directly at the front where power is usually located. The seat is so that you the facilitator can be interviewed. When the social interactional dynamics change like this in a different *structural* format (e.g., room layout) this can empower people (sometimes called *liberating structures* – see Lipmanowicz & McCandless, *The Surprising Power of Liberating Structures*, 2013).

These ideas also link to Q & A approaches at end of session or programme, to create confidence in asking more questions, so that participants can discover more about what they want to know.

Thinking Faster

Lakoff and Johnson (1999: 3) argue that "the mind is inherently embodied. Thought is mostly unconscious. Abstract concepts are largely metaphorical." The brain has many processing regions: higher and lower, left and right, and back and front. All these areas are variably *connected* and *integrated*. The integrative processing is millisecond fast and therefore occurs mostly in the subconscious. The following brief account highlights just how much fast processing is carried out in the simple acts of recognising something. A flowering rose is recognised as follows. Based on past experiences, together with the sensory information of the basic shape, form, smell, contours and angles, information is integrated to generate a "categorisaton" that what is being seen are "*flowers.*" The processing continues and sub-categorisation and differentiation occur, to further identify the flowers as *roses*. This upward-downward part-whole processing moves from the *general* to the *specific*, from "lower" level analysis (*parts*– shape, form, petals) to higher analysis levels (*whole* = flowers) and back to lower levels (parts) to subsequent analysis (these are roses) (see *Big Brains*, Lynch & Granger, 2008 for an excellent, detailed neural explanation). Interestingly, in mindfulness training the reflective focus and attention is on opening-up the sensory gates "rather than grasping onto the top-down invariant judgements" (Siegel, 2007: 107).

In *Thinking Fast and Slow* Kahneman (2011) discusses two major processing speeds, though the boundaries are not clear-cut. The fast subconscious processing route is responsible for the "emotion-based response" required for survival-based decision making. Kahneman calls this System 1 thinking that involves quick judgements and a quick response. System 2 is the slower "rational" thinking response. Examining some of the myths associated with the supposed benefits of slow rational thinking over fast emotion based-thinking, Kahneman suggests that much of our life operates on System 1 autopilot, with little control, with the subconscious mind influencing our thinking with considerable bias. The slower

Experience Design: Feeling~Thinking **129**

rational response system 2 however is not as reliable as we think: system 1, the emotion-based response, is the hero of his book.

Motivation to Learn: Purpose and Pleasure

Several processing areas in the brain create *emotions*, as a state of mind that prepares brain-body for action, to evoke *motion*. The innate need to learn, create new things, better ourselves~world, and direct our lives, are important forces that motivate learners. *Passion* and *positive* emotions, along with *purpose*, are particularly important in learning. Positive emotions are linked to health, well-being, and resilience.

People (1) seek *pleasure* and avoid pain, (2) seek *hope* and avoid fear, and (3) seek *social acceptance* and avoid rejection, and these three motivational forces significantly influence learning. Emotions are *relational* in that they link with and influence self and others, and positive emotions occur when there is an appropriate *integration* and alignment of the external and internal world: to create "positive emotional states, the individual is both internally and interpersonally more integrated" (Siegel, 2015: 338).

Motivation is about *why* we do things, that is, what *drives* us to do what we do. They satisfy our needs and desires. There are many different motivational layers that, to an extent, reflect the major processing areas of the brain. At a "lower" level there are rudimentary drives such as food and water, defending territory (options for fight, flight, or fright), reproduction, the need for rest and activity, and for safety. Maslow (1954) produced seven layers: (1) physiological (food water), (2) safety (security, protection, shelter), (3) belongingness (giving and receiving love and affection), to higher level needs of (4) esteem (respect, achievement, self-esteem), (5) cognitive needs (curiosity, understanding, knowledge), (6) aesthetic (beauty, order, art), and (7) self-actualisation (realising one's potential – a higher order motivation).

Motivation is divided into intrinsic and extrinsic forces. Intrinsic motivation essentially involves the internal dynamics driven by enjoyment, curiosity, relevance, ambition, fascination, a desire to help others, or to be creative. Extrinsic motivation on the other hand involves external factors or rewards. There are different forces operating in learning, such as the motivation to *get* or *have*, for example, a good grade, to receive praise, appear competent, or impress.

Motivation by Design

Motivation is influenced by a need for achievement, competence, self-actualisation, self-worth, autonomy, and relatedness. Major motivations include the need for *achievement* and a sense of *belonging*: when satisfied, both can create pleasurable emotions. A positive mind is said to *broaden* out (rather than *narrow*) thought–action

130 Experience Design: Feeling~Thinking

options, resulting in creativeness, play, joy, and curiosity, for example (see Barbara Fredrickson's *Broaden-and-Build Model of Positive Emotions*). "Positive emotion arises with increases in integration, whereas a negative emotion occurs with decreases in integration" of the self (Siegel, 2015: 338). Positive learning experiences can reinforce positive habits of learning, that in turn influence future goals and aspirations. However, Beaumeister et al. (2001) present an excellent review of the way that negative emotions can dominate and have a very powerful undesirable effect on our lives. They outline how we focus on negative issues more readily, and point to the fact that there are more negative words in all languages.

Basic internal drives (the need for food, survival) have been coined "Motivation 1.0" processing by Daniel Pink in *Drive* (2010). "Motivation 2.0" relates to the extrinsic (external) motivators such as rewards or punishment (also a form of conditioning), which can work well for rule-based, routine tasks. Powerful, advanced intrinsic motivational forces, referred to as "Motivation 3.0," are said to produce *mastery, purpose,* and *engagement.* Pink suggests that only through engagement can this mastery be produced, and engagement is linked to purpose. Behavioural psychology professor Paul Dolan (2014) in *Happiness by Design,* similarly, argues that pleasure and purpose are important motivational forces for achieving happiness. Happiness is underpinned by three Ps: *pleasure* and enjoyment (in contrast to pain), *purpose* (in contrast to pointlessness), and being *productive* (rather than leading an unproductive life). These Ps are important for learning experience design: to create Pleasure, enjoyment and fun, through Passion and Purpose in a focus/goal/target, by being Productive by making or creating something, and achieving success/goals. If these are crucial to being happy, they are surely crucial for learning. In the previous chapter the experience of pleasure in learning was discussed in some detail.

Well-being and *flourishing* are terms that are used interchangeably. *Flourish* is the name of a book based on positive psychology by Seligman (2011), who suggests the building blocks of optimum flourishing are five specific categories of experience: *positive emotion, engagement, relationships, meaning,* and *accomplishment* (PERMA). These five categories present a useful experiential learning design framework for the consideration of positive learning experiences. Positive emotions from learning derive from *focus and engagement, being absorbed, thinking, pondering, moving, building, wanting,* and having immersive *flow* experiences. These are enhanced by social relationships including the design of a feeling of *belonging within the group,* of *safeness, security, being connected, being able to speak freely and being listened to, feeling liked and loved.* The job of experiential learning designer is to find ways to create memorable experiences that create (mostly, not always) positive emotions, so that people can be engaged, build relationships, develop autonomy, find meaning in life, and become skilled and competent at something (see Chapter 10 for research on the importance of the integrative nature of life competences). These emotional states generate positive memorable experiences.

The Pleasure of Learning

In 1921 Austrian scientists took two frog hearts and put one in a saltwater chamber connected to a second chamber by a fluid-filled tube. When they stimulated the vagus nerve of one of the hearts it slowed down, and after a few minutes the second heart also slowed down without any stimulation. This was the beginning of evidence that chemicals were transmitting information (messages) in the body fluids. They were awarded the Nobel Prize in 1936. The previous chapter explored how pleasurable states are similarly derived from electrical and hormonal stimulation of areas of the brain. Positive emotions in the form of a pleasurable "high" derive from the chemical neurotransmitter called dopamine. Positive states that result in a calming effect derive from natural opiates/endorphins (Gilbert, 2010). These two types of positive feelings originate from (1) a sense of *achievement* (the incentive, resource-seeking, drive-excitement system —"high") and (2) the sense of *affiliation* (sense of belonging, soothing, connected, safe, calming, contentment system). The opposite negative emotions are (3) "threat" based emotions that give rise to, for example, aggression, feeling stupid or bad, under attack, rejection. All three make up the fundamental emotional rollercoaster of everyday experiences. I refer to the two positive states as the AA Batteries (A*ffiliation* and A*chievement*). The experience of learning should charge these AA batteries as they oppose the negative emotional states which are based on fear: life is unsatisfactory when there is insufficient lightness (joy) to dispel the darkness (pain and rejection).

The Fear of Thinking at the Edge

> Although the notion of transformative learning points to a desirable destination for educational endeavours, the difficulty in the journey is often neglected. Our intention is to map the experiential micro-processes involved in transformative learning. . . . We employ the notions of liminality, comfort zone, and edge emotions to elucidate the transformative process.
>
> *(Malkki & Green, 2014: 5)*

In this extract learning and life are portrayed as a *journey*, towards a *destination*, using a *map* (as a navigational tool). Learning experiences tend to journey through recognizable territory, rather than the unknown, for comfort and self-preservation (Malkki, 2012; Beard & Malkki, 2013). When journeying through *difficult* terrain there is a tendency to return to our *comfort* zone to avoid potentially transformative though unpleasant emotions that occur at the *edge* (precipice). Cognitive *dissonance* refers to a situation involving conflicting values, beliefs, attitudes, or behaviors, that produces a feeling of discomfort that can also lead to the alteration in values, beliefs, attitudes, or behaviors that

132 Experience Design: Feeling~Thinking

reduce discomfort and restore balance. Whilst positive emotions reduce anxiety and increase performance, dissonance and discomfort can foster change by enabling difficult circumstances to be faced in ways that can create profound shifts in belief systems, values, or meaning perspectives. This can come about through critical reflection and exploration of uncomfortable emotions, and their origins. In the long term, confronting "edge emotions" can help people accommodate and be comfortable with difficult terrain (see the transformational phase of a learning design in Chapter 10).

The Thinking Areas in the "Head"

As the brain evolved it retained older neural wiring and structures, such as the reptile wiring that evolved around 300 million years ago. Old wiring remains at the base of the human brain, responsible for *instinctive* survival behaviours and bodily functions associated with hunger, breathing, movement, temperature regulation, posture, balance, and territorial instincts such as flight or fight. The mammalian brain evolved around 200 million years ago, when "competencies for complex thinking, reflection, theory of mind and having a sense of self-identity, began to emerge" (Gilbert, 2010: 29). The human brain evolved only 200,000 years ago yet it possesses a collective capacity of two million miles of neurons and one billion connections. It is estimated that the storage capacity of the brain is around a thousand terabytes of information, equivalent to about 500,000 hours of movies.

The human *brain*, consisting of three pounds of wrinkly flesh located within the 22 bones that form the human skull, never rests from processing. It does not make sense to suggest that the extensive neural processing network has clear-cut boundaries: much of the processing is *distributed*. Recently evolved processing capacities lie in the area known as the cerebral cortex, which consists of six thin, tightly sandwiched layers that form a wrinkly outer covering immediately below the skull. Called the *executive* functioning area, it operates to *integrate*, and make *coherent* the part-whole relationships: *spatial relations, audition, olfaction, movement, emotion, memory,* and *communication* to name a few. The newest parts are located in the forebrain, where complex mental tasks are processed, including thought, judgement, and long-term planning. In *Big Brains: The Origins and Future of Human Intelligence*, Lynch and Granger suggest "the forehead tells the story; only humans have them" (2008: 93), though knowledge of the great apes will tell you that this is not quite the case!

Whilst *evolution* and *experience* influence who we become, what we direct attention to will influence what we experience. The brain has many interdependent functional areas, with both symmetry and asymmetry, a clear separation of the left and right hemispheres, a basal and dorsal area, fast and slow processing areas, and old and new wiring. We possess a brain that over thinks (*ruminates*), and brains that try not to think (meditative states), and we refer to the social brain, emotional brain, and rational brain. Although the "brain" is regarded as being within the skull, the brain is *embodied*, and we also have a *head brain*, and a *gut brain*. The nervous system around the gut in humans is said to be equivalent to the brain of a cat. We speak of "gut feelings," and in the majority of animals the brain is located very close to the entrance to the gut, which suggests that the brain evolved as a way of controlling what was taken in (or not) in terms of nutritious foods and toxins. There is also a *heart brain* with the heart communicating with the head in four distinct ways: *neurologically* (transmission of nerve impulses), *biochemically* (hormones and neurotransmitters), *biophysically* (pressure waves) and *energetically* (electromagnetic field interactions). These distributed processing systems are vertically integrated, linking the brain with the whole body.

Thinking in Movement

Much has already been covered on the important role of movement in the development of human thinking. The body and brain have co-evolved to function in an exquisite, optimising partnership resulting in much of the brain being devoted to "vision, motion, spatial understanding, interpersonal interaction, coordination, emotions, language" (Lakoff & Nunez, 2000: 1). Movement has been particularly significant in the evolution of brain capacity, and the reason for this is interesting. Sharks are formidable predators, and as fish they have relatively large brains. The non-predatory basking shark has a comparatively smaller brain. The brains of fruit eating primates, such as the spider monkey, are larger than those that eat leaves, such as the howler monkey and the gorilla. Moving to catch prey or navigating space to find maturing fruit has played an important role in brain development, but the trade-off is that large brains take longer to mature, and offspring are nurtured for longer.

Sheets-Johnstone (1990, 2009) presents substantial *phylogenetic* (evolutionary), and *ontogenetic* (developmental – from foetus, to infant, to adult) evidence to demonstrate how the bond between human *thinking* and human *evolution* is cemented by the *sensing, feeling, moving* body. Her phylogenetic exploration shows how all animals, from single-celled creatures to mammals, exhibit a kinetic, bodily logos (body intelligence), in that they move towards food, and away from predators (to avoid being eaten), and that these abilities are not just *instinctive*. The ontogenetic analysis shows how infants think primarily through movement, by *tasting, grasping, crawling, reaching*, and *touching*. Sperry (1968) concluded in his Nobel prize winning research on the functional differences in brain hemispheres, that the brain is an organ *of* and *for* movement. Similarly, in *Evolving Brains*, Allam (2000: 2) suggests "there would be little need for a nervous system in an immobile organism or an organism that lived in regular and predictable surroundings."

134 Experience Design: Feeling~Thinking

Evolutionary developments	Short Notes on Some of the Key Evolutionary and Experiential Influences on the Development of the Brain
	Sheets-Johnstone highlights the indissoluble bond between hominid *thinking* and human *evolution*, a bond cemented by the living *body*. Our evolutionary past is important as it points to several major influences on capacities to learn that have become refined in humans over long periods of time. '*The brain and body co-evolved so that the brain could make the body function optimally. Most of the brain is devoted to vision, motion, spatial understanding, interpersonal interaction, coordination, emotions, language, and everyday reasoning*' (Lakoff and Nunez, 2000:1).
1. The impact of Warm bloodedness, and myelin sheaths: allowed increased processing (thinking) speeds enabling greater integration, and coherence.	Warm bloodedness creates the optimal temperature for the stability, balance, and efficiency of chemical reactions, to regulate the body and brain using neurotransmitters and hormones, acting to *block* or *activate* neural networks (e.g. *serotonin, dopamine, oxytocin, acetylcholine, glutamate, noradrenaline,* and *endorphins*). These chemicals contribute to *feelings,* pleasure or the sense of *security and calmness* (belonging), or anxiety, and *fright, fight, or flight responses.* The chemicals allow *fast processing* of *messages* within the body. All these function better in optimum temperatures. The myelin sheath is a crucial vertebrate evolutionary innovation that has resulted in *faster processing* (judgement) speeds. They first emerged in early vertebrates that possessed jaws, that is, they had *active*, predatory rather than *sedentary* lifestyles. This required fast response wiring (nerves), *functional diversity, efficiency,* and *density, that is, masses of cabling.* Myelin sheath enables dense neural networks, that doesn't interfere with neighbouring cables which is important in the more complex human brain (cephalisation), which allows for the neuronal density required for *association, integration, comparison,* and *contrast,* through complex mental maps. This resulted in the significant advancement of the human capacities to learn. Warm bloodedness requires more food to maintain the consistent temperature: searching and predator-prey pressures also accelerated brain evolution.
2. The improvement of sensory capacities	Sensory capacities have developed over a long period of time. All animals *move* away from or *towards* predators or food. The most basic of organisms such as bacteria possess highly developed sensory systems for the *detection* of nutrients and toxins (Allman, 2000: 5). Primitive animals had *photoreceptive cilia* that responded to the *contrasting* light of day and night (*daily activity cycles*) keeping some animals *away* from water surfaces during the day to *avoid* predation. Smell developed early. In mammals *major sense of vision* then became very important. *Colour* is especially important as it allows a focus on *differentiation.* '*Good sensory skills, such as colour vision, are needed to recognise ripe fruit in a tree, and good motor skills are required to reach and manipulate it. Good spatial skills are required to navigate to trees that contain fruit. Good memory skills are required to remember where fruit trees are, when they will be ripe, and in which trees the fruit has already been eaten'* (Kolb & Whishaw, 2014:25). The *senses* enhance *arousal, awareness,* and *focus. Sensory* experiences enhance *memory.* The MRT-London Underground Maps are a classic example of effective colour use. Humans capabilities include *Sensory Intelligence.*
3. The impact of movement	Living things move. *The roots of thinking lie in movement.* Thinking is linked to the body. Concepts are generated by animate form and the tactile-kinaesthetic experience (displayed in language). Brain evolution is linked to *predatory movements* behaviour. *Movement* towards or away from predators or prey is significant for all animals. Movement is important for overcoming *challenging environmental conditions,* such as searching for food. Movement requires *faster processing speeds.* Neural systems developed that allowed fast movement, reduced reaction times and problem solving. The nonpredatory basking sharks have *smaller brains* than other sharks. There are many other similar examples (the Howler Monkey which chews leaves, has a smaller brain than the Spider Monkey that eats fruits). Movement and other circuits are stabilized and co-ordinated by *serotonin* systems – serotonin modulates the connection strength. Following physical activity there is a *sense of well-being.* *Movement* is central to brain function and processing. *Movement creates attention.* That is, movement of objects for learning, movement of ourselves, the brain is instantly focussed on moving things, movement within the places where we learn, and movement of the environment (furniture, desks).Outdoor learning, focus on movement, engaging for many learners. Kinaesthetic intelligence.
4. Upright posture freed the hands, changed perspectives, and impacted on human capacities.	About 4.4 mya early humans became bipedal, standing upright enabling them to see a different view of the world. *Upright stance gave new perspectives, angles, distance, dimensions, part-whole picture.* Resulted in the *hands* being freed to *communicate, feel and do things* whilst moving and hunting in social groups. Body form changed and freed so that 'the entire grid of spatial orientations of an upright hominid creature became fundamentally distinguished from that of a quadruped' (Sheets-Johnstone, 1990: 77). The upright orientation increased awareness of *spatial binaries* increased the awareness of up/down, side/side, front/back, top/bottom. The hands became free as they were not needed to support the body. Manipulation of objects became possible. Hand and brain feedback loop developed. More *expansive visual capacity.* The *hands,* freed from supporting the body, gradually develop exceptional manipulative capacities. Touch and feel become an important function. Rotation and *manipulation* of *objects* is a powerful way to learn.
5. Tool creation and use enhanced capacities for learning.	Around 2.5 mya early stone tools were crafted. Hands freed to craft tools, to hunt and *manipulate objects.* Hand developed co-ordination capacities including *holding, rotating, squeezing, grasping, striking, shaping, crafting,* all linked to *imagination and visualising* an end-product. Also involved muscle co-ordination, mind-body interactions, resulted in complex co-ordination of several parts of the brain by the *cerebral cortex.* Co-ordination of movement of the body, rotation of stone objects, and striking of object with an object, in a spatial dynamic. *Visual-spatial sketchpad* memory is said to be the oldest working memory system. Crafting multi-dimensional tools by humans is said to have taken us beyond ape grade spatial cognition. *Creative production. Manual skills. Visual-spatial relational* dynamics are particularly important for learning. Kinaesthetic-Spatial awareness/intelligence.
6. Searching, navigating, and foraging for food enhanced several human capacities.	Ten times more food had to be found in order to operate as a warm-blooded animal. Brain function requires considerable food resources. Significance of food finding in challenging environmental conditions became more important, requiring *navigation, memory, colour* differentiation and other *sensory discernment* to detect ripeness of fruits and nuts on certain trees, in certain locations, at certain times: requiring an understanding of *space and time.* Catching prey requires faster *movement.* The gorilla has a relatively *small brain* in relation to its size c. to many other primates, *low levels of movement,* feeds on static bamboo plants. Movement for hunting developed in *social groups.* Darwin proposed that the *evolution of intelligence is related to living in social groups.* The larger the size of the *neo-cortex* volume relative to the rest of the brain, the larger the social group size in primates (see Allman, 2000: 174). Expression through *gestures* and the reading of *facial expressions/emotions* advanced. Sharing hunting, and *food* meant also sharing *information/knowledge/skills.* Powerful sense of *spatial awareness,* part-whole *relationships* became important (the bigger picture, and smaller elements).Understanding *distance .*
7. Social grouping and the evolution of language had a significant impact on our ability to learn from others.	*Collaboration,* and *competition.* Bigger brains meant *longer maturity* time: parenting and bonding time has lasted longer, and humans depended on the establishment of the *extended family. Sharing, protecting, planning, and organising became more complex: thinking abilities advanced.* Communication capacities develop further. *Gestures and other movement of the body became important, especially the facial muscles. Language* developed from gestures and basic onomatopoeic sounds (mimicked natural sounds and movements). Language, both spoken and written allow for the *transmission of complex ideas.* Communication included a complex array of facial expressions of emotion.

FIGURE 6.2 Seven adaptive developments that have influenced the human ability to learn from experience.

Experience Design: Feeling~Thinking   **135**

Movement is also important for experiential learning designs: moving *objects* and *data*, moving *hands*, moving *self*, moving *groups*, moving within *space*, movement of *furniture*, and interacting with moving plants and animals. However, movement is just one of several significant evolutionary forces that have greatly influenced the human capacity to learn. The chart in Figure 6.2 presents a brief analysis of several major *evolutionary (experiential)* influences on the development of the brain, including sensory focussing, movement, upright posture, hand use, new visual perspectives, searching and navigating in time and space, production of objects and tools, language creation, emotions, and complex social interactions. All point to important human capacities that are significant to experiential learning design, and there is a clear degree of alignment with the seven experiencing modes within the holistic experiential learning model (HELM).

Upgrading Mental Capacities: From Foraging to Taxi Driving

Searching and foraging for food led to increased capacities for understanding and navigating space and time, and these capacities are now adapted to new forms of learning. London taxi drivers memorise over 25,000 streets, and over 1,400 landmarks before gaining accreditation. Maguire, a neuroscientist, wanted to find out what impact this had on their brains, and she and her colleagues discovered that these taxi drivers have an enlarged right posterior hippocampus, an area of the brain known to be involved in *spatial navigation* (Maguire et al., 2000). This notion of *neuroplasticity* is important (rather than "fixed brain" theories that promote the idea that humans are all genetically born either slow learners or faster "gifted" learners). Genetic differences do occur yet *experience* also accounts for the development of brain capacities: in experienced violin players the brain area that directs the fingers of the left hand is five times larger than that of those who don't play an instrument (Swaab, 2014: 259).

Maguire went on to study world memory champions and discovered that whilst these mental athletes were learning many three-digit numbers, two specific areas of the brain lit up: those responsible for (1) *visual* memory and (2) *spatial* memory. These memory specialists were converting numbers into visual images and placing them in a spatial sequence along a familiar journey (Maguire, 2000; Foer, 2011). This ancient recall method is called the "Method of Loci," used by great orators to deliver long speeches since ancient times. Winston (2003) refers to this method as the *marriage and burial* approach (marriage is the association with something, burial concerns where information is placed within a location). Foer (2011) suggests memory is more about creatively using visual images to link disparate ideas and form new associations. *Visual*, *spatial*, and *temporal* schema help learners navigate and remember their learning experiences (see *complex representations*, Chapter 10).

136 Experience Design: Feeling~Thinking

Mapping the Processing Areas

Back in 1848 a one metre metal rod shot through the eye socket and brain of Phineas Gage as the result of an explosion that occurred whilst working on the railways. Everyone was amazed that he survived. Initially he appeared to carry on as normal despite the damage to his frontal lobe (linked to emotions). Over time the result was debilitating: his personality began to change dramatically, his life fell apart, and he was unable to make judgements or sustain relationships. The link between cognition and emotion becomes clear through this well-known story which signifies early functionality mapping of damaged brain areas. Modern brain research now includes brain scanning and other high-tech approaches.

Whilst the brain carries out different functions in many different areas, integrative processes are important. Feelings and thought are so integrated that without adequate access to emotional, social, and moral feedback, learning cannot be reliably informed about real-world functioning when the *emotional rudder* is absent (Immordino-Yang & Damasio, 2008). Indeed "surgeons now make every effort to leave the hippocampus and related brain regions intact, at least on one side of the brain, when operating on the temporal lobes so that these devastating effects can be prevented" (LeDoux, 2008: 159).

Mapping all the functional areas of the brain is immensely difficult: the cortex alone contains between 50 and 100 distinct functional areas though the boundaries are not clear cut. Vast brain *networks* use electrical signals to communicate, and the speed and density of the signals is enhanced by a fatty *myelin sheath* surrounding the cables enabling signals to travel long distances uncontaminated by adjacent cables. The consequence is that neural networks can be tightly packed together without signal interference.

External representations are extensively used to facilitate and support understanding and *ways of thinking* (e.g., objects, maps, diagrams, graphs, and pictures). Complex internal firing patterns are also thought to internally *replicate* and *represent* what is going on in the outer world using complex neural networks.

Intelligence, Attention, and Privilege

The following quotation was introduced earlier in the book. It is reproduced again here to highlight historical notions of intelligence and privilege:

> The lower classes ought to be educated to discharge the duties cast upon them. They should also be educated that they may appreciate and defer to a higher cultivation when they need it, and the higher classes ought to be educated in a very different manner, in order that they may exhibit to the lower classes at higher education to which, if it was shown to them, they would bow down and defer.
>
> *(Curtis, 1963: 5th edition, p. 256)*

Experience Design: Feeling~Thinking **137**

This quotation, taken from the *History of Education in Britain*, reflects the prevalence of erroneous ideas about intelligence in the 19th century. In the Victorian era, with a penchant for maths, Galton believed that mental ability was inherited, and that society was structured the way it was for "natural" reasons. For Galton "women, blacks, and the lower classes occupied inferior positions because of their lack of innate talent, and he published graphs illustrating this" (Murdoch, 2007: 14). In *IQ: A Smart History of a Failed Idea* (2007) Stephen Murdoch chronicles a century long, turbulent, and appalling history of attempts to identify a single measure to establish someone's intelligence. Beliefs about intelligence, developed to segregate people, have profoundly affected public policy over many years, and flawed "intelligence test" scores have damaged so many lives. These tests privilege and value certain neural processing areas, despite each person having immensely complex and unique neuronal processing structures and personal circumstances.

Research on a person called "Kim," who was born with unusual brain features, including a lack of two fibre bundles that are typically very large in most humans and serve to connect quite large regions of the left and right sides of the brain is reported by Siegel (2015). Kim can read a full page of text in about 10 seconds, or an entire book an hour. He can remember all of it and recall upon request any part of thousands of books, including several telephone directories. What is significant about this story of Kim is that whilst this person is capable of tremendous mental feats that most humans would struggle with, by other measures this person is considered as impaired in that they have difficulty with abstract concepts, and social relations.

There is growing evidence of the privileging of hemisphere functionalities. DeSalle (2018: 149) quotes Roger Sperry as saying: "*What it comes down to is that modern society discriminates against the right hemisphere.*". The left hemisphere is said to support linear, sequential processing, associated with reading, writing, and speaking, whereas the right hemisphere supports holistic (wider picture) thinking and pattern detection, for example. Sperry's left-brain, right-brain theory (1968) is controversial, though the brain certainly does have different processing areas in the left and right *side* (for a comprehensive account on the hemisphere differences, based on a critical review of over 5,000 independent pieces of research, see Gilchrist, 2009; for a short version, see Gilchrist, 2019). Mistakenly the right hemisphere used to be regarded as the minor hemisphere, though Gilchrist notes that over a 10-year period between his book being first written and later expanded, there has been substantial research that has created "increasing respect for the capacities of the right hemisphere" (2009: xiv).

> Forget everything you thought you knew about the difference between the hemispheres, because it will be largely wrong. It is not what each hemisphere does – they are both involved in everything – but how it does it, that matters. In the prime difference between the brain hemispheres is the

138 Experience Design: Feeling~Thinking

manner in which they attend. For reasons of survival we need one hemisphere (in humans and many animals, the left) to pay narrow attention to detail, to grab hold of things we need, while the other, the right, keeps an eye out for everything else. The result is that one hemisphere is good at utilising the world, the other better at understanding it.

(McGilchrist, 2009, on the rear of his book Ways of Attending: How Our Divided Brain Constructs the World*)*

Separation and Integration

To understand why the brain is separated into two hemispheres it is important to go back in time to look at evolutionary clues. "If you are a bird, in fact, you solve the conundrum of how to eat and stay alive by employing different strategies with either eye: the right eye (left hemisphere) for feeding, the left eye (right hemisphere) for vigilant awareness of the environment" (Gilchrist, 2009: 26). The location of eyes on either side of the head in early animals created a *dual-attention processing system*, and such lateralisation brings evolutionary advantages in humans just as it does in many other animals. It turns out that each hemisphere attends to the world in a different but consistent way. The right hemisphere processes things in ways that create a context of the "whole," a *global perspective*, whereas the left hemisphere sees things abstracted from context, and broken into detailed parts, that is, a *local perspective* (Gilchrist, 2009: 27) (try out Geometric Psychology, Chapter 7 to see some of your own design preferences). Both hemispheres, however, function to integrate some processing functions, whilst separating other functions (separation~integration).

The diverse brain architecture is responsible for processing equally diverse *modes of experiencing*. Siegel highlights that "we have circuits responsible for visual processing and others for processing more abstract representations of ideas" (2015: 221). The earlier case of Kim warns against privileging specific networks, with variations and differences regarded as a deficit or disability. Human brains aren't neuro*typical*: the term *neurodiversity* is more inclusive. Human brains have both similar and dissimilar characteristics, and so what is attended to is likewise going to be different and similar. This has implications for *inclusive* and *pluralistic* approaches to experience design.

Understanding the basic brain processing architecture leads to an appreciation that a diverse range of "intelligences" must exist. Gardner (1983) regards intelligence not as a single unitary thing, but a collection of intelligences. The notion of processing "capabilities" constituting intelligence is reflected in Gardner's Multiple Intelligences Theory (MI Theory) (see Figure 6.3).

There are more intelligences. Lombard (2007) for example argues the case for the recognition and development of *sensory intelligence*. This broad range of "intelligences," to an extent, reflects the major brain processing areas (see Figure 6.4).

Experience Design: Feeling~Thinking **139**

1 mathematical–logical – the ability to organize thoughts sequentially and logically;

2 verbal–linguistic – the ability to understand and express ideas through language;

3 bodily–kinaesthetic – the gaining of knowledge through feedback from physical activity;

4 musical – sensitivity to tone, pitch, and rhythm, and the ability to reproduce them;

5 visual–spatial – the ability to learn directly through images and to think intuitively without the use of language;

6 interpersonal – the ability to notice and make discriminations regarding the moods, temperaments, motivations, and intentions of others;

7 intra-personal – the ability to access one's own feelings;

8 naturalistic – the ability to understand and be in tune with one's relationship with the natural environment;

9 creative intelligence – the ability to be creative and innovative;

10 spiritual intelligence – interconnectedness with the inner and outer world and the abi lity to sense the higher -self;

11 moral intelligence – the ability to act for the wider benefit of society, to have good principles and values.

FIGURE 6.3 Design implications of multiple "intelligences."

Integration: Simple and Complex Thinking Patterns

Figure 6.4 illustrates *integrative processing* across multiple, distributed functional areas, at different levels. The brain sorts, filters, organises, and classifies through up~down processing, from physically lower areas that process mostly sensory inputs, to higher processing areas that create complex meaning by "*sequencing, hierarchical classifications, part-to-whole, causation, comparing and contrasting, describing, analogies, and defining in context*" (Hyerle & Alper, 2011: 14). Different firing patterns create similarities, differences, generalisations, categorisations, associations, and new combinations (a useful list for thinking skills design). This type of processing also occurs in the interactions between and within the left~right hemisphere, and the front~back areas: all three complementary processing pairings (up~down, left~right, and front~back) are important for separation, integration, and coherence. Bloom's Taxonomy explores the vast range of processing (thinking) capabilities at different *levels* of complexity. In the revised taxonomy *creativity* was added to the top of the hierarchy. The verbs and

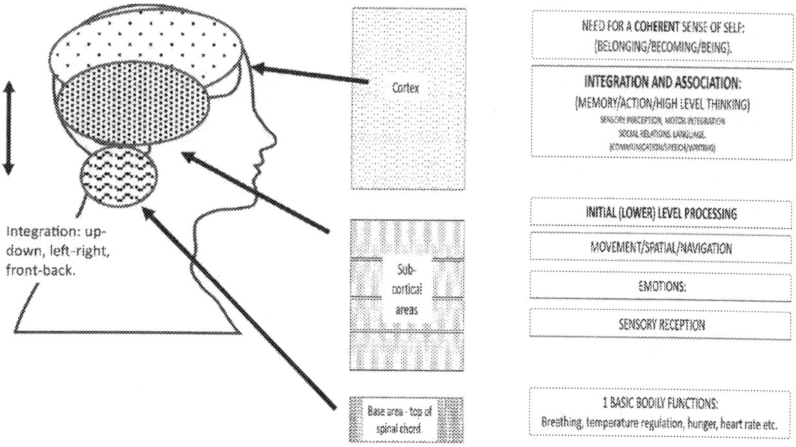

140 Experience Design: Feeling~Thinking

FIGURE 6.4 A simplified representation of the major processing ("thinking") areas of the brain.

nouns highlight the cognitive processing capacities of the brain, and they are also useful in providing design ideas for active thinking experiences. *Create* involves identifying new patterns, new concepts, innovating, generating, producing. *Evaluate* involves judging, critical evaluation, selection, recognition, and conceptualisation. *Synthesis* requires an ability to synthesise, summarise, argue, relate, précis, organise, generalise, conclude. *Analysis* requires an ability to select, compare, differentiate, contrast, break down, integrate, deconstruct. *Application* requires an ability to carry out, implement, predict, select, assess, find, show, use, construct, compute. *Comprehension–Understanding* requires an ability to classify, identify, interpret, illustrate, represent, formulate, explain, contrast. *Knowledge–Remembering* requires an ability to state, recall, identify, retrieve, recognise, select, reproduce, measure (adapted from Bloom's Taxonomy).

Memory, Recall, and Reflection

Ringer (2002) suggests three purposes of experiential learning: to affect the learner's *thinking*; to modify the learner's *attitude*; to expand the learner's repertoire of possible *behaviours*. Thinking, behaviour, and attitudes are affected by large neural networks that create what are known as *internal working (mental) models* or *representations*. To recall and reflect on something requires the same networks/connections to fire again to "trace" the "gist" of the experience. How we *remember* involves specific groupings of firing networks called "engrams" (think of *engraved*), as memory traces, that represent the underlying "gist" of the experience; memories are best understood as *re-firing* "potential," rather than fixed or permanent. The retrieval process using *refiring* of networks does not, however, result in an identical firing pattern to the original. It is important to remember that "confusing experience with the memory of it is a compelling cognitive illusion" (Kahneman, 2011: 381). Recall is therefore only approximate to the original firing network. In the refiring processes the brain also discards, makes links, and creates chunks of memory in the reflective processes, and these processes are also influenced by the refiring of past experiences, and potential future experiences. Learning and forgetting are closely related! One method that helps to overcome memory limitations (explored earlier) is called the "Method of Loci," as practiced by world memory champions. They use episodic memory and association to support the recall of substantial amounts of factual material (semantic memory).

There are multiple ways of thinking and knowing. *Factual* knowing involves the basic facts and figures. *Conceptual* knowing concerns the interrelationships in the basic elements. *Procedural* knowing involves how to do something, for example, methods of inquiry, or the criteria for using skills, techniques, or methods (also called *procedural memory*). *Metacognitive knowing* is an awareness and knowledge of one's own thinking and learning, involving learning to learn. Different ways of remembering are also processed in different parts of the brain. Computer terminology is useful to explain memory: working memory is the RAM, and the long-term memory is the hard drive capacity. Memories are essentially split into *implicit* (subconscious) and *explicit* forms (recalled, conscious memory), and consciousness is understood to occur through working memory. Some aspects of memory are deeply buried and not accessible to the conscious mind: subconscious elements that have potential to be accessed through greater awareness are also referred to as the *preconscious*. Conscious memory has two types: "*semantic*" memories, and "*episodic*" memories. The exact number of memory systems is contested and there are thought to be several: *procedural* (mostly preconscious, riding a bike or patterns of behaviour learned as a child), *perceptual* (sensory memories), visual spatial sketchpad memory (VSSM/spatial awareness) *semantic* (facts, figures, general knowledge, concept-based knowledge unrelated to specific experiences), *episodic* (re-experience specific episodes from one's own personal past), and *long-term*, and *short-term working memory*.

 DESIGN ILLUSTRATION 18 RECALL, REFLECTION AND REFIRING POTENTIAL.

If our brain fails to remember to retain arithmetic facts, that is because the organisation of human memory, unlike that of a computer, is associative: it weaves multiple links among disparate data. Associative links permit the reconstruction of memories on the basis of fragmented information.

(Dehane, 2008: 282)

The Stand-Up review experience enhances recall by using the notion of remembering as a mental "video" replay of experiential *episodes*, from the start to finish of a specific reflective period. Episodic memory is easier to recall than semantic remembering, though episodic memory can lead to the recall of semantic memories. The review takes an internal representational form of a movie, made visible using a dialogic process. On arrival to a second day, for example, participants stand behind their chair. The rules of the video replay are explained, and the process started. Anyone can start the process and everyone contributes. People can challenge the sequence or interpretations of events. After a contribution that is agreed by the group is correct, that person is seated and simply observes the review. What becomes clear is the significance of spatial (where), and temporal (when) and other memory associations, that is, associative memory.

The video replay highlights how behavioural, perceptual, somatosensory, and emotional aspects of experiences are often the first descriptions to surface, followed by specific details of the learning that occurred (e.g., conceptual deductions). Many participants refer only to what they *did*: the experience of *doing* appears to increase the refiring potential: they are often prompted to develop their memory further by the *so what* question. Where the activity took place, and in what context seems to increase refiring potential. This reviewing approach suggests that the experience of *doing* things, in *places*, with *others*, with *objects*, using *signalling* to focus *attention*, lays a powerful *engram* that is more easily retraced by the refiring of previously fired neural networks. *Experiential* learning appears to create more neural networks that have potential to fire on recall.

Cognitive Load

Short-term working memory systems have a limited processing capacity that can be overloaded with extraneous elements. The concept of *cognitive load* is an important principle in experiential learning design. Good *representational designs* (e.g., graphs, objects, images, maps) for example are known to reduce working memory load because much of the mental effort is *offloaded* and so less processing is required for a given task. In contrast, low offloading will necessitate higher cognitive effort to perform a given task.

Design Illustration 19 is a simple illustration of a *representational* design used to support the development of higher thinking skills (see Chandler & Sweller, 1991).

 DESIGN ILLUSTRATION 19 THE DEVELOPMENT OF HIGHER THINKING SKILLS — A SIMPLE DEPICTIVE REPRESENTATION.

Experience Design: Feeling~Thinking **143**

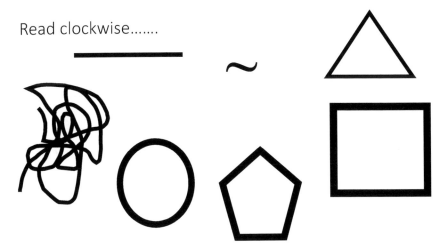

FIGURE 6.5 Points of view: Language as a design clue.

The visual images in Figure 6.5 illustrate how a very simple visual *representation* can explain the development of complex *levels of thinking*. These shapes can show that higher thinking skills are based on more complex themes, arguments, and *points of view*. The linguistic notion of *"points of view"* contains a metaphorical *design cue*. In the images in Figure 6.5, the "points" (of view) gradually become more complex (to be read in a clockwise direction).

Take, for example, the simple accounts on the topic of racism. The development of complex thinking is illustrated across the five images to be "read" in a clockwise direction: the images change from two opposite but simplistic points of view (colour: black versus white), to three (involving colour, culture, and class), five (fear, threat, colour, power, culture, and class), six, then the infinite-neat circle, then an infinite complexity of points of view (messy squiggles). The last image represents the messy complexity of real life, inherent within society today. On closer inspection, nodal clusters are revealed exposing several significant interrelated issues.

The same shapes visually illustrate how design can develop the kind of complexity illustrated in the final Chapter 10. Instead of a squiggly line a spider's web could be used. The final, rather messy, ill-structured visualisation follows the thinking of Jonassen (2011: 210) on problem solving: "designing instruction to support ill-structured problems requires that the ill-structuredness should be conveyed, not eliminated."

This visualisation has been further developed, to turn it into a group activity (see a video on https://youtu.be/mkKGhDcYOvc).

(For more on complex issues associated with racism training see Swan, 2007, who critiques three overlapping race equality training interventions: multi-cultural awareness training, anti-racist training, and diversity training to examine the kinds of experiences that are being created.)

Thinking Through Representations

A "representation" is also a re-presentation of something. It helps with communication, problem solving, and understanding. An iconic example is the London Underground Map (or MRT map), upon which many global transport maps are based. The designer, Harry Beck, got the idea from looking at the colour coding of electrical wiring. He is said to have remarked that because the details were located underground, the *connections* were more important than the *geography*: the success of this cartographic representation is largely due to the *reduction in extraneous load*. Reality is simplified in a colour coded spatial layout that is easy to navigate. The most effective maps are visually stimulating creations that use colour, symbols, lines, emphasis, novelty, icons, images, and keywords. (For the design of a complex representation see Chapter 10).

Due to the increased focus on multi-media, *"the use of external representations in learning, teaching, and communication has increased dramatically"* in information and communication technology (Verschaffel et al., 2010: 1). Designing effective representations is particularly important as information and concepts can be *re-presented* in numerous ways: they can be *descriptive* (e.g., words/symbols) and/or *depictive* (show using, e.g., images/miniature models/graphs). Multi-media research presents a diverse range of essential principles related to the representational use of words and images and their effect on working memory load reduction (cognitive load), especially in computer-based environments (Figure 6.6). Underlying these principles are two core theoretical positions: (1) Paivio's (1986) dual coding theory, relating to how we understand words and pictures, and (2) Baddeley's (1986) concept of working memory.

Processing Areas: Multi-Media Principles

The interpretation of the term "medium" as concerned with only words and pictures is limiting. It is aligned with notions of *instructional* methods, rather than a broader experiential focus on the complex *interactional* dynamics of learning that includes, for example: touch, gestures, pointing, handling, manipulating of objects, and bodily movement. Skulmowski et al., for example point out that there have been *"recent efforts to expand these models to include movements and related aspects of embodiment"* (2016: 65); they also point out that there are clear advantages when learners *construct* their own representations and then interact with them. The building of representations generates much *thinking*, which is made *visible* and *shared*, to create other perspectives.

Principle	Design Implications
Multiple Presentation Principle	Uses different sensory modes when presenting (sensing).
Signalling principle.	People learn better if experience design includes cues, pointers, and signposts for navigation, and drawing learner attention. Focus of attention (sensing).
Voice principle	People learn better when a friendly human voice is used rather than one generated by a machine. The human voice arouses (sensing).
Personalisation principle	People learn better when words are presented in a conversational style rather than formal style.
Spatial contiguity principle *Temporal contiguity* principle. *(also known as split attention).*	Temporal contiguity: people learn better if corresponding words and pictures are presented simultaneously rather than one after the other. Spatial contiguity: people learn better when words and visuals are presented close to each other. Split attention: referring to two or more different sources of information simultaneously creates excessive load. A common example is when, in presentation slides, the audience have to *process* the visual, the text, and the voice of the presenter simultaneously.
Worked example principle.	People learn better if the design includes the provision of a worked example.
Collaboration principle.	People learn better if the design includes collaborative online activities (Social interaction).
Drawing principle.	People learn better if they create drawings (doing) as they read explanatory text. This encourages cognitive processing such as *organising*, *structuring*, and *integrating*.
Modality principle.	People learn better if design includes *graphics* and *narration*, rather than *graphics* and *printed text*.
Learner Control principle	Design experiences that allow the learner to make choices about pace and order of instruction.
Extraneous Cognitive Load	Relates to the mental effort required (by the working memory). Extraneous load distracts, due to unnecessary or excessive material. Harder to turn working memory into long term memory.
See Mayer (2014) for a comprehensive review. See also Ginns who used a meta-analysis of over 50 instructional design experimental studies mostly in science subjects, especially STEM subjects (science, technology, engineering, and mathematics).	

FIGURE 6.6 Basic multi-media design principles.

The expansion of research on multi-media design principles is highlighted in the work of Mayer (2014): in 2001 Mayer outlined seven design principles, expanded to 12 by 2009, becoming 30 plus by 2014 (see Whitton for the relevance to digital game design – *Digital Games & Learning*, pp. 170–171). Textual-visual boundaries are becoming less clearly defined: icons, for example, are increasingly used as a form of *picture-text*, and Microsoft introduced a suite of icons in *Word* in 2016. The alphabet is another example where letters contain remnants of the original pictographic form: we forget that written language is also a form of *thinking in images*.

To create "higher" levels of thinking, the brain notes similarities and differences, makes generalisations, categorises, associates, analyses, and creates new combinations of information and so Design Illustration 20 highlights a basic presentation design related to some of these thinking skills. Note the *textual*, *visual*, and *conceptual* congruence (correspondence-equivalence).

 DESIGN ILLUSTRATION 20 THINKING THROUGH ALIGNMENT AND ASSOCIATION.

The notion of research as *investigation* conjures up the design ideas of research as a form of detective work. In research design the exploration of *detectives*, and their different research approaches, can be *metaphorically* productive in terms of creating design ideas. Similarly the notion of *categories* can be depicted as shown below.

Descriptive Explanatory-Concept LINEAR TEXT	Depictive Experientially Embedded Imagery VISUAL NON-LINEAR IMAGE
Explanatory Text Compare and contrast. Q: What is similar? Q: What is different? Q: How and why are they different?	Noodles and spaghetti Similar/sameness, but also different. **Differentiate**.
Explanatory Text Divide up the literature/research findings into themes. Cut and paste themes *into* containers, to identify differing categories.	Image of several different **coloured waste bins** **Paper, plastics, metals, glass, fabrics**. Bins are 'containers', they contain, and categorize. Things belong there because of their *characteristics*.

* Having explored this chart on *comparing, contrasting, categories* and creating *themes*, now close your eyes and see what you can remember.

This alignment of visual and textual representations can improve understanding. The representations in the previous image offer inclusive approaches to ways of *thinking* and *understanding* using *reading*, *seeing*, and *visualising*. Ken Robinson, in *Out of Our Minds: Thinking Creatively* (2001), outlines the predominant use of linear text in education, despite the need for non-linear thinking in order to solve many of the current complex global problems. Non-linear, visual thinking tools, maps, and other representations that communicate and develop rich patterns of thinking are found in other sections of this book (see also Hyerle, 2009; Hyerle & Alper, 2011). Design Illustration 21 focuses solely on words; however, the thinking processes involves creative *production*, *social interaction*, the use of *hands/bodily movement*, and *spatial sequencing* to *construct* a definition. Creative desings can generate creative thinking!

DESIGN ILLUSTRATION 21 THINKING THROUGH WORD WEAVING.

The "*Word Weaving*" experience involves *making meaning* involving the *construction* of a *definition* to demonstrate knowledge and understanding from a basic collection of words. It was first used to develop skills associated with "giving feedback" with consultant anaesthetists in the UK, who mentor junior anaesthetists. The design involved *deconstructing* (unpacking) the word *feedback*, to identify the basic elements that make up the term. The same deconstruction process can be used for other words, like *happiness, assertiveness,* or *fear*.

Early in the development programme little awareness of the defining parameters of feedback existed, and this activity generated considerable discussion, *making thinking visible*, such as the *foundational underpinning reasoning*. The following words were presented on separate cards:

> Deficit, Development, Constructive, Critical, Feedback, Criticism, Judgements, Observations, Ideas, Answers, Feelings, Needs, Requests, Demands, Transmission, Transaction, Transformation, Destructive, Problem, Person, Subjective, Objective, Task, Process, Outcome, Solution, Problem, Opportunity, Intuition.

These words are used by groups to create their interpretations of feedback, that become available for further group discussion. A set of three or four blank cards give the freedom to add other words. The construction process utilises *conversations, selection, elimination, sequencing, deciding, collaborating, capturing, comparison, co-production*, and other skills to create a definition of "*giving feedback.*" This design process involves the freedom to create new thinking, and the sense of *production* was enhanced by creating "take-away" recordings. Two consultant teams generated the following:

Feedback necessarily evokes feelings as it involves a series of observations which may be a subjective analysis of performance, often, but not always, involving judgement (implied or inferred). It is an opportunity to identify problems or deficits to help trainees generate or own ideas and answers in order to transform their practice, change their behaviour, and solve problems. (Group 1)

Feedback is an ongoing process that acknowledges the feelings and needs of both parties. Feedback is based on direct observation, and objectives, and represents an opportunity to share ideas for development. It should not be based solely on deficits or problems, rather it should be part of a series of transactions that aims for a transformation of that person, that both parties have carefully reflected on. (Group 2)

Extending the Mind: Tools for Learning

In Chapter 4 the quotation at the beginning stated that "the first mathematical experiences that children have are with concrete objects" (Bryant & Squire, in Gattis, 2016: 175). When asked to calculate 6 x 5 the answer will come into mind with little effort. When asked to calculate 568 x 149 most people would consider using pen and paper, or a calculator, to speed the process and offload working memory demand. The Extended Mind Theory (EMT) (Clark & Chalmers, 1998) provocatively challenges the assumption that the demarcation of skull and skin determines the boundaries of cognition, an idea that prompts a radical rethink of the nature of learning. The concept that the mind *extends* into, and *interacts with*, the body and into the environment is intriguing. The understanding of the use of tools to extend capacities of the mind is certainly useful for experiential learning design. Einstein is reputed to have said that his pencil was cleverer than he was!

The evolution of humans over five-plus million years resulted in an important development for one of our most important abilities. Understanding space and spatial relations was extensively enhanced by the crafting of tools such as axe heads around five million years ago (see Wynn, 2010), as a process that required complex co-ordination by the cerebral cortex, notably shape recognition, shape imagination, imposition, and striking of blows, and body co-ordination. This is said to have taken humans beyond ape-grade spatial cognition. Evolutionary theorists, and proponents of embodied cognition, now suggest that our experience of and in space, and the cognitive structures we develop to perceive, navigate, and remember space, are the essential foundations of complex abstract cognitive tasks (Gattis, 2001). This has significance in relation to Extended Mind Theory: Barbara Tversky (2016: 79) in her research on spatial cognition, remarks that "less noticed is the fact that we craft tools to augment our mental capacity as well." The printing press influenced the Renaissance, the microscope gave rise to microbiology, and the telescope encouraged astronomy. Only humans seem to make advanced tools to make things such as robots and cars. Objects, tools, and other artefacts are important tools for learning in *experiential* learning designs (see the Design Illustration 13 on Industrial Ecology), and technology is increasingly being used to create different realities (virtual, enhanced, and mixed realities).

The Implications for Agency

The 80-millisecond gap between *action* and the *consciousness* of that action is intriguing. In *We Are Our Brains* (2014) Swaab argues that we don't just *have* brains, *we are our brains*. His main argument is that the free will and agency that we think we have is not quite as extensive as we believe it to be (see the quotation at top of this chapter). Swaab examines the brain from prenatal development to old age, and concludes that "everything we think, do, and refrain from doing is determined by our brain. The construction of this fantastic machine determines our potential, our limitation, and our characters; we are our brains" (2014: 3). In contrast, Siegel declares his position in the sub-title of his book *How Relationships and the Brain Interact to Shape Who We Are*. Siegel explores the links between the individual minds, the minds of others, social interaction, and social relationships.

Interpersonal and intrapersonal relationships directly influence the development of the brain, and the ways people make sense of the world, to construct their own realities. The importance of social relationships in experiential learning design will be explored in the next chapter.

7

BELONGING

Social Interactions in Social Spaces

Introduction

The previous chapter focussed on the way emotions influence how we *think, understand*, and *remember*, highlighting several significant evolutionary developments that have increased human capacities to think, reason, and learn, particularly those affecting the brain and the mind. Indeed, "*collective knowledge and individual understanding are dynamically co-emergent phenomena*" (Davis & Sumara, 1997: 119). The focus of this chapter is the **H** for "Home" and/or "Habitat." *Home* and *habitat* are where we *belong*. This includes belonging in a social, digital, and physical world. Belonging in the natural world will form the focus of the next chapter (Chapter 8).

This chapter focuses on the importance of social relationships, affiliations, and interactions with other individuals in terms of how they influence the human capacities to learn. Critical thinking, empowerment, power and control, choice, voice, and self-authorship are briefly considered. The way we humans occupy and engineer spaces and places (*where* learning takes place) are also explored in this chapter.

We humans are relational beings, engaged in complex and diverse relationships with others. Ringer (2002) points out that in a group of just 10 people there are 90 relationships: 9 directly involving yourself, and 81 others. Through the individual~collective group dynamic of multiple social relationships, knowledge and meaning are constructed. Minds and bodies work with other minds and bodies, and knowledge becomes distributed across and between these multiple relations, co-determined by people, tools, and artefacts. Conversations between the group become a social action through the symbolic tool of language. As in the crafting of tools such as axes, the tools of language have also had a profound effect on the human ability to learn.

DOI: 10.4324/9781003030867-7

Groups also function through their individual and collective "working models," which operate in the consciousness and subconscious, in the mind of individuals, and in the collective mind of the social space of the group. As Ringer notes *"participant patterns of mental representations are the most significant aspects of a group"* (2002: 240).

Humans collectively construct group identities, values, beliefs, and culture, which contribute to group *being~belonging*. Individuals, and the group-as-a-whole, possess powers of self, agent, and actor in and through these complex social interactions. What *determines* agency, however, is the subject of much controversy. Are free agents capable of socially creating change or choice, or (highlighted in the last chapter) are we influenced by our biology? Agency is not derived from one or the other: it is determined by multiple factors.

Daniel Siegel highlights an important link between this chapter and the previous chapter by suggesting that *"the mind emerges from the substance of the brain and is shaped by our communication with interpersonal relationships"* (Siegel, 2012: 1). Siegel explores these links by synthesising *"information from a range of scientific disciplines to explore the idea that the mind emerges at the interface of interpersonal experience and the structure and function of the brain"* (2012: xii). He notes that:

> in my own field of psychiatry, the tremendous expansion of neuroscience research seems to have been interpreted in the extreme by some as a call to "biological determinism." . . . Recent findings of neural science in fact point to the opposite: interactions with the environment, especially relationships with other people, directly shape the development of the brain's structure and function.
>
> *(Siegel, 2012: xiv)*

In *Relational Being* (2009) Gergen similarly reconstitutes the mind as a manifestation of social relationships. He adopts a *social-relations* perspective to suggest that all meaning grows from coordinated *action*, or *co-action*, and that our understanding of the world very much depends on the well-being of our human relationships. What is common to both these writers is the notion we are *relational beings*. This has considerable significance for experiential learning design.

Secure and *insecure* patterns of *attachment*, developed with caregivers early in life, are carried forward into adulthood. Secure patterns are characterised by the person seeing themselves as likeable and good, exhibiting flexibility and durability in a range of circumstances, with the world essentially experienced as a safe place. Insecure attachments lead to a range of *defence* mechanisms, against pain and anxiety. Ringer (2002) presents an interesting comparison of what he refers to as traditional, outdoor activity based experiential learning, and psychoanalytic group work (it is worth remembering at this point that much of the early work by Lewin, on which the experiential learning cycle was based, involved group reflective analytical work using dialogue to look back on past experiences). Activity based experiential learning uses physical activity as the personal "concrete experience": just sitting around talking isn't seen as constituting a concrete experience by outdoor activity designers. The psychoanalytic perspective, in contrast, regards physical activity as a means of avoiding verbal expression of cognitive or emotional material, and that physical activity is a group *defence* mechanism.

Designs for social interaction centre on *what* is *expressed*, or *done* together, with *whom*, and *where* and why? Group learning is said to not only promote achievement, and interdependence, but also the development of "*social skills such as communication, presentation, problem solving, leadership, delegation and organization*" (McWhaw et al., 2003: 69). Gillies and Ashman (2003) present an historical review of the use of groups to promote socialisation and learning, including an interesting account of experiments conducted by Lewin with 10-year-old boys. Lewin divided the boys into an *authoritarian* group, and a *democratic* group: the former exhibited considerably more aggressive behaviours. Lewin went on to explore the dramatic impact of different leadership styles by the boys. These experiments created interest in group learning, which then re-merged in the 1970s, stimulated by findings that showed the positive impact of children assisting other children to learn, reducing incidents of disruptive and deviant behaviours. Increases in learning resulted from these co-operative approaches to learning experience design. The authors note that research on co-operative learning has burgeoned over the past three decades, becoming a significant feature in pedagogic design.

> **DESIGN ILLUSTRATION 22 MOMENTS OF COLLABORATION.**

This experience can be created in both physical and digital learning environments.

The lecture theatre is a space designed for *transmission* approaches to learning. One experiential approach used by lecturers for some years is explained by Bovill (2020) who labels the design as a "*notetaking relay.*" The lecturer breaks after approximately 20 minutes and the students have a couple of minutes to write down what they think were the most important ideas from those first 20 minutes. These ideas are then passed on to the student sitting next to them. After another 20 minutes this can be repeated. There are various mechanisms to allow people to keep several notes or to copy some of the best ones that are being passed around. Bovill presents other ideas relating to student collaboration in large groups, including one called the "two-stage examination." The first stage involves a typical individual exam or test followed by a second stage where students are actively encouraged to work in groups to do a repeat test answering the same questions or a subset of questions that were used in the first test. This tends to produce better grades and enjoyment of the process, leading to a high level of knowledge in the group.

In the Holistic Experiential Learning Model (HELM) presented in Chapter 3, *belonging* is one of the seven core modes of experiencing, because humans have a deep desire for positive *interpersonal* and *place* attachments. The need for *acceptance*, as opposed to *rejection*, is an important underlying principle within *attachment theories*, pointing to the importance of emotional bonds with other people, and in particular the early childhood *emotional* bonds with primary caregivers (Bowlby, 1969). The need to *belong* is also said to be a fundamental human *motivational* force (Baumeister & Leary, 1995).

Belonging has considerable significance to the lives of all people, affecting interpersonal *relationships, behaviour, emotion, thought,* and *action* and therefore the ability to *learn from experience*. Maslow's (1968) hierarchy of needs ranked *belonging* and *love* in the mid layers of the hierarchy, indicating that the need for love and belonging is a precondition to achieve the higher order needs of *self-esteem, self-authorship,* and *self-actualisation.*

> Attachment to place runs deep in us. In neurological terms, the evolutionary roots of the integrated emotional system involved in the formation of social attachments may lie in more ancient and primitive animal attachments to place. Some animals bond as much with their nest sites as with their mothers. "Belonging" comes from the Old English word *langian* which forms the root of longing.
>
> *(McGilchrist, 2009: 390)*

Attachment and Social Bonds

The human capacity to communicate thorough language, including the reading of emotional messages, is particularly important in social learning. Social signals emanate from several thousand facial expressions: there are more muscles in the face than anywhere else in the body. People are extraordinarily social beings, craving *doing* things with, and *relating* to, other people. Social interactions shape who we are and who we become, and our long history demonstrates the advantages of working collaboratively with others. Our lives are intricately intertwined with other humans, indeed we have talk of *tightly knit* communities. The brain has evolved to maximise the power of these relationships: Gergen refers to the *social brain* (2009) that is shaped by the environment, and, together with social relationships, influences emotional health and well-being. Learning is also strongly influenced by the complex interactions of social, intellectual, and emotional experiences.

If the *brain* is the hardware, then *mind* is the processing. The work of Thomas Scheff (1997) in social psychology is particularly relevant: his most central

154 Belonging: Social Interactions

concept is the notion of the *social bond* (a term borrowed from attachment theories, Bowlby, 1969). Scheff argues that social bond theory asserts that these bonds generate *primary motivations*, as a cognitive and emotional attuning that occurs when people meet: the interactions affect the quality of the social bonds. In terms of learning design these bonds are especially influenced by issues of *equality*, *power* relations, and the need for freedom to learn.

Experiential learning has significant foundational roots located within *human relations training*. Early work by Kurt Lewin and others in the 1940s, on which the later work by Kolb (1984) was based (see Seaman, 2008) involved *human relations* work, concerning racial and religious conflict within communities. Lewin sought to develop community *solidarity* and personal *agency* through *critical reflection* on their experiences. Using *discussion groups* within expert facilitated *laboratory* workshops, social conflict experiences were explored and reflected upon to develop new skills that would lead to *empowerment*. Kolb built on these ideas, establishing the importance of reflective processing, bringing it to the forefront of experiential learning designs.

Learning with others involves the *relational* dynamics of collaboration, co-operation, listening, participation, competition, action, and acting. These social interactions create greater awareness of the rich complexity inherent in any discussions. Individuals, groups, and whole communities can benefit from the multiple perspectives, values, and beliefs that surface through these interactions.

Learner Control

The idea of the learner taking greater control of the design of learning is certainly not new. Ten years after developing his client-centred therapeutic work (developed in the early 1950s), Carl Rogers applied the concepts to create the notion of *learner-centred learning* (1969). A considerable body of literature has emerged that addresses dependency, power, and authority, and critical feminists, for example, have developed renewed interest in the role of emotions in social control, power, and gender relations (Boler, 1999: Hughes, 2011).

There are now several experience-based theories associated with learner-centred practices: *action learning* is concerned with solving problems in real work situations (see O'Neil & Marsick, 2007), and *active learning* is a process that has learner at its core, focusing on *how* they learn, not just *what* they learn. Other educational designs encourage learners to "think" for themselves, rather than passively receive information from the "expert" teacher. These include *collaborative learning* (involving the design of joint "intellectual effort" by and between students, and students and teacher), *cooperative* and *participatory learning* (the design involves a co-operative/social approach to learning, e.g., where members complete a component of bigger tasks that requires a joint co-operative effort), *students-as-partners pedagogies* (SaP – students involved as *partners* in many stages of the learning experience – shared goals, shared responsibility, shared power, etc.), *critical pedagogy* (where designs involve issues associated with social justice and democracy that are not distinct actions separate from teaching and learning), and *project-based learning*, and *problem-based learning* (PBL designs involve a student-centred, active exploration of real world projects. It is a form of inquiry-based learning). All these approaches have similarities and all incorporate several experiential learning design principles.

Andragogy is a term related to *self-directed learning* (Knowles, 2015), *heutagogy* is concerned with *self-determined learning* (Hase & Kenyon, 2013; Stoten, 2020). The linear progression from pedagogy, to andragogy, and heutagogy typically presents differing aspects of control, power, and authority: in the latter, power and control is very much the responsibility of the learner/s. The term *pedagogy* essentially concerns the practices of teaching children and young adults, whilst *andragogy* refers to the methods and practices of facilitating *self-directed* adult learners. *Heutagogy* is a non-linear design approach that focuses on what and how the learners want to learn: learning is *self-determined*. These three approaches do not have clear boundaries, however, in simplistic terms there is a role shift from *teacher*, to *facilitator*, to *guide* as the balance of *provision* is *progressively determined by the learner*. The locus of control, related to *internal* and *external* power, authority, and dependency is fundamentally changed. Experiential approaches to learning, where learning experience takes centre stage, can be applied to a greater or lesser degree within all these practices.

Critical Thinking About Social Relations

The experience of empowerment is associated with equity, diversity, emancipation, democracy, agency, and social change aligned with the freedom to *learn*, to *think, become*, and to *be*. These are the central issues associated with *critical pedagogy* (Freire, 1970). Freire emphasises that learning is also political and can act as a means for all people to be liberated. There is a long history of discrimination and oppression linked to the freedom to learn and the right to be educated. Aristotle (c. 384 BC to 322 BC), regarded as an early proponent of experiential learning (Stonehouse et al., 2011), "explicitly excluded women and slaves from higher stages of education" (Palmer et al., 2001: 18). Fast forward to the late 18th century when Jean-Jacques Rousseau published a controversial book titled *Emile* in 1762 in which other aspects of oppressive schooling were exposed. It is suggested that Rousseau's revolutionary ideas about the need for a more "natural," developmental education, influenced the work of Dewey and other writing about experiential education as a way forward to a democratic society. Yet Rousseau felt that the poor, and girls, should not be educated other than to look after their house and children. Fast forward yet again to the late 19th century and a passage introduced earlier in the book illustrates the oppressive ways of thinking about schooling of the "lower classes."

156 Belonging: Social Interactions

> The lower classes ought to be educated to discharge the duties cast upon them. They should also be educated that they may appreciate and defer to a higher cultivation when they need it, and the higher classes ought to be educated in a very different manner, in order that they may exhibit to the lower classes at higher education to which, if it was shown to them, they would bow down and defer.
>
> *(Curtis, 1963: 5th edition, p. 256)*

Hierarchies and social divisions at that time meant that the mind-body dualism reflected the lives of people: bodies were used in the work of women and labourers and assigned lesser value than those whose status was bestowed through intellectual achievement. French sociologist Pierre Bourdieu (1930–2002) researched the ways that societies reproduce themselves and how the dominant classes maintain their positions in society through the strategic application of *economic, social,* and *cultural capital.* He applied these notions to explain social inequalities. The *field* is the space in which there is competition over resources, and *cultural capital* concerns the ways that the higher classes use their cultural knowledge to shore up their place in the social hierarchy. *Social capital* refers to the ways that networks of social relationships operate to establish and maintain one's place in the social hierarchy. It is now argued that social and cultural networks are not always the exclusive tools of the elite, suggesting that Bourdieu's arguments might be limited and deterministic. The idea of "social capital" can be of value and be utilised by all people, including the powerless and marginalised. Gauntlet suggests that human capital:

> such as a secure sense of self-identity, confidence and expressing one's own opinions, and emotional intelligence, enables young people to become better learners, and so helps them to be more successful in the education system and in society. This human capital emerges out of social capital because this kind of development depends on relationships, most obviously within the family (or other support network).
>
> *(Gauntlett, 2018: 130)*

Social capital relies on the existence of functioning networks of people, and Gauntlett refers to two elements within social capital: *bridging* and *bonding.* The former, *bridging,* is open, drawing people in by embracing diversity and generating links between different people and different groups. *Bonding* social capital, however, is more exclusive, and closed, in that it ties people together who are similar, for example in their interests.

Liberatory characteristics have roots in experiential learning. Tony Saddington, in his paper *The Roots and Branches of Experiential Development* (1999), proposes that there are three core traditions that lie within adult experiential education and experiential learning: (1) the *progressive* tradition, he suggests, taps experience

Belonging: Social Interactions **157**

as an additional source of knowledge; (2) the *humanist* tradition pursues and values personal wholeness; and (3) the *radical* tradition sees deep, critical reflection on experience as a means of resisting oppression, to give empowerment, and to generate social transformation. Usher suggests that it is these traditions that explain why experiential learning is often quoted as an approach that is "central to the theory and practice of adult education" (Usher, in Hager, 1991: 169). However, experiential learning can also restrict and restrain, particularly when uncritical minds unquestionably accept given "truths," when the freedom of discovery learning is negated. The development of an internal identity and authority for self-expression and engagement in mutually interdependent relationships in ways that generates critical assessments of the expertise of others is of considerable importance. Hodge et al., 2009: 2) note:

> these capacities cannot be cultivated solely by engaging actively with the raw materials and tools of the Academy or by participating in a student-centred classroom, although these are essential. Instead, they emerge gradually when educators foster students' holistic growth through continuous self-reflection, seamless and authentic curricular and co-curricular experiences that steadily increase in challenge, and appropriate levels of support.

Narratives, Power, and Politics

In Chapter 1 the use of hand-held "experience enhancement" devices in museums were explored, and much can be gleaned from the way that museums have advanced their designs of educational experiences in the 21st century (for a more complete history of museums, see *Learning in the Museum*, by George Hein, 1998). Museum resources may not have changed, but the way resources are utilised for learning experiences has fundamentally changed. The way resources are used is important in experiential learning designs.

> At the beginning of the 21st century, museums are re-orientating themselves through imagining afresh what they can become; familiar practices are being reassessed and tired philosophies are being overturned. New ideas about culture and society and new policy initiatives challenge museums to rethink their purposes, to account for their performance and to redesign the pedagogies.
>
> *(Hooper-Greenhill, 2007: 1)*

These design changes are being brought about against a backcloth of demands for social and cultural justice. The resources used by museums for learning are always active agents in that they *mediate* the message, and the narratives are always interwoven with culture, politics, and power, and so museums' educational texts

158 Belonging: Social Interactions

are being sensitively re-examined, revised, and rewritten (Coxall, 1999). One 150-foot stone monument in Edinburgh, Scotland, now has a new plaque commissioned to more fully explain the impact the person perched high on its summit had on society. He delayed the abolition of the slave trade (I have excluded the person's name), and so the plaque now includes the following additional words:

> he was instrumental in deferring the abolition of the Atlantic slave trade. Slave trading by British ships was not abolished until 1807. As a result of this delay, more than half a million enslaved Africans across the Atlantic . . . (*this person*) also curbed democratic dissent in Scotland, and both defended and expanded the British Empire, imposing colonial rule on indigenous peoples. He was impeached in the United Kingdom for misappropriation of public money, and, although acquitted, he never held public office again. . . . In 2020 this plaque was dedicated to the memory of the more than half a million Africans whose enslavement was a consequence of (*this person's*) actions.

Design Rewritten

Educational texts are being rewritten to make excess words redundant Ekarv (1999). Gilmore and Sabine (1999) explore the core design principles for writing texts in museums and their advice is to use simple language, to provide one main idea per line, to use active verbs, to test read texts aloud to consider natural pauses, and to state the subject matter early in the sentence. In the process of revision and refinement, they suggest that text is read aloud first to identify natural pauses so that the wording can reflect the natural spoken rhythm. Museum *education* is shifting to museum *learning*, with more emphasis given to the visitor's perspective rather than institutional convenience. Museums are also acknowledging that learning is not always purposeful; rather, at times, it occurs in an unintentional, haphazard, and idiosyncratic way. Like outdoor learning, museum-based learning experiences are very much concerned with bodily-physical engagement, involving multiple facets of movement, including the design of the personal or group journey of discovery within inside or outside spaces. Hooper-Greenhill (2007: 12) notes that "learning in museums emerges as embodied, immersive, holistic, individualised, performative and identity-related." She notes that the term *"edutainment"* is an expression that brings together the terms *education* and *entertainment* to conceptualise and characterise the learning experience within museums. Figure 7.1 highlights the binary opposites that differentiate learning in museums.

Every word is more than is first apparent. Words and sentences are like suitcases that need to be critically *unpacked*, to see what is inside, and expose their multiple meanings: language, when examined from this sociological perspective, is a form of *performance*, a social action. Individuals, groups, and organisations

Belonging: Social Interactions **159**

Education and Entertainment: binary opposites	
Education	Entertainment
Hard Work	Pleasure
Cognitive	Affective
Instructive Mode	Discovery Mode
Experts and Novices	Friends and Family
School Days	Holidays

FIGURE 7.1 Education and *edutainment*.

(From: *Museums and Education*, Eilean Hooper-Greenhill, 2007: 34, Reproduced with permission).

create, interpret, and manipulate knowledge through language, and knowledge is always moulded by history, power, and politics. Words are never innocent: knowledge and social action go together.

Critical "unpacking" is a skill that is developed, and valued, in academic institutions. However, unpacking is also problematic, as McGilchrist (2009: 178) notes:

> Philosophy shares the trajectory I have described as typical of the relationship between the hemispheres. It begins in wonder, intuition, ambiguity, puzzlement and uncertainty; it progresses through being unpacked, inspected from all angles and wrestled into linearity by the left hemisphere.

McGilchrist, drawing on a substantial body of research, talks of the primacy of "wholeness" processing by the right hemisphere, before the left hemisphere separates, divides, analyses, and represents it. The significance of hemisphere dominance is illustrated by the geometric psychology in Design Illustration 23 where participant conversations about their learning preferences reveal how different people make meaning depending on hemisphere dominance.

 DESIGN ILLUSTRATION 23 GEOMETRIC PSYCHOLOGY – CONVERSATIONS ABOUT "DIFFERENCE."

Why is the brain divided? Brain hemisphere dominance is regarded by some as a myth, yet a substantial amount of research (see Gilchrist, 2009; Gilchrist, 2019) suggests not. Try this practical activity and listen to the conversations of learners when they experience this activity. Try it on yourself too and talk with others about your choices, and how this might affect your design approach.

How it works. The session is good to establish the different ways that people report how they prefer to learn, and to recognise *difference*. In my version, groups of people are asked to choose a first and second preference from four shapes: *a circle, a triangle, a square, and a squiggly line*.

When people have chosen, I ask them to talk with others who made the same choices, and I refer to each group as a tribe. The tribes are given a specific space to talk to each other (corners of a field, or corners of a room) and each tribe answers two questions together: *why did we chose our shape*, and *what does it tell us about how we like to learn*? After a period of discussion two groups are asked to meet each other, one going to the territory of the other, that is, being *invited* by the other. The arriving tribe is listened to first. The square and the triangle meet (representing left brain preferences/characteristics), and the circle and the squiggly line meet (representing right brain preferences/characteristics). They share their *similarities* and their *differences*. Then, when this is completed, the four tribes all meet and listen to each other. The differences emerge in a much stronger way in this final gathering: the two tribes of the square and the circle have many similarities, but it also emerges just how very different they are to the other two tribes. The square and triangle tribes remark on how they need order and like to work in a systematic way, and say they regard the squiggly line preferences as messy and chaotic. The squares need to know exactly what is required, and what the boundaries and details are. The squiggly tribe comments about seeing the messiness as *artistic*, and *creative*, with the fact that there is no line, no rigidity, no predictability which is seen as confined and bounded. The circles like the idea of the flowing wholeness, the big picture, and the infinite points of view. They like to please people and they avoid arguments. Like Susan Dellinger (see Dr. Susan Dellinger, 1996, *Communicating Beyond Our Differences: Introducing the Psycho-Geometrics System*), I have found that the conversations show remarkable levels of consistency across many groups around the globe. Dellinger holds a doctorate in communication and reveals the findings of significant amounts of interesting data collected from thousands of people across the globe.

 DESIGN ILLUSTRATION 24 STARTING OUT – ACKNOWLEDGING POWER AND CONTROL.

Setting the Emotional Climate

In the development of the emotional climate at the start of any session a facilitator can ask participants what they want to know about the facilitator, as part of the *introduction* process. The group can be asked to *decide* and *design* the significant questions *they* want to ask, and so experience an initial level of control. The nature of participant questions (e.g., categories) can be analysed and discussed after the facilitator has responded. Issues such as power and control (at group

Belonging: Social Interactions **161**

and individual levels). This design is covered in detail in DI 18 in Chapter 6. To further develop empowerment, a group introduction process can involve choices. The best questions from Part A (previous) can be collected from several sessions, and converted into an *Introduction question card set* of 30+ credit card sized laminated cards. Sitting in a circle, the cards are passed round, and quickly read (they can be passed around in both directions to speed up the process and create fun!). After a short period of time, when everyone has had a chance to read most of the cards, an announcement is made that each person can keep only one card to answer, though a card can be swapped if a better question comes along. This experience gives *personal choice*. Some questions that have been asked of me in the past have included:

1. Who is one of the most interesting individuals who have ever met and why?
2. What is one of the best gifts that you have received?
3. What is a characteristic in others that you admire?
4. If 10 people you know were asked to choose the one adjective that they feel best describes you, what would be the most common word?
5. What is the kindest thing you have done for somebody else?
6. What qualities do you look for in a friend?
7. If someone was looking for you in a bookshop, what section would they find you in?

Another design for introductions introducing choice, power, and responsibility is called "20 seconds of fame." The facilitator does not need to be involved except to give participants the resources to complete a task: a tripod, a simple recording device such as a camera, or smartphone, and a very simple brief that needs interpretation. The group produces a short film. Each individual contributes 20 seconds of self-introduction. *Responsibility for design, organisation, and distribution lies with the group.*

Individual participants tend to develop their own short script or narrative to introduce themselves. The narrative should focus on significant positive aspects of participants' lives. Participants set up the camera, and a seat in front of it, at the right height for a presenter to sit. The group forms a line and when all agree they are ready to "shoot," one after another, each person sits in the recording seat for their own 20 second "film" about themselves. The next person in the queue sits down, and this sequence continues to create a group film. This allows a facilitator to learn participant names and other information later (permissions to use any video clips are of course required). The group can do an end commentary and a group finishing "photo" if they wish. After this experience, or variations of it, a conversation can follow about *power, control, and responsibility.*

Choice

Learning journey route maps can, as part of the design, offer a choice of routes. From the image, options are designed to allow choices. Different experience "routes" can be shared afterwards, which can enhance the overall group experience. Creating options for what is available to read in the experience called *Coffee and Papers* is an example in Chapter 7. A complex design relating to power and control is offered in Chapter 10.

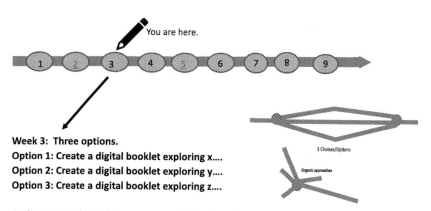

Week 3: Three options.
Option 1: Create a digital booklet exploring x….
Option 2: Create a digital booklet exploring y….
Option 3: Create a digital booklet exploring z….

Each group to share their resources with the two other groups.

Critical Reflection Through Conversation

Chapter 2 highlighted the use of *touch screens* (or touch cards) to develop *sensitivity* and personal *awareness* of social interactions during conversations, meetings, or group work. Behavioural awareness touch cards can be adapted to allow other interpersonal interactions to be *surfaced*, *unpacked*, and *critically reflected* upon. The touch card (physical/digital) in Figure 7.2 can also be used for example to reflect on group behaviours that unfold during discussions about power and control.

Vince and Reynolds (2007: 3) in *The Handbook of Experiential Learning and Management Education* note that "*reading, researching, or taking part in discussion is itself an experience which can confront behaviours and beliefs.*" Significantly, they note the importance of acknowledging "*the unreliability of experience as a concept because this encourages us to question assumptions about the nature of experience*" and they argue "*that the very value of experiential learning is in its unreliability and instability,*" because "*the value of experiential learning is that it can discourage and disrupt our tendency to produce prescriptions for learning.*" Their book presents 25 examples of experiential approaches to management education, highlighting how the design of meaningful conversations is difficult and complex.

Belonging: Social Interactions 163

Human Relations Sensitisation Cards: Power, control, and self-authorship			
PUSHING APART		PULLING TOGETHER	
Telling/giving information.	**Blocking**/shutting out.	**Listening**	**Merging** others' ideas/pulling strands together.
Disagreeing	**Arguing** a specific point.		**Building** on alternatives.
		Clarifying& Seeking Information	
Countering Opposite views	**Pushing** out your own view.	**Agreeing**	**Paraphrasing**

FIGURE 7.2   The design of touchpad awareness cards.

Voice and "Self-Authorship"

Covey (2004) in *The Eighth Habit*, explores the idea of "voice" as having personal significance about *hope, resilience, intelligence,* and the limitless *human potential* to influence positive change. Greater *awareness* and *consciousness* of *conditioned* ways of interacting tend to influence *conduct* through voice, behaviour, and action. Baxter Magolda (2011) suggests that the "self-authorship" voice comprises three inter-related dimensions: trusting the internal voice, building an internal foundation, and securing internal commitments. She notes that developing self-authorship is an arduous task because:

> navigating the complexities of 21st century life requires self-authorship, or the development of an internal voice to guide one's beliefs, identity, and relationships. Competing demands of adulthood introduced the limitations of uncritically following external authority and help adults realise that although they cannot control reality, they can choose how to respond to it. Establishing their internal criteria for what to believe, how to identify themselves and how to relate to others yields an internal voice to coordinate external influence.
>
> *(Baxter Magolda, 2001: 76)*

Self-authorship derives from learning experience designs that promote *interdependent* as opposed to *dependent* partnerships. Baxter Magolda argues that such capacities are crucial to the successful navigation of adult life.

164 Belonging: Social Interactions

> **DESIGN ILLUSTRATION 25 SELF-AUTHORSHIP, INTERNAL AUTHORITY AND SELF-AWARENESS.**

The "Ideal" Student – Creating Self-Authorship Through Conversations

Design Illustration 25 highlights an intentional transference from external to internal authority. This experience involves card playing to generate conversations about what makes an "ideal university student" (the design can be easily modified to cover other topics). The experience facilitates: (1) *choice* through self-selection of personal statements, (2) the generation of both private *internal* (self) and *external* public (social) *conversations*, and (3) *increased self-awareness* about self-authorship about personal and professional development. This card playing experience, called *"Creating Conversations,"* has been designed in this example to help higher education students reflect upon their personal strengths and areas for developmental through "learning conversations."

In the first part of the experience of playing cards, each student chooses a set of six card statements which they feel best characterise their perceived self, as a student. This results in a "hand" of cards with preferred statements that they feel are ones that reflect their strengths or areas for development. Each person places their "hand" of cards on the table, discusses them with other students, and makes a brief note of the cards chosen. In the second part of the experiences when the playing of the game and sharing is complete, all the students place all the cards on the table and mix them up. The whole group then collaborates to select a set of statement cards that they perceive would represent an *"ideal student."* These experiences were designed to generate student conversations about this notion of an idealised student, and at some stage there is usually a comparison of individual selections and "idealized" selections.

In the design of this playing cards experience careful consideration was given to the final list of personal statements chosen and the language used. This resulted initially in 120 statements which were then refined to 36. These 36 offered a clear pedagogic structure in that they were from six self-awareness themes as follows:

1   Emotional intelligence (coded red),
2   Own strengths and weaknesses,
3   Personal values (coded green),
4   Motivation,
5   Drive and energy,
6   Transition and transformation (coded purple).

Example set of GREEN coded cards associated with aspects of Personal Values:

1   I have a strong sense of right and wrong.
2   I value honesty.
3   I am empowered by my beliefs.
4   I always try to respect the beliefs of others.
5   I rarely compromise my values.
6   I can often be single-minded.

The pack consists of 72 cards, that is, 36 designs duplicated twice. The cards are coded with icons printed in the centre of each card, and the shape and colour are significant. The icons provide a structure for the reflection by students at the end when their own set and an "idealised student" set are analysed in terms of the six colour coded areas. This experience design embraces "positive psychology" (statements are mostly positive). The game is specifically aimed at students in the first-year *transition* stage of Higher Education. The card game was developed over a period of a year. Research funding enabled the development of the self-awareness statements, including prototype testing within HEIs. The cards are essentially used to generate reflective dialogue and facilitate personal development within an informal, friendly, and private peer group setting. This design was funded by the Higher Education Academy in the UK (for a more detailed explanation see Beard, *The Experiential Toolkit*, 2010).

Putting Positive Relationships at the Heart of Design

Bovill (2020: 3) notes how *"relational pedagogy puts relationships at the heart of teaching and emphasises that meaningful connection needs to be established between teacher and students as well as students and their peers, if effective learning is to take place."* New thinking about "relational pedagogy" presents useful insights that guide social interactions in ways that enhance developing learner-centred designs. The focus is on removing aspects of *subordinate* and *superior* roles. Building good quality, caring relationships between and amongst teachers and students, and facilitators and learners, be they individuals, organisations, groups, or communities, lies at the heart of co-creative design, where all stakeholders are regarded as *partners* in the learning processes, including design.

Without mutual trust or respect there is unlikely to be positive learning experiences. This is the central topic of *The Emotionally Intelligent Lecturer* by Mortiboys (2002), who recommends that facilitators and teachers establish and question assumptions in relation to their values and beliefs that underpin the creation of the emotional "climate," to question the *metaphors* that frame their actions: as *helper, gardener, sage,* or *travel guide* for example. Finkel (2000), in *Teaching with*

166 Belonging: Social Interactions

Your Mouth Shut, argues that the predominant mode of education remains that of *telling*, as a *transmission* approach: indeed he offers an alternative book title: *How to Think Through, Design, and Take Control of What You Might Want to Teach So That Your Students Actually Experience It* (xi). Finkel uses the strapline: *providing experiences, provoking reflection*.

Within experiential learning a foundational principle is to recognise that the most valuable resources for learning lie in the learners themselves: learners bring their own experiences, and offer a multitude of perspectives. A co-creative design approach challenges the notion that a teacher or facilitator possesses all the necessary knowledge, skill, or range of perspectives. This fundamental design change can be emancipatory, shifting power relations in a way that creates new insights, outcomes, and lines of enquiry.

The way knowledge is understood influences design. If knowledge occurs within a *relational web* that is in a permanent, intersubjective state of flux, then consider what happens if:

> we reject the pervasive knowledge-as-object (as "third thing") metaphor and adopt, instead, an understanding of knowledge-as-action – or, better yet, knowledge-as-(inter) action? Or, to frame it differently, what if we were to reject the self-evident axiom that cognition is located within cognitive agents who are cast as isolated from one another and distinct from the world, and insist instead that all cognition exists in the interstices of a complex ecology of organismic relationality?
>
> *(Davis & Sumara, 1997, 110)*

This rejection of knowledge as residing solely within individual minds is liberating. Gergen (2009) suggests that we should shift from the notion of a bounded sense of being to that of a *relational being*, from the *I* to the *We*. Hughes and Lury (2013: 797) view knowledge as an ephemeral "event": "*we think the term ecology is helpful insofar as it enables us to acknowledge the ongoing and dynamic interrelation of processes and objects, beings and things, figures and grounds.*"

Co-creation of learning recognises that all participants are *partners* in the process of learning and so have something to contribute to discussions, understanding, outputs, and design. Co-creative design includes discussions about choice, and the provision of opportunities for negotiating and challenging design decisions, including planning and evaluative processes. Co-creation increases motivation and confidence. In the context of Higher Education, Bovill (2020: 4) defines co-creation as occurring "*when staff and students work collaboratively with one another to create components of curricula and/or pedagogical approaches.*" Here the notion of *distributed cognition* is both liberating and empowering: "*collective knowledge and individual understanding are dynamically co-emergent phenomena*" (Davis & Sumara, 1997: 119).

Many people are familiar with the idea of *lifelong* learning, that is, that people learn throughout their lifespan. Less well known is the concept of *lifewide* learning that occurs beyond formal institutions of learning: *"formal education is just one part of an individual's whole life"* (Jackson, in Jackson, 2011: 2). Running a home, being a member of the family, being involved in a club or society, travelling, taking holidays, and looking after one's own well-being mentally, physically, and spiritually, means that people live their lives in different ways, and have the freedom to choose *which* places they want to occupy, what to be *involved in*, who they *meet* and *interact* with, to form different kinds of relationships.

People adopt different roles and identities. They think, behave, and communicate in different ways, encountering different sorts of challenges and problems. They seize or miss opportunities in their aspirations to achieve their ambitions and live a useful and productive life (see Jackson, 2011). It is in the spaces that we create, with others, where meaning emerges in life. Gergen refers to these complex relational interactions as *"circles of participation"* (2009: 201).

Service Learning and Creation of Value for "Others"

Service learning is a form of experiential learning that involves civic engagement, using "real" projects that benefit communities and/or the environment. These designs create outputs of value for multiple stakeholders. Participants often express feelings of being highly motivated, perceiving these projects as *doing* good work. Popular environmental projects include learning about teamwork, by for example installing a public footbridge across a stream using a kit provided by local authority; planting, felling, and extracting trees in the management and improvement of a community woodland. The surveying of nature reserves by professional cartographers/mapmakers is illustrated elsewhere. Student fundraising for charities by designing and delivering real events as part of their degree experience are another example. Dry-stone walling projects in the National Parks have also been designed for addiction rehabilitation (Beard, 2010).

Belonging: Attachment to Place and Space

> *"Just as landscape defines character, culture springs from the spirit of place."*
> *(Davis, 2009: 33)*

If you were a fish the last thing you might discover would be the water. Places and spaces we live and work in are often taken for granted in terms of their impact on life and learning, yet the impact can be profound. We shape them and they shape us. Learning "spaces" embrace an ecology of natural, physical, digital, emotional, mental, social, spiritual, and metaphorical form. The term *learning environment* is in common use, and I define this as a diverse and varied physical, digital, or virtual, natural, or artificial place and/or space that facilitates the engagement of people in a wide range of learning activities.

168 Belonging: Social Interactions

In previous chapters the importance of spatial perception and cognition has been emphasised. The movement of the body in space has resulted in the evolutionary development of powerful navigation skills. Place is not just a physical entity: *space* becomes *place* when it is occupied, when a sense of belonging develops. Place generates identities, as occupants become interwoven within the social, environmental, and spiritual fabric. Wenger-Trayner & Wenger-Trayner (2020) refer to the notion of *"social space"* as the field in which social interactions occur, but social space is just one important element within the broader landscape involving physical space, emotional space, thinking space, collaborative space, solo space, virtual space, and writing and reading space.

Space and place present exciting opportunities for design. Kayes (2007: 430) in the concluding chapter on institutional barriers to experiential learning in *The Handbook of Experiential Learning and Management Education*, comments:

> as I walked up the aisles of the multitiered classroom to move the chairs of the new lecture hall into a more experiential friendly arrangement, I notice something both odd and expected. Here, in the brand-new, technology-enhanced classroom, the chairs were bolted to the floor. No matter what configuration I wanted, I was trapped by the institutional barriers from moving things out of order.

Spaces and places similarly reveal ownership, power, and authority. The layout of spaces reveals a lot: linear designs usually place the facilitator at the front, where the technology is situated and controlled, indicating where power lies. Terms like "front" and "back," and "higher" and "lower" are spatial concepts that are strongly charged, possessing long held significance in terms of social status, power, and influence. Space and place are terms that can represent freedom or threat, or security or stability. "Superior" is a word derived from the Latin word for "high" (Tuan, 1977). Front and back are unequal in social value (going backwards, forward thinking, important people sit at the front, trades people using the back door) (Tuan, 1974). Yi-Fu Tuan suggests that spaces are terms that are merged, though "'space' is more abstract than 'place'" (1977: 6): space becomes place when inhabited; it is where we dwell, and where we feel at "home." The terms work*space* and work*place* highlight different usage: *workplace* is regarded as the place of an organisation, with *workspace* being the desk and work zone of an individual. Away days is a term referred to as away from the workplace (home~away/dwell~escape).

Learning Environments and the Experiencescape

Much can be gleaned from the service sector (e.g., hospitality, tourism, events) where design focus has shifted from investigating "everything that a consumer senses, feels, and experiences" (Pizam & Tasci, 2019: 26) which was essentially the "*atmospherics*" (Kotler, 1973) to the broader notion of "servicescapes" (Bitner, 1992). *Atmospherics* involves the design of reactions and interactions that result from lighting, colours, size and shape of artefacts, and smells of the built architecture and interior designs. These sensory experiences are known to impact on consumer purchasing. The broader term, of *experiencescape* (see O'Dell, 2005), embraces the idea of the design and choreography of the learning experience *land*scape. The term *experiencescape* represents a shift from specific sensory focussed atmospherics towards a broader holistic approach that includes aspects of physical, social, cultural, sensory, functional, and natural design elements of the experience of learning.

Experiencescape design differs according to different stakeholder perspectives: facilities and estates staff at educational institutions have long been concerned with safety, flows of people, occupancy statistics, longevity and durability, and investment life cycles, whereas teachers and lecturers are concerned with what might support better teaching, student engagement, and student learning activities. As a result, different stakeholders speak different design languages.

 DESIGN ILLUSTRATION 26 DESIGNING THE EXPERIENCESCAPE.

Kadoorie Farm & Botanic Garden (KFBG) is based in the rural New Territories of Hong Kong (website: www.kfbg.org). The organisation is located on the northern slopes of Tai Mo Shan, Hong Kong's highest mountain. These are their seven headings in the organisational values: *sustainable living, justice, love, participation, professionalism, learning,* and *happiness*. These values influence the experiences of staff and those visiting. KFBG offers a series of public experiential learning events each year that work with the four Hs: *Head (thinking), Hands (doing/sensing), Heart (feelings),* and *Home (belonging)*. All the events work with experiences that involve different levels of interaction with the "more-than-human world" (MTHW). The programme includes, for example, a half-day and a full day such as a "Day of Mindfulness"; Working with Sustainable Farming Methods (that use the 24 solar rhythms of the Chinese calendar); a "Talk to Plants" programme, and many other experiential "encounters" with the more-than-human world.

The two-day Master Class in Experiential Learning that I run each year with KFBG is an open public course. The whole experience is carefully crafted by the Education Department staff, who pay close attention to the design of the wider *experiencescape* (the whole experience). Participants in the Master Class are offered a chance to stay at the Old Police Station which is now a peaceful residential Green Hub in downtown Hong Kong. When all participants arrive at the KFBG centre in the countryside on the first day they are welcomed in the beautiful glass sided, single storey training centre located on the slopes of Kwun

Yum Shan overlooking Hong Kong. This is a spiritual mountain, and the road to the summit has long been a journey of pilgrimage for more than 1,000 years. The views of the surrounding forests, and of Hong Kong and the surrounding seas in the distance are stunning. The mood is one of welcome and relaxation. The two days are intense and short refreshment breaks are frequent, allowing for social interaction or quiet solo reflection. Monkeys will often come down the slopes to investigate, especially if lunch is ready. In the *Coffee and Papers session* (see Design Illustration 27) people scatter to find suitable reading spots, on outside lounger chairs, on the lawns, and other special places. Each year someone notices my hammock rigged in the forest and uses it for their quiet reading.

On the first night participants venture out into the dark. They experience a night walk journeying slowly down the mountain from the top to the centre, stopping occasionally to listen to, and observe wildlife under the guidance of expert staff. Participants walk together and chat about their first day, and they are encouraged to swap partners at set intervals during the walk to get to know other participants. On arrival back at the centre in the dark of night, the outside of the venue has been surrounded by candles, and there is a lovely smell of hot vegetarian food that is beautifully laid out on tables outside. Drinks are served, and the experience is uplifting yet tranquil. Participants report experiencing a quieting of the mind, a special closeness to nature, an inner peace and well-being. At the end of the second day everyone is given a booklet about the centre and a USB stick with support materials to take away. These are beautifully gift wrapped in plain brown paper. While everyone says their farewells, the minibus waits outside ready to take everyone down the mountain to multiple drop off points.

Space to Learn in Higher Education

Mortiboys (2002) acknowledges the significant relationship between the physical environment and the learning climate. He asks lecturers to evaluate their emotional intelligence, asking 19 questions, two of which include:

- *How far did I succeed in creating a positive emotional environment?*
- *Did I create the best physical environment in the circumstances?*

If you were to be asked about the design of your ideal learning space, what would it look like? Usually it is a struggle to answer this question, and the responses are diverse. Research on the impact of physical space on the accomplishments of those who occupy them remains disappointingly low and the important consideration of the *optimal places to learn* remain, for the most part, unknown. It is said that students in higher education will have spent over 20,000 hours in "classrooms" by the time they graduate (Fraser, 2001). Time spent learning may be more productive if a diverse *ecology* of places and spaces were available. The "traditional linear classroom," which has colonised the psyche of educational institutions over many years, dictating teaching and learning behaviours, is now becoming scarce.

The Evolving Spatial Ecology

Different stakeholders understand space and place in different ways, and so dialogue is much needed between architects, facilities managers, designers, and users of learning spaces. The latter are increasingly making more contributions to learning space design. Tuan notes, *"what begins as undifferentiated space becomes place as we get to know it better and endow it with value"* (1977: 6). In examining why students go to university we see that seminars and lectures and other face-to-face experiences are highly valued, and physical areas are linked to identity, as places to be seen, to just "be," to "belong," and to meet. Social dynamics coalesce with spatiality in the educational experience.

I have come across some very interesting developments in recent years, including: seat hammocks in lecture theatres in Turku polytechnic in Finland, large Mongolian style tents on a University campus used for teaching outdoor education and outdoor adventure, moveable indoor "igloo walls" for private quiet space in a learning centre, classrooms located in department stores in Thailand, and the education and training of Omani senior civil servants on a tall ship that travels the world. Learning is moving beyond the classrooms, into informal spaces, and into cafés and corridors, and out to outdoor spaces. Nature is moving indoors, with plants and other "landscaped" spaces on the increase, as well as wooden decking, water features for calming, beanbags and sofas for relaxation, straw bales to sit on (with removable plastic covers), and floor coverings with numbers, grids, and letters built into early years classrooms.

Form usually follows function: sometimes the reverse is true as students modify "given" space arrangements to suit their own needs. They appropriate, occupy, colonise, and modify spaces, particularly in uncontested, unclaimed informal spaces within and around universities. The evolving landscape of spaces and places for learning is interwoven with learner practices. In educational institutions the informal occupation of spaces by students is sometimes encouraged by providing additional furniture (tables, chairs, sofas, and technological enhancements) in ways that support the occupation of underused spaces.

The Coffee and Papers design illustration highlights one very simple approach to the use of informal space (cafes, secluded corners, hotel window seats, and a vast array of outdoor niche spaces) for the development of relaxed alertness. It can engender the pleasure of reading and excitement about this aspect of learning.

 DESIGN ILLUSTRATION 27 FINDING A SPECIAL SOLO SPACE: THE READING EXPERIENCE OF *COFFEE AND PAPERS*.

172 Belonging: Social Interactions

Finkel (2000) in his book *Teaching with Your Mouth Shut* says that great books can engender great experiences. One chapter is titled *Let the Books Do the Talking*, and his design strategies suggest that we should also: *Let the Learners Do the Learning*, *Let the Learners Do the Talking*, and *Let the Learners Make Choices*. Finkel notes however that we don't automatically learn by just reading: a great book needs to provoke engagement, and reflection on its contents.

In this design illustration, both solo-reflective and collaborative-social-reflective experiences are important parts of the design. The broader *experiencescape* involves the creation of a positive ambience of *relaxed alertness*, and participants are invited to select their own special spaces to read.

Several "papers" are laid out in a newsagent style on a large table. People select two items to read. Once they have been selected, individuals find a quiet and comfortable personal space to read and *be* alone. The level of reading and the topic focus has to be appropriate to the specific group: this is an important part of the design. Information on the content of the range of papers can be given. This can include academic papers, book chapters, or newspapers.

The session is about providing a relaxing period of learning in a peaceful environment, and one that changes the energy and pace of group dynamics for learning.

Refreshments can be provided to add to the ambience.

When the group finishes and returns for a plenary session at a fixed time, a collaborative discussion follows which is facilitated in a light touch way. The findings can be very enlightening, including the number of people who comment on how they enjoyed the whole process.

The session design can include "splitting" so that *choice* is an option. Choice can generate discussion that covers a broader area.

Underlying Principles

- Choice of personal spaces to quietly read and relax (around the globe I have witnessed people sitting by hotel pools in India, under a bamboo tree in China, lying on lawns, under the shade from a hedge, and in a hammock in the forests in Hong Kong).
- This session uses the principle of mood setting and relaxation to create a pleasurable flow experience of reading (of articles) for a specific period of time.
- Learners are given (or can bring – or both) a large choice of "papers" to be read.
- The session uses informal learning spaces in a creative way and the mood setting metaphor is taken from the idea of relaxing on a Sunday whilst reading the papers.

What It Achieves

- That reading is a pleasurable and informative experience.
- That using space (e.g., university cafe, atrium, outdoors) in a creative way supports the positive feelings of pleasure during the (critical) reading, and the notion of different spaces for different learning purposes.
- Improvements in knowledge and understanding by using collaborative discussion after the solo reading experience. Deeper thinking and reflection following reading. This develops critical reading and debate.
- The session can introduce a broad literature base to a topic/subject. Some groups have even examined newspapers and critically examined reporting of a topic.
- Higher cognitive processing skills are developed within a short space of time because of group collaborative sharing when the starting knowledge base is high because of the reading experience.

The *coffee and papers* experience in this design illustration triggered a response from participants in one programme. They reflected on their experience and realised just how important reading is to gain knowledge, and so made a request when they returned to work for innovation funding. It became a subtle campaign by staff in the medical health professions to recognise the importance of the allocation of time and space, *at work*, to read in order to maintain and update their clinical practice on an everyday basis. They needed to keep up with the shared, collective, scientific knowledge of the medical profession. The bid was successful. The request could be seen as also linked to voice, workplace politics, and power.

(See also Reading for Pleasure Pedagogy – RFPP.)

Space to Think

Outdoor educationalists are familiar with the role of the "solo" and its role in learning from reflection. Space to read and think in silence is important, and research into the pedagogy of silence (Bethuniak, 2005) explores the provision of solitude experiences for learning. She expresses concerns about the space provided for solitude within educational learning environments, as public spaces are diversifying whilst private spaces are declining:

> given the need for solitude, it is ironic that what most universities do is to create an environment in which students are rarely alone. Intent on forming a campus community, campus architecture creates communal spaces: classrooms, student living quarters, outdoor quads, dining halls, recreation centres, and now even libraries are places to be designed to be with others. Where, then, do they go to be alone . . . Where is the private space?
>
> *(Bethuniak, 2005: p 11)*

174 Belonging: Social Interactions

Paradoxically, contemporary educational thinking calls for greater student reflection about personal and professional development within formal education. Quiet reflection can be significantly enhanced by the provision of private thinking space. The lack of such space is being addressed by the design of pods, and informal spaces, landscaped areas, and other retreat areas are evolving. Going for an "away-day," is about relocating in a *different* space to think, and writing retreats offer similar experiences.

Digital Space

Physical and digital spaces have both similarities and differences. Physical space contains real objects, furniture, walls, and floors that can be utilised for learning. Digital experiences can create experiences that simulate or go beyond the physical: when physical and digital merge this is referred to as the *phygital* experience. Previously I have mentioned how The Titanic Museum enhances an old sepia photograph by digitally projecting real people, dressed up in Victorian clothing, walking across the photograph: visitor attention is drawn to this experience. In *Everywhere* Adam Greenfield, who works in a design consultancy, explores ubiquitous computing, and more specifically, the ways that humans interact and connect with the digital world of software embedded into (*smart*) buildings, objects, clothing, furniture, and even bodies so that "computers per se effectively disappear" (Greenfield, 2006: 1). This type of expansion of the digital presence can provide masses of information and knowledge whilst lying below awareness in ways that can "transfigure our notions of space and time, self and other, citizen and society in ways that we haven't begun to contemplate" (Greenfield: 3). The Octopus card used in Hong Kong is an example of a late 20th century digital technology that can be used "at vending machines, libraries, parking lots, and public swimming pools. It's quickly replacing keys as the primary means of access to a variety of private spaces, from apartment and office buildings to university dorms" (p. 216). Back in 2004 there were eight million transactions a day.

Many other types of spaces can be created within the digital world: the outdoors for example can be brought indoors through virtual~reality simulations. Saunders, back in 1988, described several examples of indoor "simulation gaming" under the umbrella of experiential learning, and he includes the well-known game called Island Escape, where participants are stuck on a volcanic island that is about to explode. He comments that "whilst this is a fantasy game, participants rapidly introduce themselves to other people, and reveal their backgrounds, interests and skills" (136). Saunders notes that simulation gaming combines the features of *games* (rules, players, competition, co-operation) with those of *simulation* (incorporation of critical features of reality). He suggests that these can be used very effectively for encouraging communication, both as a diagnostic and prognostic instrument. "Diagnostics" involves detective work to identify issues for

Belonging: Social Interactions **175**

people to work on, with case studies that replicate the essential features of real-life situations, while "prognosis" involves predicting people's future performances.

In researching the design of immersive video gaming, Turner (2005) suggests that gaming design principles offer education new forms of literacy within a virtual learning environment interface. Video games, she suggests, can engross players in complex and challenging activities. E-learning designs are undergoing dramatic changes, particularly in terms of social networking. There is also an increased interest in using experiential design principles for virtual-real interfaces, leading to the emergence of new term, e^2-learning environments (electronic-experiential learning environments) (see Beard et al., 2007). (For a comprehensive exploration of a wide range of technology generated consumer experiences including Virtual-Reality, Augmented-Reality, and Mixed-Reality, see Flavián et al., 2019.)

The next chapter explores digital tools in terms of whether they *connect* or *disconnect* us to the natural world. The next chapter also explores *belonging* in the non-social or *more-than-human world*. The human relationship and connectivity with both the living and physical world is particularly important, not least because global warming and species and habitat decline are the responsibility of everyone.

8

BELONGING

The Human Connection with the More-Than-Human World

A Focus on Home~Habitat

This chapter focuses on the complementary and interdependent relationships involving the social~natural world. This is represented by the *H* for *Home* (or *Habitat*), where human beings *belong*. This chapter examines learning experience design ideas that strengthen the human connection of *belonging* in a more-than-human *habitat* that we share as *home*. The chapter emphasis is on specific issues related to human connectivity with the natural world, such as: (1) organisations that lead the way in experiential learning design by making clear their intentions and concerns about the natural world through their mission, core values, and everyday practice; (2) unpacking the contested term *natural;* (3) exploring why traditional indigenous ways of knowing, learning, and wisdom really does matter; (4) whether technology *connects* or *disconnects;* (5) a consideration of what happens when the stories we tell are wrong; (6) healing and being in nature; and (7) creating change through *action*.

> There is a fire burning over the earth, taking with it plants and animals, ancient skills, and visionary wisdom. At risk is a vast archive of knowledge and expertise, a catalogue of the imagination, an oral and written language composed of the memories of countless elders and healers, warriors, farmers, fishermen, midwives, poets, and saints – in short, the artistic, intellectual, and spiritual expression of the full complexity and diversity of human experience. Quelling this flame, this spreading inferno, and rediscovering a new appreciation for the diversity of the human spirit as expressed by culture, is among the central challenges of our time.
>
> *(Davis, 2009: 34)*

DOI: 10.4324/9781003030867-8

This quotation highlights the threats that are simultaneously denuding the socio-cultural and intellectual diversity of the planet (*ethnosphere*) as well as the biological diversity of the planet (*biosphere*). As species and habitats decline so does a considerable amount of the wisdom of our ancestors: much has already been lost, devalued, or forgotten about the deep human connection with the earth, as many more people become disconnected from the living forms that we humans share the earth with. Richard Louv coined the phrase "*Nature Deficit Disorder*" in his book *Last Child in the Woods* (2005). The journey from awareness to intention, and on to action is routinely interrupted: other things gain attention and priority. Simple solutions include processes such as *re*cycling, *re*fusing, *re*pairing, *re*imagining, and *re*designing (re's). *Reconnection* goes deeper: Design that reconnects is the central thread of this chapter.

Species *de*cline, *de*forestation, *de*sertification, and *de*struction (de's) continue, yet we all have choices about the extent to which we learn to be *aware* of these environmental issues and choose to *understand* them. We can develop *intentions* to act, but it is better to *act*. It is now more important than ever that experiential designers provide frequent opportunities for people to reconnect with the other-than-human world: disorder of ecosystems mirrors disorder of the human world. This is partly due to a crisis in education concerning how we don't learn and what we don't know. Donella Meadows, one of the great minds on holistic systems thinking, who co-authored *Limits to Growth* published in 1972, suggests that we cannot control or figure out the complexity of the earth systems, but we can listen to its wisdom, and watch how it behaves, feel the beat, and dance with the earth (see *Ecological Literacy*, Stone & Barlow, 2005). The human relationship with the earth should be one of *reciprocity* (see Design Illustration 1, Chapter 1). The earth cares for us and provides life support. It heals and contributes to our well-being. It touches us and offers us special moments of inner peace and joy.

Organisations That Lead the Way

Oikos is a Greek word, referring to *household* or living *place*, and it is the basis of the word *ecology*. *Place, home*, and *ecology* are all *connected*. Kadoorie Farm and Botanic Gardens (KFBG) is a remarkable organisation located in a special place known as *The Garden in the Sky* (see KFBG "*experiencescape*" design illustration, Chapter 7). Their mission, vision, and core values create the context for this chapter. Their *mission* is to harmonise our relationship with the environment. Their *vision* is a world in which people live sustainably with respect for each other and nature.

Their *core values* present much more detail about their underlying approach to ways of *working* and *being* in the world. Having worked with them for many years it is clear to me that this organisation has given much thought to the values that underpin everything they do: (1) *Sustainable Living*: Appreciating the impact of our actions with regard to current and future generations. Having awareness

178 Belonging: The Human Connection

of our connection with the environment. Valuing simple and responsible lifestyles. (2) *Justice*: Being fair and accountable. Valuing socially equitable systems that protect the health of the planet, the people, and their way of life. Protecting future generations. (3) *Love*: Having self-awareness and understanding of the inter-relationship of all things. Having compassion and respect for all life. Recognising that outer discord is a reflection of inner discord. Striving for inner silence. (4) *Participation* is about: Engaging mentally, physically, emotionally, and spiritually; fostering respect for different viewpoints, openness, dialogue, and teamwork. (5) *Professionalism*: Being a role model of caring, integrity, commitment, professional standards and best practices for partners, organisations, individuals, and communities. (6) *Learning* is about: Being adaptive and flexible to changing circumstances. Having a holistic outlook. Being practical, objective, creative, and insightful. (7) *Happiness*: Appreciating that our happiness lies in creating and sharing happiness with others. Working on the slopes of the mountain forest where KFBG is based it is noticeable how the natural surroundings influence interest and awareness, creating positive conditions for learning. How many organisations have the word LOVE in their core values?

These statements represent important principles for ways of reconnecting with the earth. KFBG recommends that education should be informed by the same *wholeness* and *harmony* that is found in nature, by applying *relatedness and interconnectedness of all subjects*: for example, science is connected to intuition, economics to ecology, and philosophy to practice. Their educational programmes encompass ecology, art, farming, economics, culture, and *connecting with nature from the heart*. Their website explains that *separation* and *disconnection* is at the root of the environmental, economic, and social crisis facing the world today. It says that the world is, unfortunately, commonly seen as a collection of objects, each separated from the other. Mainstream educational systems could do more to recognise the *interconnectedness of all things, including the values of humanity*.

An organisation not too far away from KFBG is Outward Bound Hong Kong. Their core values are also worthy of note. Their mission statement says that Outward Bound helps people to discover and develop their potential to care for themselves, others, and the world around them through challenging experiences in unfamiliar settings using four pillars (based on the work of Kurt Hahn): self-reliance, physical fitness, compassion, and craftsmanship. Their programmes are based on the following six core design principles: *experiential learning* (a sequence of activities; facilitated learning opportunities – action, reflection, and transfer); *challenge and adventure* (unfamiliar settings, uncertain outcomes); *safety* (supportive approach, managed risk, clearly defined expectations); *outdoor physical activities* (environmental awareness, peak experiences); *team learning* (working to achieve a common goal, co-operation, interdependence, group independence); and *service* (community, belonging, interdependence, assisting or helping others, volunteering).

Nature: *A Contested Word*

In *Wild: An Elemental Journey* (Griffiths, 2006: 3) Griffiths comments on problematic *constructions* that influenced her adventurous journeys across the globe:

> I wanted nothing to do with the heroics of the "solo expedition." There was no mountain I wanted to "conquer," no desert I wanted to be the "first woman to cross." I simply wanted to know something of the landscapes I visited and wanted to do that by listening to what the members of those lands could tell me if I asked. I was exasperated (to put it mildly) by the way that so many writers in the Euro-American tradition would write reams on wilderness without asking the opinions of those who live there, the native or indigenous people who have a different word for wilderness: *home*.

Nature is a term that means different things to different people. It is often used to refer to the non-human living species and physical forms found in urban, rural, and wilder landscapes. Terms like "nature," "natural," and "wilderness" are all contested: they are social constructions (see *Uncommon Ground*, Cronon, 1996). Sociologists encourage us to unpack such terms that have been constructed and reconstructed within particular social and cultural frameworks. This can open minds to alternative constructions such as living on and with *the land*.

By unpacking the sociological contribution to the understanding of the more-than-human world the frequent use of anthropocentric paradigms that promote a view of the world as consisting of (1) the social and (2) the *material* is exposed. Classifying living species as "*material*" contributes to a rupture of the human connection with the world around and beyond the human. Dillon (2007) suggests investigations across and between disciplines can generate much more creative and integrative ways of thinking *at, between,* and *across* restrictive boundaries. Burns in *Nature Guided Therapy* (1998: xv) expresses a sadness "*that each body of knowledge has kept its wisdom within its own boundaries.*" Multidisciplinary and transdisciplinary understanding may help address many of the complex issues arising in the world we all inhabit.

Macnaghton and Urry (1997), in *Towards a Sociology of Nature*, contend that social scientists should decipher the social implications of the fact that nature has always been elaborately entangled and fundamentally bound up with the social. Benton and Redclift critique the relationship of social theory to the natural environment: the sociological heritage has made a slender contribution to the study of the environment:

> culture, meaning, consciousness and intentional agency differentiated the human from the animal, and effectively stemmed the ambitions of biological explanation. . . . In one move the opposition between nature and culture

180 Belonging: The Human Connection

(or society) made room for social sciences as autonomous disciplines distinct from the natural sciences, and undercut what were widely seen as the unacceptable moral and political implications of biological determinism.

(Benton & Redclift, 1994: 3)

Nicol (2003) advocates an *interconnectivity* and *interdisciplinarity* that is derived from both the social and natural sciences (social~natural), and there are others calling for experiential learning to be "envisioned within broader perspectives" (Fenwick, 2003: 22), with some arguing that many theoretical underpinnings to experiential learning are also "socially over-determined" (Michelson, 1998: 227). Payne (2002: 19) suggests a "sorely needed reparation of first, human-environment, second, community/society-land/sea/town/cityscapes, and third, culture-nature relations." "The" could be replaced by ~ thus avoiding the:

> interlocking system of overlapping dualisms that guide our thought and actions in environmentally significant ways; and these include civilised/wild, modern/primitive, culture/nature, mind/body, and so on. In each case, the first term of each pair represents a preferred state or entity, whereas the second indicates something that we try to distance ourselves from, composing a value system that gives the impression of being based on "factual" distinctions.
>
> *(Kidner, 2001: 10)*

Experiential learning needs more integrative design approaches. The more-than-human world is after all "prior to human existence or activity – historically, ontologically, and materially." The world beyond the human is a "condition of social life rather than a consequence of it" (Kidner, 2001: 20).

Moving beyond *humanist* frameworks enables the creation of a holistic understanding of *knowing* and *being* that connects the human experience as integral to the complex *multispecies world*. This opens up new possibilities for experiential learning designs. Writing from a perspective of cultural events design, Dashper and Buchmann comment that design: "as with most other areas in the social sciences, is strongly anthropocentric, and sees events as solely human domains; designed, managed and experienced by and for humans alone . . . we need to recognise that (those) collective experiences often involve not just other people, but also other species" (Dashper & Buchmann, 2020: 294). *Knowing* and *being* in the world are not an exclusive privilege merely bestowed on humans.

Social Interactions in the Outdoors

Important social, cultural, biological, and evolutionary bonds still exist between humans and the natural, spiritual, and physical world. We have long been influenced, and educated, *by* a reciprocal relationship, referred to as *biophilia* (Wilson,

1984). Spending time with family and friends is frequently a core motivation to visit the outdoor spaces, particularly as they contribute to the sense of belonging, and improve health and well-being. We humans have much to benefit from by simply (1) *being in* and *present*, (2) *viewing/observing*, (3) *actively participating/being involved* in *action*, (4) and by *developing a deeper understanding* of the world beyond the human. Palmer (2006) speaks of the need for education to be orientated "towards" the environment; as education *in* the environment; education *for* the environment; and education *about* the environment. These are all significant design principles.

In *A Pedagogy of Place: Outdoor Education for a Changing World*, Wattchow and Brown (2011) call for outdoor educators to be much more responsive to the connections that people have with their local conditions and cultural traditions in the places where people live and spend most of their lives: where they *belong*. The authors note that traditional outdoor education practices are based on theories and cultural ideas of risk and adventure (where the human connection with nature is often combative), or psychological theories of personal and social development. They note a significant shift towards outdoor education activities that have greater emphasis on the natural environment, to generate respect for *self*, *others*, and *nature* (see also Mortlock, 1984) where learning *in*, *for*, and *about* the environment embraces the importance of attachment to "place."

 DESIGN ILLUSTRATION 28 ACTION FOR CHANGE IN THE DESIGN OF PROGRAMMES AND CONFERENCES.

Whenever I design learning experiences, I generally include choices to take personal action towards a more sustainable society. I like to discuss a three-step process that moves from *awareness*, to *intention*, and through to *action*. Awareness is a first step to raise consciousness.

"*Let's Make Waste Extinct*" is a fine slogan, but if actions speak louder than words, then the intention-behaviour gap has to be bridged. At big conferences there is much waste, including a lot of conference "gifts." So how do we change these things?

"*Please Bring Your Own Food Container and a Spork*" was the influential action message in a conference I attended in Singapore – a banana leaf wrapped food parcel was available for those who forget, and the conference gifts were small gestures, and all were recyclable.

I like to promote the purchase of pens with ink refills as it is a simple way to reduce a considerable amount of plastic waste.

Removing and reusing tents left behind at music festivals is now commonplace (sent, e.g., to homeless charities) or pull string bags made from those beyond repair (*reimagine and recycle*).

The question is: what could you do as a designer to promote *practical action* at a primary level, or *ethical action* at a secondary level?
(See the Design Illustration on the circular economy).

Many humans become divorced from the more-than-human world: this relationship, requiring reciprocal respect, has for many simply dis*integrated*. They have forgotten how to connect through *noticing, observing,* and *reading* the signs and signals of the natural world. Now is a time to *re-*learn, and to *re-*member what our ancestors knew. Do we teach our children that when a butterfly in the rainforest stays under the leaf it is telling you something – that a storm is coming? English-speaking children are not taught that the English alphabet, without which there would be no *writing*, was originally *pictures* (Q for example is a stylized picture of a monkey). Outdoor environmental educators neglect these and many other important historical connections to the *natural history* of their world. Abram (1997) explores the natural connection to the evolution of the alphabet: the roots of language lie not only in gestures, but also in sensual *sounds* of the nature (onomatopoeic sounds), and in *pictures* (pictographic).

Why Does Ancient Wisdom Matter?

Indigenous knowledge focuses first and foremost on the relational bonds built on respect and reciprocity between *beings* of the living world: *knowing* is collective, practical, cumulative, and experiential. Indigenous knowledge has frequently been interpreted in "Western" societies as idealised, or backward, and oral knowledge was bypassed when the printing press, accompanied by wealth and privilege, arrived. Printing liberated and promoted some voices, whilst silencing others. Traditional knowledge has been embedded within communities over many generations through dreams, stories, dance, visions, songs, and ceremonies. Their knowing is now being *re*visited and *re*cognised as providing new ways to change towards more sustainable way of living.

> From an ecological viewpoint, the elders' narratives reflect an intimate knowledge of the natural environment in which they lived. They were closely familiar with the behaviour, habits, diseases, predators, reproductive cycles, and migration patterns of the animals and fish.
>
> *(Levesque et al., 2016: 66)*

What happens when the stories that are told are only those we were told? What happens when a teacher only knows one story? Made in 2019, *In My Blood It Runs* is a documentary film about the impact on educational systems of colonisation. It is a moving account of a 10-year-old boy called Dujuan growing up in Alice Springs, Australia. He is an aboriginal healer, a good hunter, and he speaks three languages, yet from a Western perspective Dujuan would probably be regarded as illiterate, and a troublemaker. His teacher is filmed reading the Western version of the history of Australia to his class. They are told how Captain Cook conquered their land, which was deeply frustrating to Dujuan as he had heard a very different story by his elders. His teacher didn't know that Polynesian navigators influenced Cook with their world leading navigation skills. In *Wayfinders: Why Ancient Wisdom Matters in the Modern World* ethnobotanist Wade Davis points out that *"knowledge is rarely divorced from power"* (2009: 64). Western accounts regard Cook as *"arguably the finest navigator in the history of the Royal Navy"* (2009: 41), though Davis exposes a largely unknown story about Captain Cook's first major voyage in 1769. Cook himself reported that he had travelled with a Polynesian priest and navigator who was able to indicate at any moment in the voyage the precise direction back to Tahiti though he had no charts or sextant.

Polynesian wayfarers navigate using their deep understanding of relational elements of the earth: when voyaging at sea they stay awake for long hours, *reading* the signs offered by the stars, sun, moon, wind, waves, clouds, birds, fish, and water. Remarkably these navigators learn the movements of over two hundred stars as they emerge at sunrise and set at dusk, thus creating a 360-degree *compass*. The clouds are understood by their shape, movement, character, colour, and place in the sky. The "reading" of wildlife and their ways for the purpose of navigation is equally impressive: the dolphins and porpoises swimming towards sheltered waters can indicate storms coming, a Frigate Bird heading out to sea can anticipate calm of the seas, Petrels and Terms travel fixed distances from their nests, returning each night and a sighting of a White Tern indicates land is within 200 kilometres, a Brown Tern 65 km, the Boobies rarely more than 40 km. "Phosphorescence and the debris of plants in the sea, the salinity and taste and temperature of the water, the manner in which a swordfish swims, all these become revelatory in the senses of the navigator" (Davis, 2009: 56.) This is the finest example I know to illustrate *experiential* learning and *connectedness* at its very best: this represents a different "intelligence," a different consciousness. It is traditional knowledge anchored in *being* in the world, within a complex social, ecological, and spiritual context. It is learning from practical everyday experiencing, inherited within and across generations. Learning is accumulated and shared to create a *collective knowing*. Again, it is important to point out that in the beginning there was only experiential learning no matter what claims are made about who coined the term.

There is much for all of us to learn and understand about the dialogue that nature offers if we learn to read the signs.

Technology: Connect~Disconnect, Dependency~Interdependency

The Polynesian navigators were not reliant on technology, and this raises the question of whether technology reduces our capacity to *connect* with or *gain knowledge* from the natural world. A vast range of technologies are now available to influence learning, for example virtual reality, enhanced reality, mixed reality, social media, GPS devices, facial recognition, and touch screens. Security wristbands are a technology used by Kidzania, a global *edutainment* experience, to make sure children are safe and can be easily located. The data from these electronic devices revealed that many gender stereotypes were playing out with over 600,000 4–14-year-old children across the globe. More males chose occupations such as pilots, or surgeons, whereas more females chose occupations such as flight stewardesses or making beds in a hotel. Kidzania experimented and intentionally changed the supervisors at the Formula One racing car mechanical engineer experience, where children changed the racing car tyres. When two female supervisors were present at this station, more young females queued to try the experience out for themselves. Kidzania believe that it is important to offer more opportunities for children to broaden their experience base as they can only aspire to what they know (see TEDX talk: (711) TedX Santa Barbara–2021 – YouTube).

Hills and Thomas (2020) create a simple design framework for judging *whether* to use, and *when*, *how*, and *why* to use digital technologies in outdoor experiential learning in terms of their positive and negative impact (see the following). The authors note that "technologies" includes equipment, tools, and clothing that have become so common that they are now *normalised*, becoming perceptually transparent. History has shown tools have increased human brain and body capacities: this was explored in earlier chapters in relation to spatial cognition capacities resulting from the crafting of stone axes half a million years ago (Wynn, 2010). Smartphones and tablets, global positioning systems, and digital cameras are rapidly becoming the "new normal," as was previously the case with walking boots and the compass. Drones are being used to review swimming or kayak techniques. Digital technologies can distract and diminish experiences or create additional opportunities for learning or improve security and safety. GPS devices for example can provide *augmentation* of an experience through feedback, by confirming how accurately a person has navigated a particular bearing when learning to navigate by map and compass. Hills and Thomas investigated 70 peer-reviewed papers, 2 blogs, and 15 book chapters to create a decision-making framework for the use of digital tools in terms of *opportunities* or *threats* in five areas. Each is explored in terms of how they affect the experience. Figure 8.1 is an adaptation derived from their work.

The question of whether technology connects, or disconnects, is not easy to answer! Chris Loynes (2020) investigated map and compass use in terms of how

Belonging: The Human Connection **185**

A Design Framework for Digital Tool Use		
5 experience design technology issues to consider	Positive & Negative Considerations Of the use of digital tools (DTs).	
Learner Experience of . . .	WITHOUT DIGITAL TECHNOLOGIES THE EXPERIENCE CAN . . .	WITH DIGITAL TECHNOLOGIES THE EXPERIENCE CAN . . .
Navigation/Location	increase risk. increase the sense of adventure.	increase security and safety. reduce the adventure experience.
Awareness/Attention	create a 'direct' experience rather than a mediated one.	'mediate' an experience, experience is seen or recorded via a device.
Communicating - with others	create more face-to-face connectivity whilst learning.	enhance communication and reduce solitude.
Knowledge/Information	mean lower levels of accessing knowledge.	offer instant access to knowledge.
Presence and Reflection	offer more immediacy, *noticing*, and *presence*.	be used to enhance reflection opportunities.

FIGURE 8.1   Deciding on digital technology use.

they can negatively impact (1) *education for sustainability*, (2) *pro-environmental behaviours*, (3) *the appreciation of space and place*, and (4) *the level of connection to the meaning and beauty of the natural world*. Whilst navigational skills have persisted in educational use for over a hundred years, Loynes suggests that there is a tendency to transfer rituals, tools, technologies, and symbols into contemporary educational experiences without *critically questioning* their suitability. He built on research by Wattchow and Brown (2011) who critique orienteering for its tendency to encourage participants to rush from place to place with little connectivity to the natural environment.

Loynes suggests that critical questions about design are necessary to create new thinking about technology use in outdoor educational activities. His overarching design question for his research was: *what values do these activities and experiences promote or hinder?* Maps and compass reading were promoted by ex-military personnel such as Lord Baden-Powell (founder of the scouting movement) to develop navigational abilities of *accuracy*, *punctuality*, and *reliability* that would be needed for survival. Their use was also to encourage the values and development of resilience in citizens of post-war times. Loynes designed an interesting experiment to explore how these technologies *mediate* the experience. He established two different student groups and the results showed those with maps tended to stay in larger groups, orientated using map and compass and distant fells, and planned routes and timings, and they tended to think ahead. Those without maps used slope of the ground, and the sun, and they followed natural features, such as streams and animal trails. They intentionally did not plan routes, nor work out timings, and they tended to be in the moment. Whilst both groups saw wildlife those without maps saw these sightings as more significant and so commented on them more often (2020).

So, what do outdoor facilitators think? Research on smartphone use was conducted by Bolliger et al. (2021) who surveyed 151 outdoor instructors in one US organisation. Smartphones are multi-tools possessing a compass, camera, notepad, torch, search engines, tracking devices, and weather apps for example. The research suggests these outdoor instructors dislike smartphone use, except during travel to and from the programme or event. The instructors disliked the use of text messaging, games, phone calls, and social media; however, they were more positive about the use of GPS tracking, checking weather, and location for example. A significant number of instructors approved smartphone use for photography, and video recording, and the research showed that younger instructors, especially males, were more amenable to smartphone use.

DESIGN ILLUSTRATION 29 DIGITAL MEMORIES.

This experience design, and variations of it, can create greater awareness of special moments in the natural world by creating digital memories.

Ask participants to take lots of personal photographs of an experience in nature, then afterwards select a few images representing *special moments*. Ask participants to create a digital *"storied memory strip"* sequence of several images (as in cartoon *strip*). Speech bubbles, thought bubbles, and story boxes can be added.

Participants quietly reflect on their chosen images to consider what makes them special, why were they chosen, and what aspects create these special moments in the natural world. Are these moments ones to hold onto, remember, and be grateful for? Do their pictures have anything special in terms of their *sensory* appeal, or *feelings*? Do the pictures represent what participants saw, heard, touched, tasted, or smelled whilst in nature? (See Wiking, 2019, *The Art of Making Memories*; also Beard & Rhodes, 2002, on creating reflective cartoon strips.)

Being Connected: Awareness of Special Moments

> I paddled a canoe smoothly and quietly as possible, breathing out with each "j" and in with each recovery. I listen to the sounds of the encroaching evening as I watch the concentric circles formed from water dripping from the blade and the small whirlpools meander away after each stroke. My mind is comfortably blank, no assessing, no philosophizing – the canoe, the surrounds and the river. A kingfisher swoops past, some wallabies hop casually along the bank, I feel as though I'm a silent, invisible observer.
>
> *(Wattchow & Brown, 2011: 115)*

Paddlers feel and sense the water. Mountains create a special sense that is felt by climbers. These experiences are in places other than where we dwell (dwell~escape). They are special in an *elemental sense:* they re-connect. They are magical moments that defy description, pointing to something bigger, and potentially spiritual, often involving *emotional-sensory awareness* (felt good inside/peacefulness), *thoughts* (contemplation), and *behaviours* (ethical, purposeful, action) that appear connected with the appreciation of something bigger, something sacred.

Heintzman (2016) provides an extensive reference list of qualitative studies in which participants have identified activities they associate with spiritual outcomes, including climbing, dragon boat racing, gardening, windsurfing, yacht cruising, zoo visiting, and other activities. He explores research that found that spiritual benefits were valued less by mountain bikers than by walkers, potentially suggesting that non-mechanised travellers appeared to be more easily able to focus on nature. Tuan (1997: 59) recommends solitude as "necessary for acquiring a sense of immensity," to satisfy a felt need to leave the familiar behind and go somewhere elemental like the sea or the mountains, for renewal and the opportunity to think. Connectivity can also derive from the rhythmic, routine activity inherent in walking, jogging, and kayaking. Walking and hiking are like slow cooking: at a walking pace we experience things very differently (see Daudelin, 1996 on repetitive activities and reflection; see Francis, 2011, for the effect of 22 years of walking during 17 years of silence; see Gros, 2014 for a philosophy of walking).

Special encounters with nature often occur whilst being "alone" yet at the same time being connected with the living world. I once became lost in a large tract of Malaysian rainforest. Whilst this was potentially a frightening experience, after an initial panic it became indescribably beautiful. A strong sense of connection slowly emerged: the monkeys were watching me, and one inflated his chest to let me know this was his territory. I sat to observe the beetles and ants going about their everyday business. Immersed in the intense sounds of cicadas and frogs, it became a calming experience.

Later in life another profound experience occurred. I worked with the RSPB in an estuary with my own boat with a small outboard motor. I remember well the night when the full moon and spring tides created real danger for the birds. I decided to go out in the semi-darkness late at night in my small boat in strong winds and flowing tides to see what was happening. I noticed many baby chicks had been separated from their nests and parents, and many had been washed into the tidal waters. I managed to save several chicks by scooping them out of the water into the boat, putting them in my jacket on the floor, and taking them back to higher, dry land. Despite being out at sea "alone," I was surrounded by natural beauty, and driven by some existential force, concerned for fellow living creatures. Words cannot do justice to my experience.

Just Open the Gate

What are our capabilities of developing these deep connections with the natural world? In a remarkable book *Beyond the Doors of Perception–Plant Intelligence and the Imaginal Realm: Into the Dreaming of Earth* (Buhner, 2014), the idea of being able to open our "gates" of *perception* is explored. When we pay attention, we "notice" and the gates of perception are opened. We have an ability to influence the amount of sensory data that is processed by learning to open or close these gates. We can do this by becoming more aware of our bodily sensory states being altered, such as when we experience the special moments described previously.

Musicians and artists, for example, have different gating capacities towards what they hear and see. Children experience less perceptual gating than adults, and newborn babies have minimal gating (see also Chapter 5). Many children who exhibit negative behaviours are labelled as having sensory processing deficits (SPD): interestingly, a high proportion of "gifted" children are also deemed to have similar deficits.

These gating processes generate different levels of sensory consciousness, and therefore different realities. This gating mechanism occurs through the creation and release of neurotransmitters in unique combinations. The chemicals within these neurotransmitters used to regulate human sensory processing existed in plants long before the humans species evolved. Shamans around the world have used natural plant chemicals to create hallucinogenic experiences for spiritual rituals, to access the ancestral world (see Schultes et al., 1998; Davis, 2009): the analysis of the various plant processes used to create such concoctions reveals astonishing levels of alchemical genius that is beyond the understanding of modern science.

 DESIGN ILLUSTRATION 30 FINDING SPACE AND TIME TO CONNECT.

Find time to let people experience being silent. Let people sit in special places on their own. When they go for a walk ask them to listen out for the *sounds* and *signs* of wildlife.

Design an introduction that sends pairs on a slow walk to get to know each other.

Design a "coffee and papers" experience of silent time *reading and thinking* alone in an "outside" setting – in nature if possible.

Chilean outdoor educator Rod Walker (1999) offers other simple activities that improve interconnectedness with the earth, and awaken our senses to the beauty of the world we live in. Many experiences involve *sitting*, being *still*, or walking *slowly*:

- self-introductions (respect for diversity of individual stories, how you got there);
- sitting on the ground or on natural materials (simple contact with the earth);

- sitting to talk in circles, not lines (cyclic nature of life processes and natural things);
- being inactive and alone (quietening down, going inwards, inviting nature in);
- walking differently from in the city (e.g., slowly, silently, blindfolded – unfamiliarity);
- walking barefoot (direct contact with dewy grass, rock, wood, earth, leaves);
- walking in unfamiliar places (gorges, undergrowth, logs, snow);
- leading, giving help (risking, reaching out, human care and contact);
- being led, receiving help (expecting understanding human care and contact);
- focusing on natural rhythms (tide, wind, sunset/rise, stars, moonrise/set, night sky);
- focusing where possible on wood fire (natural processes, history of life, universe);
- telling, inventing, and listening to stories, legends of the earth (images of other ways of life);
- sleeping on the ground, if possible outside (expanding awareness, dreaming);
- sitting silently observing together (sharing different perceptions of the world).

The term *biophilia* describes the very important bond and the kinship that exists between humans and other living species. A substantive body of research exists that shows the positive impact of the natural world on humans. A well-known impact is the shorter patient surgery recovery times in hospitals when patients are exposed to *natural surroundings* (Ulrich, 1984). Burns (1998) outlines many sensory awareness activities in nature for integrative therapeutic purposes connected to health and well-being (see previous). As a therapist he designs visual experiences such as "watching the sunset or a moonrise, observing a stream, looking at a seascape, studying a natural panorama, looking at the forest, watching a waterfall, looking at the park, watching animals in nature, and observing the starry night sky" (41). He notes that it is important to consider how the client experience facilitates "movement towards the therapeutic goal: how, having achieved the task, they may be thinking differently, feeling differently, or doing things differently" (41). What these experiences do is help us to learn to increase our sensitivity by focusing on incoming sensory information. These experiences help shift levels of consciousness.

Overstimulation of the senses can be breathtaking, and for some, exhausting. In experiential learning design it is important to create opportunities for people to reconnect by *returning to their senses*, to their *feelings*, that is, to our experiencing *bodies*. We can learn much from the *reciprocal* relationship with nature, by bringing mind and body back into balance. *Experiencing* the fragrance of a flower, the texture of bark, the calls of the owl, the stars in the sky, or the spectacular views from a mountain top, can provide *inner peace*.

190 Belonging: The Human Connection

Become More Aware: Animals~Plants

"A child who appreciates a plant as a miracle approaches the study of plants differently from a child who 'engages in a task'" (Caine & Caine, 1994: 7). As discussed earlier eminent scientist Barbara McClintock approached plants in this way in her Nobel Prize winning research. Despite years of ridicule and the trivialisation of her work, her research created new insights into plant genetics and plant intelligence (see Keller, 1983). This was "despite the restrictiveness of the times, of being a woman in what was primarily a man's profession, she became one of the world's most distinguished cytogeneticists" (Buhner, 2014: 321). It did not help that she worked on plants, specifically corn, which was regarded as not an exciting species.

> The living kingdom used to be divided into animals and plants. So far as I can ascertain, the division was based on the simple idea that all the interesting things moved and all the non interesting ones did not.
>
> *(Trewavas, 2015: 4)*

Plants evolved so they didn't need to move. They do move, but on a different timescale. This influences views about the intelligence of plants, a subject of growing interest. Plants communicate through an extensive neural network found in the roots of the soil and leaf canopy. This system is not unlike the neural networks found in brains.

> A unique part of the plant root, the root apex is a combination sensitive finger, perceiving sensory organ, and brain neuron. . . . A single rye plant has more than 13 million rootlets with a combined length of 680 miles. Each of the rootlets are covered with root hairs, over 14 billion of them, with a combined length of 6,600 miles.
>
> *(Buhner, 2014: 120)*

Plant behaviour and plant intelligence are fascinating subjects, not least because the neurochemicals that regulate the human mind were utilised by plants within the networks described previously long before humans evolved. Early plants provided the foundation for the evolution of all later life forms, including humans. The question of whether plants are intelligent is complex: if we regard intelligence as possessing a brain, then we won't find "brains" as such in plants. Animals evolved neurons to send messages speedily down its cables, whereas plants evolved similar systems to send messages far more slowly though roots, stems, and leaves.

Zoos are much more popular than botanical gardens, yet the earth is dominated by plants, and the earliest forms of life on planet earth were plants. Plant fossils have been found that date back to 3.2 billion years: plants predate humans

Belonging: The Human Connection **191**

by millions of years, and "whereas plants could happily dispense with animals, we could not happily dispense with plants" (Trewavas, 2014: 72). Humans require the oxygen that plants produce, and plants require the carbon dioxide that we humans and other animals produce. Before the 18th century there was no accepted classification or naming of plants. Modern botany is relatively new and the estimates of the number of "plants" on earth varies widely from three hundred thousand to several hundred thousand species. We have still so much to discover about these remarkable living forms.

It is often thought that plants are pollinated by bees. They are, but many plants have special relationships with other creatures. Plants can be pollinated by:

> bats, to mosquitos, to mice, to ants, to opossums, to bees, to monkeys, to beetles, to lizards, to flies, to birds, to butterflies, to flying foxes. Perhaps 80% of all the flowering plants are pollinated by beetles. . . . The 700 to 900 fig species in the world, for the past 40 million years have each been pollinated by its own individual kind of fig wasp. Their lives are often mutually interdependent; neither can survive without the other.
>
> *(Buhner, 2002: 191)*

There is much to still learn from and about the plant world. Many people do not know that: birds weave nests with specific plants that can prevent infections; bears emerging from hibernation dig for the roots of certain plants and eat them to cleanse the digestive tract and protect their fur from fungal infections; wild boars eat roots that contain anti-worm chemicals to prevent their intestines becoming infested; dogs eat certain grasses to regulate their intestines; chimpanzees will select and eat plants for a wide range of health purposes and their plant knowledge is extensive. Many animals know which plants to feed on during pregnancy to assist with birthing. Researchers have monitored pregnant Africa elephants towards the end of the pregnancy walking many miles to a specific tree to consume its leaves and bark. The same plant is used by Kenyan women to help childbirth (Buhner, 2002). Out of about 300,000 species of plants growing on the earth about 20,000 are listed as having human use. The natural world is full of remarkable phenomena and there is still so much to experience: much can be gained from perspectives other than the biological previously explored, including emotional and spiritual knowing derived from the humans' interdependency with animals.

Connection in Action

Naming living things requires careful observation and reasoning. Wanting to know what a plant or animal is called can create the early stages of interest and engagement: identification requires careful observation as a problem-solving activity. Naming is a way of *noticing* and *connecting* as it involves identifying the

192 Belonging: The Human Connection

characteristics or visible features (morphological) that make it what it is: how an animal flies, what it sounds like, how it is adapted to live in a specific place, or whether it is endangered.

Citizen science projects are on the increase, involving members of the public who don't necessarily have any training in scientific work, doing research. The "Lost and Found Fungi Project" managed by the world famous Kew Gardens for example involves people in identifying fungi. The project report information, "State of the World's Fungi," says fungi are as beautiful as orchids and just as important to protect. They are a hidden part of our biodiversity. The organisers say they need to teach people and invite them in to admire fungi. Fungi are a whole kingdom that is equal to if not greater than in diversity than both the plants and animals. The project, involving over 100 scientists from 18 countries, found that more than 2,000 new fungi are discovered each year, from a variety of sources, including a human fingernail! Hundreds of species are collected and eaten as food, with the global market for edible mushrooms worth £32.5bn a year. Only 56 types of fungi have been evaluated for the IUCN Red List, compared with more than 25,000 plants and 68,000 animals. At least 350 species are consumed as foods including truffles (which can sell for thousands of dollars apiece), quorn, marmite, and cheese. Plastic car parts, synthetic rubber and Lego are made using itaconic acid derived from a fungus. Fungi are also being used to turn crop waste into bioethanol. Products made from fungi can be used as replacements for polystyrene foam, leather, and building materials. 216 species of fungi are thought to be hallucinogenic.

Go on a different adventure down a less trodden path. Learn about fungi and beetles, a hidden "world" out there that is such a vital part of *our* biosphere. Eco-adventure travel has increased in popularity over the last decade to become one of the leading income generating themes within tourism. Greenforce, Frontier, and Earthwatch are three organisations that offer a new and unusual combination of learning journeys that might be termed "*edventure*" (education plus adventure). These organisations design learning experiences for young people, using a subtle mix of educative features for self-development, including adventure, travel, environmental or community development work, and skills in scientific wildlife monitoring. These organisations are usually charities recruiting paying volunteers to support wildlife projects around the world.

Learning from experiences that utilize *real* environmental or community projects to engage, motivate, and create change is popular. Community projects include the building of playgrounds for children, the delivering of hospital radio programmes, or choreographing theatre performances. The design options are endless. With creativity the benefits can be considerable to many stakeholders. Some environmental organisations even have specialist staff to help coordinate such projects. Design Illustration 31 describes this type of project.

Belonging: The Human Connection **193**

DESIGN ILLUSTRATION 31 MAKING CONNECTIONS.

A major supermarket chain that regularly puts their supervisors and junior managers on outdoor management development programs, noticed that other supermarkets were doing the same outdoor activities, and sometimes they saw their competitors, in similarly cheap and brightly coloured waterproof clothing perched on nearby mountains and peaks in a National Park. They had experienced traditional outdoor activities for many years but now asked if it would be possible to design something different.

As Director of Training for a large practical environmental charity I set about designing a different approach. One involved a dry-stone walling building program for them (dry stone walls have for hundreds of years separated the farmed fields in the northern National Parks of the UK). We set up a complex management scenario as part of the experience design: they had budgets to work to and they had to buy in expertise from professional walling experts (at a standard rate per hour – though not "real" money!). Their work would be judged based on the national walling standards, and so they would achieve financial benefit from high standards of work. Walling can be a highly social occupation as people can work and talk on either side of the wall as they carefully select and place stones to create a solid, high stock proof boundary.

Fifteen years later one of the world's biggest map-making organisations, known as the Ordnance Survey (OS), also asked for something "different" for their staff development programme. Over 5% of the OS revenue comes from the production of maps for outdoor walking and outdoor activities. As I had previously worked for many wildlife organisations, the design of a new creative program was relatively easy: my contacts within several wildlife charities would help me by doing most of the work! I wrote to them and asked them to send me no more than two sides of A4 containing an outline of how approximately 20 of the most skilled surveyors might be able to help their charity.

Three weeks later some impressive projects arrived. This experience design was about joining the dots by *connecting and matching* people (including communities and organisations) with different projects to suit their needs. It was a matchmaking process! I simply took all the proposals down to London to the headquarters of the Ordnance Survey and presented the projects to them. The choice was difficult, but the organisation involved their surveyors in discussions and so ownership of the project had already begun. They chose one of the organisations I had worked for, a bird protection charity, for their learning experience project that would focus on aspects of their work as a team.

The project involved surveying land which frequently flooded due to peat extraction over many years. The project design created a detail brief, location details, transport logistics, health and safety advice, rules and regulations, deadlines and the outputs required. This "real" project was a great success.

The legacy for the charity was a series of high-quality maps for the bird protection charity. For OS the experience created fresh thinking about new products, services, and customers for the future.

An Alternative Way: A Connective Web of Ways of Knowing

Experience designs should not shy away from challenging the use of power and wealth to silence other voices. Mullins et al. (2016: 49) revisit indigenous knowledge to suggest experience designs should

> explore the problematic historical relationships that outdoor recreation education has with indigenous peoples, and to encourage possibilities for alternative ways of thinking and doing outdoor recreation education informed by indigenous ways of knowing and being.

They explore power and colonialism in their attempt to disrupt dichotomous thinking by reimagining human-environment relations in outdoor recreation and education in terms of the practical application of social, spiritual, and ecological ways of *being* in the world. These are highly valued elements of indigenous knowing: "the experiential nature of Indigenous knowledge allows for empirical understanding through continued close attention to, and dialogue with, particular phenomena within one's lifeworld" (Mullins et al., 2016: 52). The indigenous knowledge of Polynesian navigators illustrates this kind of deep, experiential way of *knowing* through *being*.

Aboriginal leadership tends to *serve* those they lead, rather than *command*. Research on the problems associated with the design of an aboriginal youth leadership retreat programme have been explored by Gartner-Manzon and Giles (2018). They highlight what happens when cultural diversity, and traditional knowledge is neglected. They found that most people invited to participate already displayed Eurocentric and US leadership styles before the programme, and so benefitted the most. Those who did not display the power relations associated with autocratic leadership benefitted the least. The experience design served to marginalise aboriginal culture. Western models of leadership, particularly Eurocentric and US definitions, tend to embrace a combination of *ability* plus *authority*. The latter includes decision making, and the exercising of voice and influence, by individuals utilising power and authority over subordinates to attain specific objectives. Associates, rather than subordinates, are consulted and treated with respect, as *equals*. Davis refers to this style of leadership as *acephalous* (2009).

Mullins et al. (2016: 54) note that "in order to survive and prosper as individuals, communities and nations, most indigenous people have had to learn and live within multiple worlds, often referred to as 'walking into worlds.'" They reference Mi'Kmaq and Euro-Canadian scholars who term this "*Two Eyes Seeing*," in which their students learn to approach the natural world through both Western and Indigenous eyes to form a fused and balanced whole. Lowan-Trudeau (2013) suggest this is an example of an *ecological métissage* as an active literary and pedagogical strategy for negotiating conflicting value systems. As a political praxis it seeks to uncover and reclaim the wisdom of lost or forgotten origins that lies at the intersection of the *existential* (being) and *epistemological* (knowing), as a deep ecology that embraces traditional Indigenous knowledge.

In outdoor education "over the last three decades there has been a growing awareness of alternative ways of connecting with nature other than through the physical" (Collins & Humberstone, 2018: 57). They note that outdoor education (OE) and outdoor environmental education (OEE) are often seen as separate practices. For OE the environment was a playground for physical activity. For OEE

> the outdoors was a collection of features to be studied. Because the term in popular use was "education," rather than learning there appeared to be a supposition that the leader would impart knowledge, teach about moving through the outdoors and lead participants, rather than encouraging participants to experience and explore and develop their own preferences for connecting with the outdoors.
>
> *(p. 60)*

Mullins et al. (2016: 56) offer advice to those designing outdoor programs. They suggest that:

> programs might assess critically the social and ecological acceptability of their practices, curricula (explicit and implicit), knowledge and activities. Learning would be guided by humility, inclusivity, care and compassion. Activities and programmes – and the stories told about them – would respect the specific histories, environments, places, landscapes, and inhabitants implicated, and support the desired change.

The disconnect created by the twin dialogues of *adventure* and *environment* is located within the notion of "outdoor education." Whilst both are interconnected, a split discourse disconnects. Loynes (2018: 71) refers to this as a "twin gaze": firstly, the inward gaze (self-development/character building utilising

196 Belonging: The Human Connection

adventurous activities), secondly the second gaze, directed outward towards the environment. He is hopeful that "the outer landscapes of nature and the inner landscapes of identity formation will drift back together" (81). This would represent a move away from either-or perspectives, towards a more connected, ecological paradigm. Finnish outdoor educator Jari Kujala notes that "without the ecological paradigms, OE loses its autonomy and its connection to elemental nature" (Kujala, 2018: 233).

Mies and Shiva (1993), as feminist activists and writers, demonstrate the ways in which ecological destruction disproportionately affects women, particularly so in the developing world. Gray and Mitten (2018) as editors of *The Palgrave International Handbook of Women and Outdoor Learning* explore the marginalisation of women on the unlevel playing field of outdoor learning. The many writers in the book outline the substantial but widely unknown contributions that women have made to outdoor and environmental learning and leading. In the last of the 62 chapters of this extensive edited book they outline the little-known work of Marina Ewald that was foundational in enabling and underpinning the achievements of Kurt Hahn (e.g., founding of Outward Bound). Hahn is widely celebrated, and so Gray and Mitten cleverly change "*his*tory" into "*her*story." The contribution of Marina Ewald was unknown until historical research was carried out by Veevers and Allison (2011).

Joining the Dots: Systems~Ecological Thinking

In July 2019 I was asked to deliver a keynote speech on the *Future of Outdoor Education* in Singapore, a country that substantially invests in outdoor education for young people. The conference title was: *Scaling Higher Ground: How Do We Stay Relevant whilst Serving the Community?* At the same time I was commissioned to design and facilitate an Executive Workshop for officers from the Ministry of Education and National Youth Council, senior teachers, private outdoor providers, and other invited stakeholders to discuss the future direction of OE for Singapore. Issues that were on the agenda included: ageing, youth, disadvantage, diversity, inclusivity, staffing, mental health, stratification, technology, commercialisation, and environmental issues. A tall order! So, the speech and workshop concentrated on *connecting*, using the image of a spider's web as a representation of a composite ecological connectivity. Areas that caused concern could be connected: parental time with children is frequently diminished whilst the elderly often find themselves alone. Yet the elders find great joy in watching, helping, and supporting young people. The elders sometimes struggle with technology, whilst the young are often gifted in this area. In outdoor programmes many staff are highly competent in recreational skills, though they can be low on botanical, zoological, ecological, and environmental skills despite the existence of people with such special skills. Expertise can be found in the semi-retired or retired. A lot of research exists that points to the healing power of the natural world

FIGURE 8.2 Systems thinking and the spider's web.

and so opportunities for more connectivity is important in terms of mental and physical health and well-being. Outdoor centres in Singapore often have significant areas of *land*, often based by the *sea*. Many have well-maintained areas with grassy mown areas. Here potential exists for the creation of wildlife areas, and opportunities for people to engage in nature and horticultural activities, which in turn can improve mental health. All this can occur without disrupting access to high ropes courses, kayaks, and other equipment. Many issues around the communities, outdoors, health, environment, technology, and learning are interconnected. The icons used in Figure 8.2 represent some of these interconnections.

Wilding **Through Design**

If the spirit of the wolf is to return to this land, then we'd best be prepared! This is the introduction to a tracking masterclass called *The Wolf, The Wild and Me*, that is blended with experiential enquiry and a chance to meet real wolves in the UK. In the UK the dialogue, discourse, and debate surrounding the reintroduction of the wolf is complex and controversial. Deeper questions will need to be asked about the general idea of *rewilding* the countryside, and no less importantly, what rewilding means for ourselves in our *bodies*, *minds*, and *hearts*, including those of our children.

For 250 years wolf tracking has not been possible in Britain, but the wolf has nevertheless resiliently stalked our imagination and consciousness ever since the last howl was heard in the 18th century. Now the wolf is a controversial candidate

198 Belonging: The Human Connection

entering into dreams and debates as a new indicator species that could create a healthy restoration of ecological balance and improved biodiversity in Britain. It may be time to learn wolf-tracking! The masterclass course, it is said, will teach technical tracking and fieldcraft skills. The experience will be a combination of class time and field time. The course is said to explore:

- Natural history and wildlife of the region;
- Basic wildlife physiology and morphology;
- Clear footprint identification.
- Behaviour and wildlife sign interpretation;
- Tracking.
- How wildlife interacts with landscapes;
- The fundamentals of following animal trails;
- The art of enquiry and questioning;
- There will also be an off-site visit to spend time with some captive wolves located nearby.

The wolf may have vanished from the UK, but it endures in other ways. It is embedded in our collective psyche: the wolf symbolises something mysterious and deeply wild, even if it no longer physically stalks the shadows of the land. This all represents experiential learning design in an organisation called *WildWise*. They create a camp infrastructure that supports people to live comfortably in the outdoors whilst studying tracks and signs of native wildlife.

Many other organisations are designing creative experiences in nature. S4K invites discovery of flora and fauna through play; with leaves, mud, and sticks children build dens, and create art. They learn bushcraft, fire lighting skills, tool use, and camp craft. They go orienteering and learn to use natural navigation as well as maps and compass. They learn survival skills, building shelters and cooking by living off the land. They engage in team building activities and learn to lead. The back of the brochure contains 100 reasons for spending a thousand hours outside. The reasons all have underlying research underpinning them, and the following are illustrative:

> boost the immune system, sunshine improves the function of the liver, being in nature gives an overriding feeling of peace, walking barefoot outside promotes calmness by reducing stress hormones, children with ADHD focus better after being outdoors, scores with environmental education programs score higher on standard tests in reading, and that natural environments stimulate social interaction between children.

One of the most exciting places to glimpse new ideas about connecting to the natural world is the Schumacher College, which attracts many students from across the globe. Their MA in *Engaged Ecology* is a radical new programme for students looking to reconsider their relationship with the more-than-human world, to find solutions to the environmental and social crises of our time. The advert for this course refers to the "*Call of the Wild*," is as follows:

> The formal education system is creaking under the strain of the national curriculum and our children are receiving instruction rather than a true education, within a context of reaching goals and targets that fail to address the body/mind/spirit potential within each child, or the deeper cultural need. One of the most effective ways to inspire and enrich ourselves, our communities and each other, is to find our way back to engaging whole-heartedly with the natural world and seek ways to offer this connection to others. An extraordinary syllabus is available to anyone open to spending time in nature, and our job as environmental/outdoor educators is to cultivate this "nature connection" in helpful and meaningful ways. Therefore, we invite you to become one of the new generation of change-makers.

The course has many design features similar to those previously described, including a Night Paddle and an overnight Solo, Tracking Skills, Wildlife Observation, Gaya Theory, Deep Ecology, Nature Awareness, Campcraft, Bushcraft, Woodcraft, Sensory Awareness, Naturalist Activity, Creative Interpretation, Storytelling, Nature Games, Bird Language, and more, including assignments and practice.

DESIGN ILLUSTRATION 32
SELF-AWARENESS, AUDIT, AND ACTION.

Sustainable Living: Appreciating the impact of our actions.
A self-audit increases self-awareness, and can lead to change, that is, action.
Take one sheet of lined A4 paper. Over a week on one side make a note of all the things that you throw "away." On the other side make a note of all the things you do in a week to help protect the environment such as planting trees, growing vegetables, reducing consumption, or purchasing environmentally friendly products. It doesn't have to be detailed.
If you're running a program, people can be asked to try a simple audit before (or during). Sharing and comparing can produce quite illuminating conversations. (See the *Industrial Ecology* design illustration).
The ability to lower our impact on the environment can be enhanced by the following sequence: (1) Be *patient,* simply *observe, first-hand, record* and become *aware*; (2) *Challenge* and questions about what is happening (for example sensitising ourselves to what things we throw away), and asking *should we be doing this, is there another way, can we collaborate with others?* (3) *Action,* do something by changing what is going on. Create positive benefit.

To become aware that one's own impact on the environment though self-audit is a simple way to *connect*.

The connections we humans have with the more-than-human world are vital for our health and well-*being*. It is integral to our human *being*, which is the subject of the next chapter.

9

BEING – THE DEVELOPMENT OF THE ONTOLOGICAL SELF

The focus of this chapter is the H for *H*uman, as human *beings* in the world. In a paper on the way learners either *plan* or utilize *emergent* opportunities Megginson (1994) suggests two significant questions are asked: *what do you want to do with your life?* and secondly *what kind of person do you want to be?* These fascinating questions rather nicely link *being* with what we *do* with our lives. But what is *being*?

In workshops I sometimes demonstrate speech recognition software by reading out the following statement: "Professor Ron Barnett says the wider project of higher education is not the development of the epistemological self; it is the development of the ontological self." The audience are often amazed to see the text unfold across the screen without error. The point I am making, however, is that epistemology is the study of knowing, and the ways we can know. Ontology is concerned with the study of *being* and existence. According to Kolb (1984) learning is the process of "extracting knowledge" through the transformation of a concrete experience, using reflection. According to Barnett the real purpose of learning is ontological transformation: the *self* is transformed in terms of a person's ongoing life project, the making of *meaning* in life, and/or a *quest* for *coherence* in life.

Experiential learning might be more broadly considered as providing *experiences* for the *trans*formation of the self. Another popular term is "*trans*fer" of learning: both have the root *trans*, to *change*. Transfer is regarded as a process of *continuation*, of transferring something to somewhere or something else, to change things inside or outside the self. Key questions to consider are: (1) what is the *form* of *trans-form*-ation? and (2) where is the change transferred to?

Individually we *make meaning* by bringing into focus, unpacking, and critically examining what is happening around us. Critical dialogue, debate, careful questioning, and emotional engagement all have potential to be transformative experiences. Taylor notes (in Mezirow: 303) that "based on the research it seems

DOI: 10.4324/9781003030867-9

202 *Being – The Ontological Self*

quite clear that both critical reflection and affective learning play a significant role in the transformative process."

Distracting Streams of Thought

It is easy to get caught up in the autopilot life of continuous *doing* and *thinking*. The continuous stream of everyday thoughts that swirl around in the head prevent a real awareness of "how we experience the world, who we are, and how we might improve our life and well-being" (Beard & Wilson, 2018: 277). The swirls prevent the full experiencing of experiences. But the swirls can be slowed, and experiences made more visible with sensory awareness work outlined in Chapters 4,5, and 8.

Mindfulness is also a form of focus work involving meditative reflection to *experience* the inner and outer world *experiencing*. Mindfulness is underpinned by being compassionate, and compassion involves suspending judgement. Suspending judgement typically involves "holding" the habitual tendency to *think* in dualisms: good or bad, true or false, agree or disagree, and so the complimentary ~ is important in this respect. With patient *observation* we can learn to stay with sensory and emotional experiencing and gain greater awareness of the deeper *needs* that underpin our behaviours, and those of others.

Rigidity occurs when trust~control is out of balance, and this has significant influence on the ability to be compassionate: Cell notes that "the less we are able to trust, the more control we feel we need and the more vulnerable we are to loss of control" (1984: 13). Mindfulness involves trusting and paying attention to the moment, the "now." It involves a degree of detachment from engaging with the swirl of *sensations, feelings, thoughts*, and *actions* (the outer layer in Figure 9.1). Individuals, organisations, and groups exist in a state of always going forward, always becoming. Metaphors of movement are used by Gergen (2009) who suggests that in *being* we are always carrying with us our past as we move forward through the present into a *becoming*. Movement is towards a different place than before. We speak of having *your whole life in front of you*, or to *put that behind you*: in this way changing reflects movement through time and space, so in a sense we are continually moving, changing, and *becoming* different, reconstructing the self (*self* is used in the plural – multiple selves). Something becomes a part of us through internal assimilation and accommodation. According to Mezirow "learning occurs in one of four ways: by elaborating existing frames of reference, by learning new frames of reference, by transforming points of view, or by transforming habits of mind" (2000: 19). These four ways to learning contain two important ways to transform our *being*: the *view* and the *habits*.

The Threat of Chaos

Being is a word representing the core of who we are, the sense of "self," embracing identity, values, beliefs, and the spiritual (self). In many languages (e.g., Greek, Sanskrit, classical Chinese, Hebrew, Hindi, and Latin) the word *spirit* has meanings

Being – The Ontological Self **203**

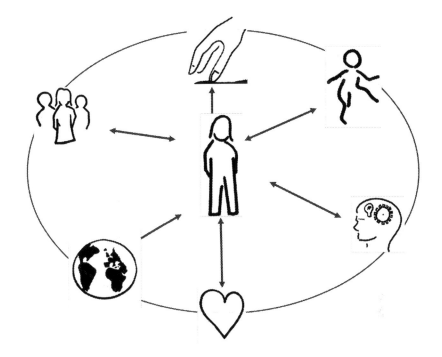

FIGURE 9.1 *Being*: Towards integration and coherence.

related to both "breath" and "life." We all breathe the same air and share a common "spirit." It is the sense of connection and attachment that is central to the development of an *integrated* and *coherent* self. These connections and attachments, shown in Figure 9.1, affect mental health, resilience, and optimal living. Siegel notes that "integration is postulated to be the central mechanism by which health is created in mind, brain, body, and relationships" and that "the field of mental health can reframe its compendium of disorders as revealing the chaos and rigidity of nonintegrated conditions" (2012: 336).

In Chapter 6 it was noted that:

> a defining condition of being human is our urgent need to understand and order the meaning of our experience, to integrate it with what we know to avoid the threat of chaos. If we are unable to understand, we often turn to tradition, thoughtlessly seize explanations by authority figures, or resort to various psychological mechanisms, such as projection and rationalization, to create imaginary meanings.
>
> *(Mezirow & Associates, 2000: 3)*

204 *Being – The Ontological Self*

Getting and Wanting

Much of the time we seek and want *things*: in doing so the mind avoids the now by projecting into the *future*. A compulsion to *do* things, *get* things, *have*, or *possess* things, to *feel* some way, to *think* or *know* something, can at times be counterproductive. The desire for *things* can allow the mind to be easily controlled and conditioned by *peripheral experiences*, that is, what we *do, think, feel*, or *sense*. This kind of wanting can lead to negative *habits of mind* that are internalized and operate in the subconscious. Much negative mental energy is generated by the judging, controlling, egoic mind: the car alarm annoys and creates negative energy because we let it. The habits of mind control through the subconscious.

The mind is an *anticipation machine* (Siegel, 2012) that needs constant feeding. The media understand this fact. They know humans look for things to worry about, or things to have, things to get excited about, or things we want to know. This is one *habitual* state, where we are always waiting for the future, because we desire "things" and this continually disconnects us from being in the present. *One day I will* . . . is a typical inner conversation about dreams of the future, but these dreams often defer life. Life waits *until*, thus distracted from *being* in the now. The things that constantly attract also distract; they easily grab our attention and focus. These things include the stuff of advertising, and regular interactions with social media. They can be replaced with alternative habits: that of learning more about self, and how subconscious reactions take over and control us.

That coloured button that you click on will take you somewhere else, to allow you to find out *who*, or *what*, or *when*. This is the stuff of social media: LinkedIn for example informs me "Colin people are looking at your profile." If I frequently press the blue distraction button I feed the *trigger* that leads to the *habit* (Eyal, 2014). These sequences underpin *experiences* of "things" we have to have, or need, or want. These are peripheral experiences that feed the mind that needs constant sustenance. "In learning to live with less self-awareness, we also diminish those distinctly human possibilities for freedom, creativity, caring, and ethical insight which are based on awareness" (Cell, 1984: 9).

In contrast to being controlled by *doing* and *thinking* there is a state within the core of our *being* that can generate fulfilment and inner peace. Eckhart Tolle (1997) reminds us that it is the "present moment" that is all we really have. He recommends that we make the *Now* a primary focus of life, by being *present* in the here and now. Inner peace requires moments of being present, in the "now." Being present develops greater levels of consciousness through greater self-awareness of *actions* (behaviours/doing), *feelings*, *thinking* (habits of mind), and *sensing* (bodily) "things." But being in this sense is not concerned with "things": it is about no-*thing*, no-form, and it takes "no time" to *be* in the now. *Being* in the "now" is about being *present* in the moment, not in the *controlling* time of future or past.

Life balance and well-*being* requires integration and coherence of the "self" (plural). If we can step out of the constant flow of the *autopilot* peripheral *experiences* of the outer layer in Figure 9.1, we can stop feeding the controlling, hungry mind. The controlling mind needs to be watched and observed in action: to be made visible. *Making visible* has been a central theme in all chapters so far. The hub of the image in Figure 9.1 represents the experience of *being* aware of the connectedness with the six modes of experiencing in the outer ring. Balance~imbalance in life is affected by the cultivation of awareness or intrapersonal attunement to these six aspects of experiencing, which leads to interpersonal attunement.

Experiencing with greater awareness can be applied to sensing, feeling, doing, thinking, and belonging/relating. Eventually we learn to become more *aware of being aware. Being* in the present, in the "now," creates greater consciousness of what we experience. This self-awareness in turn brings the benefits of integration and balance (~).

> At the center of your being you have the answer; you know who you are, and you know what you want.
>
> *Lao Tzu*

Siegel, in his book on *The Mindful Brain*, comments:

> We are in desperate need of a new way of being – in ourselves, in our schools, and in our society. Our modern culture has evolved in recent times to create a troubled world with individuals suffering from alienation, schools failing to inspire and to connect with students, in short, a society without a moral compass to help clarify how we can move forward in our global society.
>
> *(Siegel, 2007: xv)*

Self-awareness is important as it helps to avoid the dysfunctional consequences of *chaos* and *rigidity*, as opposed to *integration* and *coherence* in life which are an important focus of both educational and therapeutic endeavors.

Conditioning, Consciousness, and Conduct

On experiential education programmes in India Vishwas Parchure reminds participants that we consciously teach what we know, but we unconsciously teach who we are.

> For centuries we have been conditioned by nationality, caste, class, tradition, religion, language, education, literature, art, custom, convention, propaganda of all kinds, economic pressure, the food we eat, the climate we live in, our family, our friends, our experiences – every influence

206 Being – The Ontological Self

you can think of – and, therefore, our responses to every problem are conditioned. Are you aware that you are conditioned? That is the first thing to ask yourself, not how to be free of your conditioning. You may never be free of it, and if you say, "I must be free of it," you may fall into another trap of another form of conditioning. So are you aware that you are conditioned?

(Jiddu Krishnamurti)

The ancient Chinese philosopher Lao Tzu cautioned how our *thinking* can become our *words*, and our words become our *actions*. He suggests that our *actions* form the basis of our *habits*, and our habits lead towards the development of our *character*, who we are, our *being*. This aligns with the 3 Cs model (see Figure 9.2) showing *conditioning*, *conduct*, and *consciousness*, as developed by Vishwas Parchure. In this simple model the inner sense of *Being* is influenced by the level of awareness of the conditioning derived from the past. This conditioning influences thoughts, feelings, and actions. Conditioning derives from caregivers, general upbringing, impactful events, and schooling, for example, and from what we are told or believe is right or wrong, or from cultural and religious influences.

The conditioning of the past informs our *conduct*, in the form of behaviour and action. When we are not *aware* of past experiences, preferences, and prejudices, they seep through the membrane of *consciousness* un-noticed, regulating and

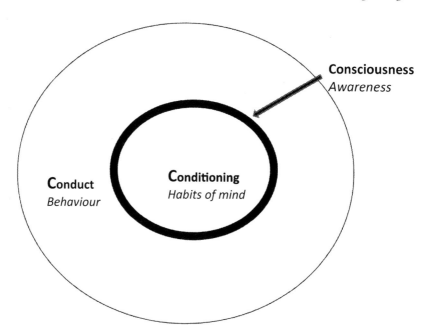

FIGURE 9.2 The 3 Cs of conscious awareness, conditioning, and conduct.

Being – The Ontological Self **207**

influencing *conduct*. The thickness of the membrane represents the level of consciousness in the model. This membrane acts like a window between the inner and outer worlds we inhabit, and it takes many years of practice to be deeply aware of what flows through it, from inside out and outside in.

The Integrated, Coherent Self

> We may see even more deeply into the meaning of being human, and so into the nature of good and evil, as we learn what invalidates and impoverishes our lives, strengthens and enriches them. We find purpose and fulfilment in the very use of these powers. Our sense of worth becomes less and less tied to having approval from others and more and more grounded in knowing ourselves to be the creators of meaning and value.
>
> *(Cell, 1984: 6)*

Integration brings balance *across* and *between* the seven modes of experiencing. We seek integration of the mind: both vertical and lateral. We seek integration of mind and body. We seek integration of the affective self. We seek integration of friendships, relationships, agency, and voice. We seek integration of the natural and spiritual world. The more *integrated* we are the more *coherent* our life is: *chaos* and *dysfunction* diminish.

> To be a person is to have the power to make a difference, a difference that we find significant, in each of our life situations. This power takes various forms, some personal, some interpersonal, some impersonal, non-neatly separated from the others, each susceptible to destructive as well as creative uses.
>
> *(Cell, 1984: 5)*

Compassion and wisdom are intimately linked: they feed each other, and "wise reasoning enables us to think about situations from different points of view" (Gilbert, 2010: 133) (see Design Illustration 18). Nurturing relationships, such as mentoring, teaching, educating, and therapy, require compassion and so I have selected compassionate communication in relation to feedback skills as the design illustration for this last core mode of experiencing.

Practical Design

Returning to experience design, the skills of suspending judgement and developing compassionate communication are difficult though particularly important to the development of self-awareness. Compassion is central to wisdom, health, and well-*being*. Siegel (2012: 387) notes:

Kindness and compassion are integration made visible. If we take on the challenge of integration across its many domains, we may just be able to make a meaningful difference in the lives of people here now, and for future generations to come.

(italics added)

Kindness and compassion promote physical and mental health, both key indicators of a coherent self. The design of experiences that have potential to enhance kindness and compassion is not easy. Design illustration 33 is just one approach. It involves two bespoke designs: (1) a design called *word weaving* (illustrated in Chapter 6) and (2) the design of a *Communication Wheel*.

> **DESIGN ILLUSTRATION 33 DEVELOPING FEEDBACK SKILLS – BESPOKE DESIGNS.**

The Narrative Weaving experience illustration is introduced in Chapter 6 but the key design features are repeated again here.

The Communication Wheel (see later image) was newly created as part of a one-day experiential learning design for training in "Giving Feedback." The participants were experienced consultants within the medical profession. A considerable body of research had been amassed over a long period of time that highlighted that this specific skill, that is, giving feedback (to junior staff) was difficult for these senior professionals, partly due to the fact that they were given little or no training.

The initial design sketch of ideas was created as a sequence of nine potential learning experiences (shown in the following chart):

Session 1: Settling in experiences and introductions.
Sessions 2 and 3: Explore topics such as assertiveness, ego states, the OK-Coral, and Transactional Analysis (TA).
Session 4: Narrative Weaving experience, which can generate high-quality discussion and several useful definitions of feedback.

Discussion and definitions to be derived from small group explorations of the following words given out on a set of laminated cards. They include words such as:

Deficit, Development, Constructive, Critical, Feedback, Criticism, Judgments, Observations, Ideas, Answers, Feelings

(for a full list see Chapter 6).

A Design Outline of a Sequence of Nine Experiences

Beginning	Middle							End
1. Introduction/s	2. Understanding ego states OK coral Sensory awareness practice.	3. Working with Assertiveness Practicing emotional awareness.	4. Narrative weaving Defining Feedback.	5. Communication Wheel Focus on judgement and compassionate communication.	6. Practice giving feedback Simple situations.	7. Extensive practice: using the wheel after seeing the film clip of a critical incident.	8. Reflection and consideration of principles.	9. Stand up review. Closing.

210 *Being – The Ontological Self*

Below are just two examples of definitions that were created and recorded by participants:

> Feedback necessarily evokes feelings as it involves a series of observations which may be a subjective analysis of performance, often, but not always, involving judgement (implied or inferred). It is an opportunity to identify problems or deficits to help trainees generate or own ideas and answers in order to transform their practice, change their behavior, and solve problems. (Group 1)
>
> Feedback is an ongoing process that acknowledges the feelings and needs of both parties. Feedback is based on direct observation, and objectives, and represents an opportunity to share ideas for development. It should not be based solely on deficits or problems, rather it should be part of a series of transactions that aims for a transformation of that person, that both parties have carefully reflected on. (Group 2)

Sessions 5 and 6: Practice the skills within the four zones of the *Communication Wheel* which can be utilised as a working model. The most difficult area is "observing without judgement" (said to be one of the highest forms of intelligence). One of the ways of enhancing these skills is briefly outlined at the end of this illustration.

Session 7: The design uses a critical incident from a film clip (with permissions – about an outdoor management development programme involving Teamwork, Leadership, and Communication). The film highlights the design of a physically tough programme by an ex-paratrooper. In the film a "critical incident" occurs when, on the side of a steep mountain in bad weather conditions, a young instructor says to the team of experienced managers "you are the worst team I have come across, and Peter you are contributing nothing."

This critical incident becomes the focus for discussion about the way the instructor gave feedback and what was said. Participants air their views in the light of what they have explored at this stage.

Session 7 continued: The next stage of experience design involves asking if people are willing to have a go at giving feedback by playing a role as the manager of the young instructor. I will play the role of the young instructor in the film. A volunteer sits in the manager's "seat" in an office (simulated). They will have a conversation with me, Julian, offering feedback (real) on the feedback (the film was real but for the course it is simulated).

Here are some examples of what happens in this experience. From the moment I knock on the door and enter the room (because the manager said "come in") the manager starts the communication process as if the situation was all real. However, to inject a little fun and humour (really important) into this joint live

Being – The Ontological Self **211**

crafting of feedback. The opportunity for humour often quickly arises. I knock on the (real) door and play the role of Julian (not real) the young instructor on the film, and often a group will decide we could do it better if the manager stood up as Julian entered as a mark of respect. So, I say "cut." The conversations stops. I go out the room, knock on the door once again, and we start again. The process often involves several "cuts" (but this is what the co-crafting process is all about) and eventually a good quality conversation evolves as a co-created, joint effort.

Other outcomes experienced are:

> Other participants can also interject and put their hand up to offer alternative scripts. For example, sometimes those playing the manager will sit in their chair and not get up to greet Julian and so another participant might say "no I would stand up, and say Hi Julian, and then say take a seat." As the coach I can thank participants, and ask someone else to take over in the seat. . . . In this way I can influence the collective crafting of good quality feedback if needed. We all learn together.

> Session 8: Open up a plenary conversation about the critical incident experience. This tends to create some interesting principles about what helps in giving feedback. One outcome is the realisation that feedback is best offered with *compassion, sensitivity,* and *respect.*

For the medical consultants, giving feedback was hard, especially when it involved and required judgement. Lives cannot be put at risk in this crucial aspect of medicine and so judgement is often involved at some stage. Feedback skills require a lot of practice, moving in and out of the four zones in the communication model in the image.

A useful guiding principle that was adopted during the event was a Zen Buddhism approach referred to as "The Grandmother's Concern" (Sogen, 2019: xx). Feedback to grandchildren by a grandmother is given with compassion, wisdom, love, respect, admiration, care, and sensitivity. This can create a mindset that guides the way, influencing the choice of words. Feedback skills can be enhanced by imagining that Julian was a son or daughter (older of course) and you were giving them feedback with compassion, but with boundaries that are expected. This mindset made a difference to our giving feedback.

Respect, care, and love play a crucial part, as illustrated by the beautiful poem written by Dorothy Law Nolte in 1972. The poem outlines how people who live with criticism learn to condemn. Other parts of the poem highlight how people who live with hostility learn to fight, and people who live with praise learn to appreciate, whilst people who live with fairness learn justice. People who live with serenity will live with peace of mind. At this point the mission and values of KFBG in Chapter 6 are worth returning to.

212 *Being – The Ontological Self*

The 4 Cs Communication Wheel: Bespoke and Original

Zone 1 No colour	**COMPASSIONATE COMMUNICATION:** Compassionate feedback starts at the base of the model, and this involves behaving in a *non-judgemental* way. It is based on being *compassionate* to ourselves and others. Compassion transforms relationships. It requires knowing, understanding and being in touch with your own *needs and feelings*, as well as the *needs* and *feelings* of others. Non-judgement behaviour is hard to achieve and requires personal commitment: humans are hard-wired to judge (the "fast" thinking mode based on survival). Four Steps: (1) *observe* and tune into what is happening, (2) consider *feelings*, (3) question the *needs*, (4) *request* change with respect.
Zone 2 Green	**CLINICAL COMMUNICATION:** Clinical feedback is where we give neutral, *pure feedback* on behaviour etc., based, for example, on our *observations* of what is actually happening or what someone is doing. This feedback is (predominantly) *non-judgemental*. The feedback is like a *mirror*.
Zone 3 Amber	**CRITICAL COMMUNICATION:** Critical feedback offers a *judgement* that is positive and constructive, and focusses on personal development. There is a focus on positive affect.
Zone 4 Red	**CORROSIVE COMMUNICATION:** Corrosive feedback is where judgemental feedback is destructive, negative and often personal in tone, and more often than not it is unhelpful.

SUB-
SKILLS

The 4 Zones of the Communication Wheel

The following image is a visual representation that has been simplified for publication. The arrows highlight the movement up and down the four zones: the zone that should be avoided is the Corrosive Zone.

Being – The Ontological Self **213**

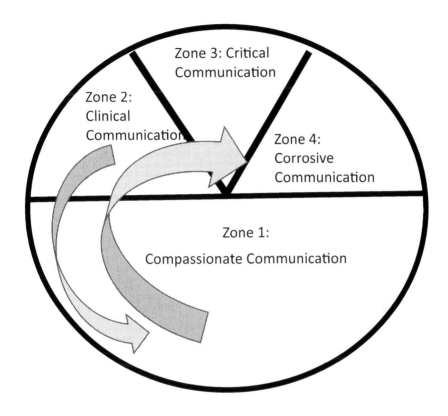

Competences for Life: Compassion, Respect, and Responsibility

In this final section I want to show how much of the thinking in this book, and in particular this chapter, is aligned with new global thinking about ways of *being* that are now being embedded in educational thinking across many parts of the globe. The United Nations *Human Development Index* is a measure of well-being. The index embraces three areas: health, education, and living standards; the expansion of people's freedoms to *live long, healthy lives*; and to actively engage in shaping development *equitably and sustainably on a shared planet*.

In the 21st century the world is changing rapidly. It is extensivly interconnected, yet also disconnected. Adaptation will require new skills, new know-how, and new competences. In May 2018, the *Council of the European Union* recommended that key competences be established for lifelong learning, to

214 *Being – The Ontological Self*

support change and adaptation so that people could achieve personal fulfilment and satisfaction, develop themselves and relate to others, and learn how to learn and keep being employable. These skills are said to be essential for *social inclusion* and for *civic participation* in society, and enable people to *cope with complexity*, be *thriving individuals*, responsible *social agents*, and become *reflective lifelong learners*.

The European Union has created nine competences that are important for everyone within formal, informal, and non-formal education. They are structured into three intertwined competence areas that relate to the integration of Personal, Social, and Learning to Learn capacities.

Personal: self-regulation (awareness and management of emotions, thoughts, and behaviour), flexibility (ability to manage transitions and uncertainty, and to face challenges), well-being (pursuit of life satisfaction, care of physical, mental, and social health, and adoption of a sustainable lifestyle).

Social: empathy (the understanding of another person's emotions, experiences, and values, and the provision of appropriate responses), communication (use of relevant communication strategies, domain specific codes, and tools depending on the context and the content), collaboration (engagement in group activity and teamwork acknowledging and respecting others).

Learning to Learn: growth (of the self) mindset (belief in one's and others' potential to continuously learn and progress), critical thinking (assessment of information and arguments to support reasoned conclusions and develop innovative solutions), managing learning (the planning, organising, monitoring, and reviewing of one's own learning).

Singapore created five socio-emotional competences:

1 Self-awareness.
2 Self-management.
3 Responsible decision-making.
4 Social awareness.
5 Relational management.

These are seen as the skills that are necessary for school pupils to develop *healthy identities, recognise and manage their emotions*, develop a sense of *responsibility, care, and concern for others, relate* to others and develop *positive relationships*, handle challenges, make responsible decisions, and act for the good of *self, others, and society*. The Singapore Minsitry of Education developed an additional set of core values. For Singapore values are at the centre of one's *character*: they shape the beliefs, attitudes, and actions of a person, and therefore form the core framework of Singapore's 21st century competences. Their core values include *respect, responsibility, resilience, integrity, care, and harmony*, and these are acknowledged as values that are foundational to shared societal and national values.

Being – The Ontological Self   **215**

Life Competences & Experiential Learning		
Outer world experiences		**Inner world experiences**
The focus is on: **Belonging (relatedness)** & **Doing (active)**	Sensing Observing	The focus is on: Feeling, Knowing & **Becoming & Being** Someone
Learning: Where, with whom, ability to act and actively do things?	Learning to sense and observe.	Learning to manage feelings, and to think at a higher and more critical level. Learning to become and be someone in society.
21C COMPETENCIES		
The focus is on: *Collaboration* *Information skills* *Civic literacy* *Global awareness* *Cross cultural*	The boundaries are artificial.	The focus is on: *Communication* *Critical thinking* *Inventive thinking*
RESULTING IN		
Concerned citizen		Self-confident
Active contributor		Self-directed learner
Core Values		
Rooted in Singapore, strong sense of civic responsibility, is informed about Singapore and the world, takes an active part in bettering the lives of those around them.		Strong sense of self, of what is right and wrong, adaptable and resilient, knows self, discerning in judgement, thinks independently and critically, communicates effectively.

FIGURE 9.3   21st Century Competences aligned with the Holistic Experiential Learning Model (HELM).

1   *Respect*: our students demonstrate respect when they believe in their own self-worth and the intrinsic worth of people.

2   *Responsibility*: our students are responsible when they recognise they have a duty to themselves, their families, community, nation, and the world, and fulfil their responsibilities with love and commitment.

3   *Resilience*: our students are resilient when they demonstrate emotional strength and persevere in the face of challenges. They show courage, optimism, adaptability, and resourcefulness.

4   *Integrity*: our students demonstrate integrity when they uphold ethical principles and have the moral courage to stand up for what is right.

5   *Care*: our students are caring when they act with kindness and compassion, contribute to the betterment of the community and the world.

6   *Harmony*: students uphold harmony when they promote social cohesion and appreciate the unity and diversity of a multicultural society.

216 Being – The Ontological Self

In Singapore the 21st Century Competences were deemed to have alignment with the Holistic Experiential Learning Model. Working with the Ministry of Education a simple overview was developed in 2015 to support teachers as shown in Figure 9.3.

In Indonesia in 2013 changes in the education curriculum called for *greater opportunities for teachers in the management of vocational learning*. Teachers were required to innovate overall learning, especially methods, approaches, and learning models adapted to 21st century learning. Singapore, Indonesia, and the European Union are just a few of the nations that have selected experiential learning to support the implementation of these globally important holistic life competences.

Having completed an exploration of seven core modes of experiencing, the final chapter of the book will return to the drawing board to explore two final designs: one simple, the other quite complex. The former highlights several fundamental principles and is in the early stages of development. The latter highlights a design that has undergone a process of continual development over several years.

10
BACK TO THE DRAWING BOARD

A Taste of Harry Potter

Now that the seven modes of experiencing have been explored, it is time to return to the drawing board. Design is never a simple task as John Dewey reminded us. If you struggle to remember the holistic seven modes design model, then use the 5Hs to get to them (5H-7M). The design of the *experiencescape* is a useful overarching concept, the choreography of which has layers within layers, offering potential for greater participation. This notion is illustrated in Design Illustration 34.

> **DESIGN ILLUSTRATION 34 FLYING BROOMSTICKS AND EXPERIENCES WITHIN EXPERIENCES.**

The Castle that was used extensively in the Harry Potter films is called Alnwick Castle, in the UK. It was here that Harry and his friends learned the fine art of flying broomsticks for the quidditch matches.

The choreography of the overarching Castle visitor experiencescape is impressive. Several "performances" and other kinds of experiences are on offer throughout the day: music of the period, expertly played by musicians dressed in *authentic* costumes of the time, scary giant dragons walking about (people walking under a plaster model), face painting, and broomstick flying lessons. The woman leading the scary dragon assures the children and parents by calling out: "don't worry she's already eaten today"!

DOI: 10.4324/9781003030867-10

The broomstick flying experience involved a young member of staff dressed up like a monk. The lessons took place several times a day. My experience, well my *memory* of this event, was as follows:

About 15 children were lined up ready to start. The young tutor doing broomstick flying lessons shouts out to the surrounding kids that he has one last broomstick left for the flying lessons. Several run as fast as they can, but only one is lucky. My son! He managed to get the last broomstick. He had a big smile on his face. The others watched in fascination, waiting patiently knowing that the next flying lesson was not too long to wait for.

All the kids in the lesson then lined up and within a few minutes of flying lessons the tutor has those participating and the parents watching laughing until their sides ached. The humour, silly tricks, false starts, pretend telling off, was brilliantly designed. Of course, no one really learnt to fly the broomstick even though the children had lots of (fake) photos that show them flying (they simply leapt in the air and their parents had to capture photos for posterity!). I began to wonder if the tutor, who was so good with the kids, was perhaps a trainee comedian or at university studying comedy!

The experience of this historical castle involved the careful choreography of several layers of *experiences within experiences*. This choreography catered to a wide range of visitor needs and expectations. I wonder what lessons can be learnt from this story of Harry Potter and the Castle? Certainly that education was merged with entertainment as *edutainment*.

An excellent chef possesses high levels of experience, and expertise. They understand presentation, timing, textures, tastes, smells, flavours, and what textures and flavours work well with other foods. To have experience and develop expertise requires a long period of apprenticeship and there is always much more to learn about experiential learning design.

It is time to return to where the book started: the art and science that underpins the choreography of an *experiencescape*. Firstly, a simple small-scale design that was explored in an earlier chapter, involving the *Packing a Rucksack*. Secondly a design that is large-scale, involving a *complex, distributed ecology of experiential interactions*. Whilst this final design is relatively complex, it also possesses an "elegant simplicity" (*simplicity~complexity*). Both designs are explored to show how the Holistic Experiential Learning Model (HELM) can be used for the purposes of experience learning design. (You may want to use the shorthand code 5H-7M.)

Back to the Drawing Board

Returning to the story at the beginning of the book about the Jaguar and the stream, that was used as a *hook* to draw the attention of the audience of young people, it is important to note the strong links between stories and learning, and memory and imagination. Sarah Parkin (1998) refers to research in the 1980s that used experiments on groups of students. Two groups were given a lecture 45 minutes long. One group experienced *stories*, *metaphors*, and *analogies*. This group showed fewer conceptual and technical errors, and they showed greater capabilities in structuring information and applying it to other novel situations than the other group. Significantly, Parkin notes that psychologists have discovered that memories work best when:

> we can see things as parts of a recognised order or pattern, when our imaginations and emotions are aroused, where we can make natural associations between one idea and another, and where the information appeals strongly to our senses.
>
> *(1998: 27)*

Patterns, part-whole relations, completeness, sensory and emotional stimulation, and the arousal of imagination and curiosity are just a few of the key design features covered in earlier chapters. So, let's return to these design ideas.

Micro-Design

Micro-design involves the choreography of the "finer details." Macro-design involves overarching design structures. The boundaries between the two are rather blurred.

The design of a session involving packing a rucksack is sufficiently simple and generic to allow several design principles to emerge. A handout on packing a rucksack is often distributed to youngsters preparing to undertake an expedition for the UK Duke of Edinburgh Award. I decided to check out the design with my friends in Outward Bound in Singapore and Hong Kong.

There were, as I expected, variations in opinion as to how to pack a rucksack. I then decided to set about designing a session on this topic to use it to highlight a range of micro design principles, particularly for the outdoor professionals I work with. Design Illustration 35 represents my initial ideas.

> **DESIGN ILLUSTRATION 35 MICRO-DESIGN – UNDERSTANDING THE DESIGN OF A "HOW TO PACK A RUCKSACK" SESSION.**

1 Small groups of outdoor staff get together and outline some of their basic principles of how to pack a rucksack.

2 Each group is given one A3 sheet of paper with a blank rucksack outline drawn on it. This is to identify common ground in terms of the major zones or areas of a rucksack. A discussion follows on where items should be packed.

3 The groups share their findings with each other.

4 Then the expedition handout mentioned earlier is given out and considered in comparison to their own principles. A discussion follows and areas of difference and similarity are discussed.

5 I then show a picture of a young expedition participant spreading out their kit on the floor and I talk about how I need to spread out my own "kit" on the floor or on the bed when I am travelling abroad.

Q: *Why do we do this?* (introduction to the significance of seeing, and spatial cognition, organisation, classification, and clustering).

6 When the groups have a relatively good level of agreement about what goes where, a critical question is introduced:

Q: *How do we "teach" the packing of a rucksack so that kids and adults know what to do and why?*

7 A list of tips, guidance, and questions is given out:

Start with the end in mind and work backwards.

Take a large sheet of paper and sketch out a timeline that includes zones for the Beginning, Middle and End.

Annotate notes alongside the "stations" that represent the main experiences (activities).

Small, coloured discs or icons can be provided to highlight *touchpoints*. Thinking focus areas of the experiences (red discs), feeling focus (blue discs), doing (black discs), sensing (yellow discs), belonging (green discs).

Use the 5H-7D code Holistic Experiential Learning Model (HELM) for design to guide the design.

Create and explore design questions:

Q: *What, how, where, and with whom?*
Q: *What, so what, now what?*

Back to the Drawing Board **221**

Q: *What do we want participants* (approx. 14 years old) *to learn?*

Q: *What kind of experience do we want them to have – and they would like to have – in this session?*

The groups then get going on their designs.

Let's Design

The groups have 45 minutes to design a detailed two-hour session called "Packing Your Rucksack."

After 45 minutes each group walks through and talks through their design to one other group going through their 3 phases of beginning, middle, and end.

In the light of sharing groups return to their design to make any changes or improvements.

Q: Did the design include elements of telling (*teaching/description*), showing (*depiction/representations*), doing (*active experimentation*), discussing (*social interaction/ different viewpoints*)?

Useful design principles that often emerge are:

1 *Let the learners pack rucksacks!*
2 The outline structures that frame the design are important. These include the "beginning, middle, and end" structure, as well as "Tell, Show, Do, and Discuss," and Head, Hands, and Heart.

   The rucksack structure is significant for framing the design. The simplified spatial layout and structure of a rucksack is key, as are rucksack "zones." They can be represented by colour, numbers, or letters, and the structure can be created using masking tape or rope.
3 The 30-point experiential design typology in Design Illustration 36 proved proved useful for getting started.
4 What is *simulated* and what is *real* might have some implications for learning to pack *real* items. The cards with kit names on them are not real and so a final check might involve the placing of *real kit* in the zones by nominating groups to show where items go. Create a design route map.
5 The collaborative construction of answers, offering incentives, and the balance of competition and collaboration are important design issues.
6 Participation, sharing, and creating a sense of belonging are all important, as is the freedom to make mistakes without ridicule.
7 The official answer might be given out as a handout, or this could also be digitally sent to smartphones so when packing this can be referred to.

The Importance of Spatial Layout.

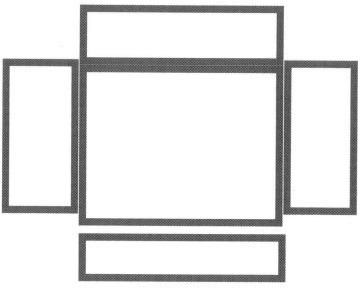

Tell? Show? Do? Demonstrate? Discuss?

Doing: Laminated Cards for Placing in Zones

Packing a Rucksack: Session design notes using the HELM seven dimensions.

Core Mode of Experiencing	Icon Visual depictive forms.	How to Pack a Rucksack Design Notes
Doing		**Doing** – possibly constructing/creating a 'representation' (a 'visual plan' of the main rucksack areas) for packing, with coloured or numbered or lettered zones representing the areas of the rucksack (M= main zone, T = top zone, S1 & S2 = side zones, B = bottom zone). Created on the floor with masking tape or ropes. Pile of real kit or for large groups large cards with the names of equipment or clothing on, with a visual/image (e.g. icon) added to the text. Questions to answer: *what* goes *where* and *why*?
Sensing/observing		**Sensing** - talking, moving/placing cards with contents that would go in the rucksack, colour coded/different rucksack areas, visualising. Use of depictive icons representing the 'type' or category of kit (clothing, cooking, sleeping, etc).
Feelings/emotions.		**Feelings** – motivated to try, feeling OK about having a go, and possibly making a few mistakes, *excited* about getting it right? Happy, and confident that they know what they can do...
Knowing/knowledge		**Knowing/thinking** - groups devise a set of questions to ask themselves about the packing. Q: What do we want to know/need to know? Q: Where does this go, why? Q: Why is it important to learn this packing skill?
Belonging Social connections		**Belonging** - interactions with others/sharing, small groups, in a large space or a small area each group. Attachment/connection/small group development/friendships. Collaboration and/or competition.
Belonging MTHW connections		**Belonging** - consider designing this experience in the outdoors in more 'natural' conditions.
Becoming, changing, transforming (views opinions, beliefs, understanding & Being).		**Becoming** - independent, experienced, knowledgeable, confident, and skilled. Growing, changing. Taking responsibility for learning. Developing opinions, voicing opinions, getting things right and getting things wrong.

At this stage I want to introduce a simple design checklist of 30 characteristics to consider in the choreography of the *experiencescape* (Design Illustration 36):

DESIGN ILLUSTRATION 36 A SIMPLE 30-POINT CHECKLIST FOR *EXPERIENCESCAPE* DESIGN.

1. Set a *target, goal, or objective*, where goals create and support an underlying "state of mind."
2. Design a sense of a *journey or destination* (for people, information – codes, data – and objects).
3. Design elements of *discovery and exploration*.
4. Design high levels of *involvement/immersion* – the degree to which active participation is required.
5. Set *time parameters/constraints*: speed dependence, quick or time-consuming experience, deadlines, etc.
6. Design, create, and sequence a *theme or plot*, embracing social, mental, psychological, and physical activities – mind, spirit, and body.
7. Design variety to the degree of *difficulty or complexity*.
8. Consider the quality of *resources, artefacts, and accessories* that enhance the experience.
9. Consider levels and timing of *stimulation*: intensity of arousal, focus, and energy.
10. Allow participants to *exercise* multiple forms of *intelligence* – MI Theory (Howard Gardner), including cognitive, social, sensory, and emotional intelligence. Allow everyone to participate, *inclusive* design.
11. Consider levels of *novelty* to avoid *boredom*.
12. *Design the key touchpoints* – knowledge, sensory, emotional, belonging, activities, etc.
13. Consider *how power and control* is exercised in the programme.
14. Design *collaboration~competition*.
15. Consider co-production/co-design by everyone (see Dramaturgy principles).
16. Design *choice* and autonomy.
17. Consider the degree of *physicality* – physical exertion.
18. Design quiet time for *relaxation and reflection*.
19. Design elements *of real~perceived risk*.
20. Consider how to deal with the emotional impact of *winning, not finding solutions, success, and failure*.
21. Consider offering *incentives* and *rewards*.
22. Does the design involve real experiences? Consider the degree of perceived *reality*: simulation, fantasy, objects, people, etc.
23. Design in *playfulness*: degree to which the experience is serious or light-hearted.

24 Design for *construction or deconstruction* in activities: a product, a physical object, or a non-physical item, for example, a model or theory, bike, phrase, poem, wall or raft, or clue.
25 Design *social/sociability*: making friends, disclosure, involvement, supporting others, solo, collaborative, or competitive strategies.
26 Design *combative and/or empathetic* approaches towards the natural environment.
27 Design *rules and procedures* (simple or complex?) *and restrictions* (sensory blocking, e.g., blindfolds, obstacles). Tactical.
28 Design for *spatial awareness:* use maps, locations, schema, navigation, routes, etc.
29 Design for *functional skills* such as surveying, juggling, map reading, knot tying, etc.
30 Design of *sorting skills* (information handling, prioritising).

The Practical Application of Complexity

From a neuroscience perspective it is known that much of the brain is devoted to "vision, motion, spatial understanding, interpersonal interaction, co-ordination, emotions, language, and everyday reasoning" (Lakoff & Nunez, 2000: 1). Complexity theories recognise that humans continually *act* and *interact* within a fluid, overlapping, interconnected, and complex ecology of experiences that are *embedded*, *embodied*, *enacted*, and *distributed*. So, how can these capacities be incorporated in experiential designs? The design of more complex *interactional dynamics* requires careful choreography. Complexity of design does not mean that the learner experience is complex: for them the experience should be one of *elegant simplicity*.

The topic for this final design concerns the development of an in-depth understanding of the evolution of the environmental movement. The topic is complex in itself: evolving environmental tactics, laws, important influencing events, milestones, extinctions, environmental disasters, influential individuals, politics, campaigning tactics, and the significant contributions of private, public, and voluntary organisations. The topic is less important than the understanding of design *principles*.

The design was originally commissioned by the Workers Education Association (WEA) in the UK for adult evening classes for a local community. Many members of the community wanted to understand and be actively involved in environmental issues. I was asked to provide a learning experience design that would: utilise and build on their existing experience, and facilitate active engagement, involvement, participation, and discovery. Initial design ideas were continuously developed over a period of 3 years. The design was *planned~emergent*.

226 Back to the Drawing Board

The initial design was subsequently expanded for mature students studying for an MA in Environmental Studies within higher education. Design ideas continuously emerged to create deeper levels of student engagement and understanding, to avoid "surface learning" (Marton & Säljö, 1976). A detailed description and theoretical analysis of the design now follows.

The overarching structure contains three distinct phases, each involving a very different experience in terms of the interactions with body, mind, objects, materials, and peers. The programme was delivered in 3-hour sessions over 12 weeks. The first four weeks were called the *informational* phase. The second four-week design was termed the *relational phase*, and the final four-week design was termed the *transformational phase*. These three distinct phases are outlined in Figure 10.1 highlighting how learners interact with *self*, *knowledge*, and *others* in fundamentally different ways.

Introductions Beginning.	Informational Middle Phase 1	Relational Middle Phase 2	Transformational Middle Phase 3	Review Ending
Week 1	Weeks: 2/3/4	Weeks: 5/6/7/8	Weeks: 9/10/11	Week 12

Initial Structural Storyboard Outline		
MIDDLE PHASE 1 Beginnings	**MIDDLE PHASE 2** Middle	**MIDDLE PHASE 3** Ending
PRIMARY FOCUS ON Peer interactions and belonging. HAVING INFORMATIONAL LEARNING	PRIMARY FOCUS ON Embodied and embedded cognition. Spatial cognition. DOING RELATIONAL LEARNING	PRIMARY FOCUS ON Transformation Ontological Self BEING TRANSFORMATIONAL LEARNING
Epistemological (knowledge focus) self Focus on 'Facts', not knowing, confusion. Surface Learning as acceptable Getting and Knowing Facts Co-production and co-creation of knowledge. Initiating peer/social relations/interactions. Positive interdependence. Individual accountability, Interpersonal-social skill development.	Spatial Schema. Spatial-Relational Understanding Critical Depth and Complexity Exploring spatial and temporal relationships of facts. Walking (movement), talking (oration), mapping (schema). Corporeal Increased depth of understanding Higher cognition becomes visible to others.	Critical work Affective/Feelings. Broad range of affect states. Working at the 'edge'. No definitive answers. Dissonance. Challenging self. Values, beliefs, and identity. Agency. Action.

FIGURE 10.1 Learning Experience Design (LED): notes on the structural framework (3 distinct phases).

The Supreme Resource: The Learners

Each of the adult learners contribute to the experience from their own life experiences. Their expertise is recognised, valued, and utilised. The learners work together in small groups to acquire information about a topic they chose, selected from a list that includes identifying when certain organisations were established, what their role is, the impact that specific environmental events had on the evolution, the development of laws, government bodies, influential individuals, and so on.

Phase 1 Design

This is the focus of the first fact-finding phase termed the *informational* phase. The substantial amount of foundational information acquired by groups researching sources of information on specific topics is all eventually shared amongst the groups. This is significant: all individuals realise the importance of sharing and contributing, and this approach adds to the development of peer relationships.

The learners document this informational work by creating booklets, and databases (co-*production*). These documents also formed foundational learning material for future cohorts to *inherit* and further develop and update each year. Over several years complex databases were created covering over 350 years of the evolution of the environmental movement. Whilst knowledge acquisition generates only a limited understanding as "surface learning" (Marton & Säljö, 1976), this initial phase serves other additional purposes, such as the development of responsibility for learning, a sense of belonging to, and interdependence with, other learners and the facilitator, group cohesion, confidence, and as a preparation and a prerequisite before proceeding to the next learning phase. Detailed critical discussions take place, which always result in a lot of unanswered questions that can be taken into the second phase.

Phase 2 Design

This second phase experience is called the *"relational"* phase of learning as it explores connections and relationships between events. During this phase, students are required to develop a greater depth of understanding beyond knowledge acquisition. The facts, figures, and other preparatory information related to the broader evolutionary narrative requires further development to understand the complexity.

The learners are asked to design a "representation" (see Wu & Puntambekar, 2012; Verschaffel et al., 2010) to highlight the way in which many of these events, organisations, facts and figures, and laws are inter-related. This is the spatial relational complexity inherent in any topic.

228 Back to the Drawing Board

Learners co-create a representation that can support their understanding and *"relational reasoning"* (Gattis, 2001: 5). The representation transforms static knowledge (facts and figures) collected during phase one into a more active approach to knowledge generation. The representation created by the learners takes the form of a large floor map not unlike the iconic cartographic design of the London city underground map by Harty Beck in the 1930s, but many times more complex. Information is presented in a creative way to slightly simplify the complex spatial relations. This design *reduces cognitive load* (Schwetman, 2014). After a period of preparation time, each research group (e.g., law group, voluntary sector group, significant events group) initially laid out their own specific key data on the floor as a map. They use colour coded (the train lines on the city underground map are coloured), laminated cards with dates and essential information printed on them.

A basic skeleton set of cards, initially created by the instructor, are added to by students. In this sense the cards were used as "objects" (see Chatterjee & Hannan, 2016) to be placed within a *chronological* (time/dates) and *spatial* (where in relation to) frame. Learners were also provided with laminated arrows to signpost important *relational connections* and flows (see Richter et al., 2016 for a meta-analysis of Signalling/Cueing Principle). Each group walks through the data explaining their part of the map.

When all the groups place their cards on the floor map, the collective visual "representation" is considerably complex. The collective representation has to "fit" together in terms of time and space (spatial and temporal connectedness) (see Kirsh, 2010). This skeletal but complex representation acts as a visual "tool" (see Verschaffel et al., 2010) to be explored and further developed in a process that can enhance thinking and reasoning by making visible the complexity of the evolution of the movement.

Learners' interactions continue as they walk amongst the representational cards (*embodied learning*), examining the map from different (*spatial and temporal*) perspectives, to articulate (*oral*) and share (*social*) what they see and interpret (*sensory/ observation/thinking aloud*). A range of possible narratives emerge as they talk, walk, navigate, and critically interrogate the final composite representation. In this phase the design involves a sophisticated partnership of *body and brain* (feet, hands, hands on, placing objects, and brain/movement/social interaction), through the physical *movement* of positioning and adjusting objects in space and time (corporeal/kinaesthesia, spatial-relational, and temporal associations of coloured cards) leading to questioning, enquiry, and abstract reasoning (social interaction/different voices/higher cognition/abstract reasoning).

The conversations begin the process of transformation, generating a reflective depth of understanding (*higher abstract conceptualisation*) (this did not occur in standard "teaching" approaches adopted before this experiential design). This relational phase generates many queries and questions. More information is added to the map. The conversations are recorded, captured, and posted online to be shared and further analysed. Light touch facilitator interventions can add challenging questions.

Phase 3 Design

The third and final phase is termed the *transformational* phase. It involves the development of a higher level of *critical reflection*. This can create *dissonance*, and at times *discomfort*: values, beliefs, and existing interpretations are challenged and questioned.

Questions might include: Why are the leading characters mostly men? (equality/gender bias); have their interpretations merely reproduced a biased representation of the truth?; how has the voluntary movement developed, or been thwarted, in terms of their changes in tactics over periods of time? (e.g., from preservationist approaches, conservation and practical action, environmentalism, global movements, and radical campaigning); what is the political backcloth to this timeline – where does the power lie, and what environmental initiatives emerged in this time period?; is indigenous knowledge and indigenous people important for protection of the environment?; what is your own personal contribution to environmental change – do you actually take positive action, or just think about action?; what differing roles have the public, private, and voluntary sector played in the evolution of the environmental movement?

The students experience a range of *feelings* during the three phases (the *joys* of sharing and self-discovery, the *unsettling feelings* that are the result of *dissonance* created by the design of difficult *questioning* which challenges the assumptions held by a group or an individual's *feelings*). The social-emotional climate is carefully designed to build resilience for this third phase. Some of the peer interactions that were considered in the design are charted in Figure 10.2.

Representations That Enhance Interactions

The co-production of a representation, and the multiple interactions that occurred in moving in and around it, is an important aspect of this complex design. Representations are increasingly being utilised by a wide range of instructional designers to support understanding, reasoning, and problem solving (Sweller et al., 1998; Verschaffel, et al., 2010). Ifenthaler notes that teachers "can influence the construction of mental models by providing well-designed external re-representations of phenomena to be explained" (2010: 83). The careful design of the way the representation is to be co-created is just one, albeit important part of the whole experience. There are clearly design layers within larger design layers, experiences within the broader experiencescape.

The use of an external schematic representation is to depict and transmit complex ideas in a physical and/or digital form, to "conceptualise, visualise, or materialise an entity into another format or mode" (Wu & Puntambekar, 2012: 755).

230 Back to the Drawing Board

Creating Interdependency Through Peer Interactions	
Peer support Dominant in Phase 1	For creating knowledge, and feelings, doing, being and belonging. For the development of the process skills for learning, achieving a common goal, and positive learning habits.
Peer pressure Dominant in Phase 1	Exposure and Visibility: not contributing, missing factsheets, poor or missing VLE materials, inability to complete the walk-the-talk activity, with little contribution to this pseudo 'viva' experience.
Peer collaboration, co-production & competition Dominant in Phase 1	Enquiry based. Cooperative booklet production, key facts. Inter and intra cohort benefits. Walking the territory together. Collectively creating and critiquing multiple/alternative narratives. Performance, levels of contribution, tutor interjections and comments.
Inheritance Strong focus in P1 & 2	Between cohorts: inheritance of materials, databases, viva voice recordings. Databases also shared with other institutions to collaborate.
Peer reflection & reflexivity Dominant in Phase 2 & 3	Continuous learning, fluid, not easy to grasp, increasing complexity and potential for the reconstruction/transformation of self.
Freedom & liberation Dominant in Phase 2 & 3	Freedom to express views and values, and freedom to struggle, tutor-less at times. Peer control of learning spaces/places, resources. Conversations relating to agency and citizenship. Comfortable to experience a range of emotional dynamics.
Peer collaboration associated on the upcoming assessment Dominant in all Phases	Critically reflective and reflexive dialogue, increasing focus on the final assessment.

FIGURE 10.2   The changing emphasis on peer relations in the three phases.

They serve to "aid cognition, give structure, and facilitate memory, communication and reasoning" (Gattis, 2001: 2). As a shareable object of thought, it does not decay like internal mental maps (Kirsh, 2010).

Wu and Puntambekar note (2012: 763) that not many studies of external representations have addressed the question of how to foster *active* processing: "without students' active engagement, affordances may not be realised, and very little learning would take place." The design of the active engagement was given considerable attention in this complex example. Research also suggests that to optimise knowledge construction in the brain, learning design should "strive to create memories containing both episodic and semantic features" (van Kesteren & Meeter, 2020: 3). The co-creation of this representation gives rise to a blend of *episodic* and *semantic* memories: facts and figures are contributed by the group and made available for the purposes of semantic memory, and the interactions that explore relational dynamics of these facts and figures generate a range of episodic memories.

The Descriptive~Depictive Dynamic

Instructional and multimedia design research (see Mayer, 2014) has a "strong emphasis on textual versus pictorial information" (Verschaffel et al., 2010: 2), which oversimplifies the design of representations in educational settings

(Wu & Puntambekar, 2012). Research should ideally focus on representation designs and the ways that learners *interact* with them. Tversky notes that when pictures developed into written words two things happened: pictures "became schematized and they lost their transparency" (Tversky, 2016: 80). The text-picture boundary becomes blurred as "pictures, depictions, and visualisations as communications are on the rise," due partly, as Tversky notes, "to technologies for creating, reproducing, and transmitting pictures" (2016: 80). The increased use of icons in communication further illustrates that the boundaries between text (as descriptive symbols) and pictures (depictive images) are not as distinct as multi-media theories (for example *dual coding* theory) would suggest (Mayer, 2014; Sadoski & Paivio, 2013). As explored earlier we are not told that the English alphabet is a symbolic form originating from pictures: whilst the descriptive text has long enjoyed an elevated status, the depictive form is on the increase.

Understanding How We Understand

As Lakoff and Nunez (2000, p. xiii) suggest, "if we are to understand how we understand" then more detailed research is needed on the ways that learners interact with representations, both individually and in groups. If the internal mental processing could be made more explicit through *in situ* talking aloud, then new knowledge about the interplay between internal and external representations might become clearer. As new technologies are utilized for learning (see Whitton, 2014: de Freitas & Maharg, 2011) further understanding of the ways technology influences these *interactional* dynamics is important. The increased use of virtual and augmented reality will necessitate multi-media research moving beyond investigations into the use of imagery, speech, and text, towards a greater focus on the *complex interactive experiential ecology* that is suggested in this pedagogically focussed case material. The suggestion here is that the representations themselves have the potential to become further "extensions of the experiencing body-mind-world dynamic" (Clark, 2011: 220).

Other underpinning principles to this design have already been outlined in earlier chapters. The following outline notes point to other sources that might be worth returning to:

1   Lakoff and Nunez (2000) note that the brain and body evolved together: the brain~body dynamic has to function in an optimal way. Much of the brain is devoted to vision, motion, spatial understanding, interpersonal interaction, coordination, emotions, and language. These are all significant to the design of these two final examples. More specifically, interactions involve brain, body, speech, text, objects, icons, and other people (social interaction/construction of knowledge). This illustrates the design of what I am calling *an interactive experiential ecology*, that is like a spider's web.

232 Back to the Drawing Board

2   Hughes and Lury (2013: 97) have coined the term *"ecological epistemology,"* to highlight the importance of the "ongoing and dynamic interrelationship of processes and objects, being and things, figures and grounds." They acknowledge the *complexity* involved in the multiple layers of interaction.

3   Dolins and Mitchell (2010) suggest spatial~temporal relations lie at heart of conceptual systems.

4   Ginns (2006) suggests that learners can learn more if complex educational materials are designed in a way that reduces the space (*spatial contiguity effect*) and time (*temporal contiguity effect*) between the disparate but related elements of to-be-learned information that in this case was found in the evolution of the environmental movement. Ginns (2006) and Mayer (2014) extensively discuss this aspect of spatial and temporal "contiguity," that is, presenting informational elements close together is a common feature of representation design that can improve understanding and memory. (See also Moreno & Meyer, 1999.)

5   Duijzer et al. (2019) highlight research showing how the creation of representations by learners themselves generates high levels of interaction. The level of control and voice is high for learners.

6   Wu and Puntambekar (2012) discuss the way external representations support the internal cognitive understanding of spatial and temporal relations.

7   Clark (2011); Pinker (1989); and Wilson (1998), all highlight how concept formation and reasoning is rooted in the rich and complex dimensions of bodily movement and interaction, as sensory and motor neural systems are now put to work in service of abstract reasoning.

Experience design is certainly not easy, and it takes time and patience to develop. It is an iterative process that involves returning to the drawing board time and time again. A team of designers, as mentioned in the early chapters, may be more able to create complex designs.

Figure 10.3 is a simple overview chart to highlight some of the principles for *structural* design, *artistic* choreographic design, and the design of *navigational tools*.

Concluding Comments

I would like to finish the book with a few things to ponder over. On one of my short writing retreats I noticed in the nearby supermarket that the store manager would have a meeting in the café with a different member of staff each morning. The meetings seemed very relaxed. The manager always made just a few notes before, and afterwards. These meetings made me ponder over how much learning occurs through *conversation*, reminding me that there are many ways to learn, and not all of them require a great deal of design.

Despite this book making it clear that the human brain has an amazing processing capacity, John Allman in *Evolving Brains*, notes that the human brain has

DESIGN PRINCIPLES - MACRO & MICRO DESIGNS		
STRUCTURAL DESIGN PRINCIPLES	**ARTISITC CHOREOGRAPHY DESIGN PRINCIPLES**	**NAVIGATIONAL DESIGN PRINCIPLES**
Ascertain the aims, Objectives &/or Experiential Descriptors. Create Structural & Functional Framework. Craft the overall Shape, Flow, & Organisation Structures. Logical sequence and shape (of chunks, topics, blocks, stages, etc). ---------------------------------- **ACTIONS** Grids, maps, & drawings. Macro – micro designs. Layers – of the experience. Parts – Whole. The bigger picture – continuity, integration, connecting to life-wide and lifelong learning. Shifts from simple to complex, known to unknown, narrow to broad & composite. Allows for planned and emergent learning. Light touch or detailed programme designs. Waves of experience: focus, energy, & intensity Consistency: icons, headings, and language.	Design is Underpinned by Personal Values, Beliefs, Principles, and Philosophies. To intervene or not, when, where, how of light touch intervention. Aesthetics: what does the experience look, feel, smell, taste, & sound like. Design with power, equity, and social justice as a core consideration. Use imagination & Creativity. Quick check: 30-point design typology (Chapter 9). Interrelating design: physical, embodied, social, relational, agentic, cultural, emotional, sensorial, situated, spatial, temporal, intellectual, and spiritual aspects of the design of experiences. ---------------------------------- **ACTIONS** Light & Fun. Atmosphere. Active - Relaxation. Flow of experiences. Challenge & support. Formal & informal learning. Reflexive. Emotional Touchpoints. Attractiveness: colour schemes, visuals, and animations.	Provide ways for learners to navigate the learning experience as a journey. Understand how different people learn differently. Activity sequences should flow. Learning for everyone. Inclusive – no person left behind. Externalise learning & thinking – more visible. Consider the degree of experiential interaction, through involvement, immersion, intensity, individual as well as group focus, innovation, & integrity. ---------------------------------- **ACTIONS** Materials, objects, props, words, numbers, colour. Movement, steps, stages, progression, touch, pointing, holding. Icons, signs, and symbols: arrows, pencils, pointers, etc. Stories, sound bites, video bites. Codes and equations. Conscious linguistics. Speech bubbles and thought bubbles. Emotional awareness, relationships and mental well-being.
	Text that can be *listened* to as well as *read* as text.	

FIGURE 10.3 Structure, choreography, and navigation.

234 Back to the Drawing Board

in fact decreased in size over the past 35,000 years! He suggests that "perhaps humans, through the invention of agriculture and other cultural means for reducing the hazards of existence, have domesticated themselves" (2000: 208). The brain needs challenges, even if at times the challenges are difficult ones.

Finally, I would advise treating this book like a sketch pad. Scribble and write notes about your ideas and what works for you. Fold the top corners of the pages if you want to. Don't try to read it all at once – you can't. If you can, get yourself in a hammock and gently rock back and forth while you read and ponder. Make *connections* (a recurring theme within this book) with what you do. Connect with your creative side, and dream about the way you want to craft *experiencescapes* that enhance the many capacities that we humans have for learning. In *Conscious Creativity: Look, Connect, Create*, Philippa Stanton offers words of wisdom:

> Creativity is about discovering your own ways of working, your own unique practice, and growing the confidence needed to accept that. It's not about learning how to create something like everyone else, it's about learning how to acknowledge the true value of what *you* do.
>
> *(Stanton, 2018: 9)*

REFERENCES

Abram, D. (1997) *The Spell of the Sensuous*. New York, NY: Vintage Books.

Allman, J. (2000) *Evolving Brains*. New York: Scientific American Library.

Arshavskiy, M. (2017) *Instructional Design for E-Learning*, 2nd edition. Yourlearningworld. com.

Artino Jr, A. R. (2012) Emotions in online learning environments: Introduction to the special issue, *Internet and Higher Education*, 15, 137–140.

Ashworth, P. (2003) The phenomenology of the lifeworld and social psychology, *Social Psychology Review*, 5(1), 18–34.

Baddeley, A. (1986) *Working Memory*. London: Clarendon.

Barbalet, J. (1998) *Emotions, Social Theory and Social Structure*. Cambridge: Cambridge University Press.

Barnett, R. (2007) *A Will to Learn: Being a Student in an Age of Uncertainty*. Maidenhead: McGraw-Hill Education.

Barrett, L. F., & Salovey, P. (Eds). (2002) *The Wisdom in Feeling: Psychological Processes in Emotional Intelligence*. London: Guilford Press.

Baumeister, R. F., & Leary, M. R. (1995) The need to belong: Desire for interpersonal attachments as a fundamental human motivation, *Psychological Bulletin*, 117(3), 497.

Baxter Magolda, M. (2001) *Making Their Own Way: Narratives for Transforming Higher Education to Promote Self-Development*. Sterling, VA: Stylus.

Baxter Magolda, M. (2011) Authoring your life: A lifewide learning perspective, in Jackson, N. (Eds) *Learning for a Complex World: A Lifewide Concept of learning: Education and Personal Development* (pp. 76–99). Bloomington: Author-House.

Beard, C. (1996) Environmental training: Emerging products, *Journal of Industrial and Commercial Training*, 28(5), 18–23.

Beard, C. (2010) *The Experiential Learning Toolkit: Blending Practice with Concepts*. London: Kogan Page.

Beard, C. (2016) Experiential learning: Towards a multidisciplinary perspective, in Humberstone, B., Prince, H., & Henderson, K. (Eds) *Routledge International Handbook of Outdoor Studies* (pp. 425–434). Oxon: Routledge.

236 References

Beard, C. (2018a) Learning experience designs (LEDs) in an age of complexity: Time to replace the Lightbulb, *Reflective Practice*, 19(6), 736–748.

Beard, C., (2018b) Dewey in the world of experiential education, in Mandell, A., & Coulter, X. (Eds) *Adult Educators on Dewey's Experience and Education* (pp. 27–38., New Directions for Adult & Continuing Education #158). San Francisco, CA: Jossey-Bass.

Beard, C., Clegg, S., & Smith, K. (2007) Acknowledging the affective in higher education, *British Educational Research Journal*, 33(2), 235–252.

Beard, C., Humberstone, B., & Clayton, B. (2014) Positive emotions: Passionate scholarship and student transformation, *Teaching in Higher Education*, 19(6), 630–643.

Beard, C., & Malkki, K. (2013) Student transformation and the interaction between the epistemological and ontological tracks: The wider project of higher education?, in Tirri, K., & Kuusisto, E. (Eds), *Interaction in Educational Domains*. Rotterdam: Sense Publishing.

Beard, C., & Rhodes, T. (2002) Experiential learning: Using comic strips as 'reflective tools' in adult learning, *Australian Journal of Outdoor Education*, 6(2).

Beard, C., & Russ, W. (2017) Event evaluation and design: Human experience mapping, *Event Management: An International Journal*, 21(3), 365–374.

Beard, C., & Wilson, P. (2018) *Experiential Learning: A Practical Guide for Training, Coaching and Education*. London: Logan Page.

Beard, C., Wilson, J., & McCarter, R (2007) Towards a theory of e-learning, *International Journal of Hospitality, Leisure, Sport and Tourism Education*, 6(2), 3–15.

Beetham, H., & Sharpe, R. (Eds). (2020) *Rethinking Pedagogy for a Digital Age*, 3rd edition. Oxford: Routledge.

Benton, T., & Redclift, M. (1994) Introduction, in Redclift, M., & Benton, T. (Eds) *Social Theory and the Global Environment* (pp. 1–27). London: Routledge.

Bethuniak, S. (2005) *Finding solitude: The importance of silence and space for thinking*. Paper presented to Design for Learning, Twelfth International Conference on Learning, 11–14 July, Granada, Spain.

Binder, J., & Desai, R. (2011) The neurobiology of semantic memory, *Trends in Cognitive Sciences*, 15(11), 527–536.

Bingham, C. W., & Sidorkin, A. M. (Eds). (2004) *No Education Without Relation*. New York: Peter Lang.

Bitner, M. (1992) Servicescape: The impact of physical surroundings on customers and employees, *Journal of Marketing*, 56(2), 57–71.

Blackie, M. A. L., Case, J. M., & Jawitz, J (2010) Student-centredness: The link between transforming students and transforming ourselves, *Teaching in Higher Education*, 15(6), 637–646.

Bloom, B. (1956) *Taxonomy of Educational Objectives: The Classification of Educational Objectives, Handbook 1*. London: Longman, Green & Co.

Boler, M. (1999) *Feeling Power: Emotions and Education*. New York, NY: Routledge.

Bolliger, D., McCoy. D., Kilty. T., & Shephard, C. (2021) Smartphone use in outdoor education: a question of activity progression and place, *Journal of Adventure Education and Outdoor Learning*, 21(1), 53–66.

Borton, T. (1970) *Reach, Touch and Teach: Student Concerns and Process Education*. New York, NY: McGraw-Hill.

Boud, D., Cohen, R., & Walker, D. (1993) *Using Experience for Learning*. Buckingham: Open University Press.

Bourg, D., & Erkman, S. (Eds). (2017) *Perspectives on Industrial Ecology*. London: Routledge.

Bovill. (2020) *Co-creating Learning and Teaching: Towards Relational Pedagogy in Higher Education*. St. Albans: Critical Publishing.

Bowlby, J. (1969) *Attachment and Loss*, Vol. 1. London: Hogarth Press.

Boydell, T. (1976) *Experiential Learning* (Manchester monograph number 5). Manchester: Department of Adult Education, University of Manchester.

Brooks-Harris, J., & Stock-Ward, S. (1999) *Workshops: Designing and Facilitating Experiential Learning*. Thousand Oaks, CA: Sage Publications.

Bryant, P., & Squire, S. (2016) Children's mathematics: Lost and found in space, in Gattis, M. (Ed) *Spatial Schemas and Abstract Thought* (pp. 175–200). Cambridge, MA: The MIT Press.

Buhner, S. (2002) *The Lost Language of Plants: The Ecological Importance of Plant Medicines to Life on Earth*. White River Junction, VT: Chelsea Green Publishing.

Buhner, S. (2014) *Beyond the Doors of Perception–Plant Intelligence and the Imaginal Realm: into the dreaming of earth*. Shelburne, VT: Bear & Company.

Burnett, C., & & Merchant, G. (2020) *Undoing the Digital: Sociomaterialsim and Literacy Education*. Oxon: Routledge.

Burns, G. (1998) *Nature Guided Therapy: Brief Integrative Strategies for Health and Well-being*. Philadelphia, PA: Brunner Mazel.

Cable, L. (2019) Playful interludes, in Whitton, N., & Moseley, A. (Eds) *Playful Learning: Events and Activities to Engage Adults* (pp. 58–70). London: Routledge.

Cain, A. (1971) *Animal Species and their Evolution*. London: Hutchinson.

Caine, R. N., & Caine, G. (1994) *Making Connections: Teaching and the Human Brain*. New York, NY: Addison-Wesley.

Cell, E. (1984) *Learning to Learn from Experience*. Albany, NY: State University of New York Press.

Chandler, P., & Sweller, J. (1991) Cognitive Load Theory and the format of instruction, *Cognition and Instruction*, 8(4), 293–332.

Chatterjee, H. J., & Hannan, L. (2016) *Engaging the Senses: Object-based Learning in Higher Education*. Oxon: Routledge.

Chen, C. M., & Sun, Y. C. (2012) Assessing the effects of different multimedia materials on emotions and learning performance for visual and verbal style learners, *Computers & Education*, 59(4), 1273–1285.

Chung, S., Cheon, J., & Lee, K. W. (2015) Emotion and multimedia learning: an investigation of the effects of valence and arousal on different modalities in an instructional animation, *Instructional Science*, 43(5), 545–559.

Clark, A. (2011) *Supersizing the Mind: Embodiment, Action, and Cognitive Extension*. Oxford: Oxford University Press.

Clark, A. (2013) Gesture as thought? in Radman, Z. (Ed) *The Hand, an Organ of The Mind: What the Manual Tells the Mental* (pp. 255–268). Cambridge, MA: Massachusetts Institute of Technology.

Clark, A., & Chalmers, D. (1998) The extended mind, *Analysis*, 58(1), 7–19.

Classen, C. (2005) (Ed) *The Book of Touch*. Oxford: Berg Publishers.

Clayton, B., Beard, C., B. Humberstone., & Wolstenholme, C (2009) The jouissance of learning: evolutionary musings on the pleasures of learning in higher education, *Teaching in Higher Education*, 14(4), 375–386.

Collins, D., & Humberstone, B. (2018) Outdoor education/studies and eco-feminism: Reflections on the last 20 years, in Becker, P., Humberstone, B., Loynes, C., & Schirp, J. (Eds) *The Changing World of Outdoor Learning in Europe* (pp. 57–70). Oxon: Routledge.

238 References

Collins, S. (2016) *Neuroscience for Learning and Development*. London: Kogan Page.

Cooperrider, D., & Whitney, D. (2005) *Appreciative Enquiry: A Participative Revolution in Change*. San Francisco, CA: Berret-Koehler Publishers.

Corballis, M. (2002) *From Hand to Mouth: The Origins of Language*. Princeton, NJ: Princeton University Press.

Corbet, P. (2006) *The Bumper Book of Storytelling to Writing*. Wiltshire: Clown Publishing.

Cornell, J. (1989) *Sharing the Joy of Nature. Nature Activities for all Ages*. Nevada City, CA: DAWN Publications.

Costandi, M. (2013) *50 Ideas You Really Need to Know: The Human Brain*. London: Quercus Editions Ltd.

Covey, S. (2004) *The 8th Habit: From Effectiveness to Greatness*. New York, NY: Simon & Schulster.

Covey, S. R., & Covey, S. (1989) *The 7 Habits of Highly Effective People*. New York, NY: Simon & Schuster.

Coxall, H. (1999) Museum text as mediated message, in Hooper-Greenhill, E. (Ed) *The Educational Role of the Museum*, 2nd edition (pp. 215–222). Oxon: Routledge.

Crawford, (2016) *The World Beyond Your Head: How To Flourish In An Age of Distraction*. New York, NY: Farrar, Straus and Giroux.

Cronon, W. (1996) (Ed) *Uncommon Ground: Rethinking the Human Place in Nature*. New York: Norton & Company.

Crossby, A. (1995) A critical look: the philosophical foundations of experiential education, in Warren, K., Sakofs, M., & Hunt, J. (Eds) *The Theory of Experiential Education,* Association for Experiential Education, Dubuque, IA: Kendall Hunt Publishing.

Cross. (2018) Expertise in professional design, in Ericsson, K. A, Hoffman, R., Kozbelt, A., & Williams, M. (Eds) *The Cambridge Handbook of Expertise & Expert Performance*, 2nd edition (pp. 372–388), Cambridge: Cambridge University Press.

Crossman, J. (2007) The role of relationships and emotions in student perceptions of learning and assessment, *Higher Education Research & Development*, 26(3), 313–327.

Csikszentmihalyi, M., & Csikzentmihaly, M. (1990) *Flow: The Psychology of Optimal Experience*. New York: Harper & Row.

Curtis. (1963) *The History of Education in Britain*, 5th edition. London: University Tutorial Press.

Dainty, P., & Lucas, D. (1992) Clarifying the confusion: A practical framework for evaluating outdoor development programmes for managers, *Management Education and Development*, 23(2), 106–122.

Dale E. (1969) *Audiovisiual Methods in Teaching*, 3rd edition. New York: Holt, Reinhart & Winston.

Dalziel, J. (2016) (Ed) *Learning Design: Conceptualising a Framework for Learning and Teaching Online*. New York: Routledge.

Damasio, A. (2004) *Looking for Spinoza*. London: Vintage.

Darwin, C (1872) *The Expression of the Emotions in Man and Animals*. Chicago: University of Chicago Press.

Dashper, K., & Buchmann, A. (2020) Multispecies event experiences: introducing more-than-human perspectives to event studies, *Journal of Policy Research in Tourism, Leisure and Events*, 12(3), 293–309.

Daudelin, M. W. (1996) Learning from experience through reflection, *Organizational dynamics*, 24(3), 36–48.

Davis, B., & Sumara, D. J. (1997) Cognition, complexity and teacher education, *Harvard Educational Review*, 67(1), 105–125.

Davis, W (2009) *The Wayfinders: Why Ancient Wisdom Matters in the Modern World*. Toronto: House of Anansi Press.

de Freitas, S., & Maharg, P. (Eds). (2011) *Digital Games and Learning*. London: Continuum.

Dehane, S. (2008) Small heads for big calculations, in Fischer, K. W., & Immordino-Yang, M. H. (Eds) *The Brain and Learning* (pp. 273–300). Chicago: John Wiley & Sons.

Dellinger, S. (1996) *Communicating Beyond Our Differences: Introducing The Psycho-Geometrics System*. Tampa, FL: Jade Ink.

Deloache, J., & Pickard, M. (2010) Of chimps and children: Use of spatial symbols by two species, in Dolins, F., & Mitchell, R. (Eds) *Spatial Cognition, Spatial Perception: Mapping the Self and Space* (pp. 486–501). Cambridge: Cambridge University Press.

DeSalle, R. (2018) *Our Senses: An Immersive Experience*. New Haven, CT: Yale University Press.

Desmond, A., & Moore, J. (2000) *Darwin*. London: Penguin Books.

Dewey, J. (1938) *Experience and Education*. New York, NY: Touchstone.

Dillon, P. (2007) *A Pedagogy of connection and boundary crossings: Methodological and epistemological transactions in working across and between disciplines*. A paper presented at 'Creativity or conformity? Building Cultures of Creativity in Higher Education', University of Wales and the Higher Education Academy, Cardiff, January 8–10.

Dirkson, J. (2015) *Design for How People Learn*. Indianapolis, IN: New Riders.

DiSalvo, B., Yip, J., Bonsignore, E., & DiSalvo, C. (2017) *Participatory Design: Perspectives from Practice and Research*. New York: Routledge.

Dolan, P. (2014) *Happiness by Design: Finding Pleasure and Purpose in Everyday Life*. London: Penguin.

Dolins, F., & Mitchell, R. (Eds). (2010) *Spatial Cognition, Spatial Perception: Mapping the Self and Space*. Cambridge: Cambridge University Press.

Dryden, D., & Vos, J. (2001) *The Learning Revolution: To Change the Way the World Learns*. Stafford: Network Educational Press.

Duijzer, C., Heuvel-Panhuizen, M., Veldhuis, M., Doorman, M., & Leserman, P. (2019) Embodied learning environments for graphing motion: A systematic literature review, *Educational Psychology Review*, 31, 597–629.

Ekarv, M. (1999) Combating redundancy: writing texts for exhibitions, in Hooper-Greenhill, E. (Ed) *The Educational Role of the Museum*, 2nd edition (pp. 201–204). Oxford: Routledge.

Ekman, P. (1994) All emotions are basic, in Ekman, P., & Davidson, R. (Eds) *The Nature of Emotion: Fundamental Questions*. New York: Oxford University Press.

Elliott, R., Watson, J. C., Goldman, R. N., & Greenberg, L. S. (2004) *Learning Emotion-focused Therapy: The Process-Experiential Approach to Change*. Washington, DC: American Psychological Association.

Eyal, N. (2014) *Hooked: How to Build Habit Forming Products*. London: Penguin.

Fenwick, T. J. (2003) *Learning Through Experience: Troubling Orthodoxies and Intersecting Questions*. Malabar, FL: Krieger Publishing Company.

Fink, l. (2013) *Creating Significant Learning Experiences: An Integrated Approach to Designing College Courses*. Hoboken, NJ: Jossey-Bass.

Finkel, D. (2000) *Teaching with Your Mouth Shut*. Portsmouth, NH: Heinemann.

References

Fischer, K. W., & Immordino-Yang, M. H. (Eds). (2008) *The Brain and Learning*. Chicago, IL: John Wiley & Sons.

Flavián, C., Ibáñez-Sánchez, S., & Orús, C. (2019) The Impact of virtual, augmented, and mixed reality technologies on the customer experience, *Journal of Business Research*, 100, 547–560.

Foer, J. (2011) *Moonwalking with Einstein: The Art and Science of Remembering Everything*. London: Penguin.

Fortin, N., Agster, K., & Eichenbaum, H. (2002) Critical role of the hippocampus in memory for sequence of events, *Nature Neuroscience*, 5(5), 137–140.

Fox, K. (2008) Rethinking Experience: What do we mean word 'experience', *Journal of Experiential Education*, 31, 36–54.

Francis, J. (2011) *The Ragged Edge of Silence: Finding Peace in a Noisy World*. Washington, DC: National Geographic.

Fraser, B. (2001) Twenty thousand hours: Editor's introduction, *Learning Environments Research*, 4(1), 1–5.

Freire, P. (1970) *Pedagogy of the Oppressed*. New York: Continuum.

Frijda, N., & Mesquita, B. (1994) The social roles and functions of emotions, in Kitayama, S., & Markus, H. R. (Eds) *Emotion and Culture*. Washington, DC: American Psychological Association

Gallagher, S. (2005) *How the Body Shapes the Mind*. Oxford: Oxford University Press.

Gallagher, S., & Zaham, D. (2008) *The Phenomenological Mind: An Introduction to Philosophy of Mind and Cognitive Science*. Oxford: Routledge.

Gallese, V., & Lakoff, G. (2005) The brain's concepts: The role of the sensory-motor system in conceptual knowledge, *Cognitive Neuropsychology*, 22(3/4), 455–479.

Gallo, C. (2016) *The Storyteller's Secret: How TED Speakers and Inspirational Leaders Turn Their Passion Into Performance*. London: Pan Macmillan.

Gardner, H (1983) *Frames of Mind: The Theory of Multiple Intelligences*, New York: Basic Books Inc.

Gardner, H. (2008) Who owns intelligence?, in Fischer, K., & Immordino-Yan, M. (Eds) *The Brain and Learning* (pp. 120–132). San Francisco, CA: Jossey-Bass.

Gartner-Manzon, S., & Giles, A. (2018) Lasting impacts of an Aboriginal youth leadership retreat: A case study of Alberta's Future Leaders Programme, *Journal of Adventure Education & Outdoor Learning*, 18(4), 338–352.

Gattis, M. (Ed) (2001) *Spatial Schemas and Abstract Thought*. Cambridge, MA: The MIT Press.

Gauntlett, D. (2018) *Making is Connecting: The Social Power of Creativity, From Craft and Knitting to Digital Everything*. Cambridge: Polity Press.

Gergen, K. (1999) *An Invitation to Social Construction*. London: Sage Publishing.

Gergen, K. (2009) *Relational Being: Beyond Self and Community*. Oxford: Oxford University Press.

Gilbert, P. (2010) *Compassion Focussed Therapy: Distinctive Features*. Abingdon: Routledge.

Gilchrist, I. (2009) *The Master and His Emissary: The Divided Brain and The Making of the Western World*. New Haven, CT: Yale University Press.

Gilchrist, I. (2019) *Ways of Attending: How Are Divided Brain Construct the World*. Oxon: Routledge.

Gillies, R., & Ashman, A. (Eds). (2003) *Co-operative Learning: The Social and Intellectual Outcomes of Learning in Groups*. New York: Routledge.

Gilmore, E., & Sabine, J. (1999) Writing readable text: evaluation of the Ekarv method, in Hooper-Greenhill, E. (Ed) *The Educational Role of the Museum*, 2nd edition (pp. 205–210), Oxford: Routledge.

Ginns, P. (2006) Integrating information: A meta-analysis of the spatial contiguity and temporal contiguity effects. *Learning and Instruction*, 16, 511–525.

Godfrey-Smith, P. (2016) *Other Minds: The Octopus and the Evolution of Intelligent Life.* London: William Collins.

Goldin-Meadow, S. (2003) *Hearing Gesture: How Our Hands Help Us to Think.* Cambridge: Harvard University Press.

Goldin-Meadow, S., Cook, S. W., & Mitchell, Z. A. (2009) Gesturing gives children new ideas about math, *Psychological Science*, 20(3), 267–272.

Goleman, D. (1996) *Emotional Intelligence: Why It Can Matter More Than IQ.* London: Bloomsbury.

Gray, T., & Mitten, D. (2018) *The Palgrave International Handbook of Women and Outdoor Learning.* London: Palgrave Macmillan.

Greenfield, A. (2006) *Everyware: The Dawning Age of Ubiquitous Computing.* Berkeley, CA: New Riders.

Griffiths, J. (2006) *Wild: An Elemental Journey.* London: Penguin Books.

Gros, F. (2014) *A Philosophy of Walking.* New York: Verso Trade.

Gross, R (2001) *Psychology: The Science of Mind and Behaviour.* London: Hodder and Stoughton.

Hadlaw, J. (2003) The London underground map: Imagining modern time and space, *Design issues*, 19(1), 25–35.

Hager, P. (1999) Robin usher on experience, *Educational Philosophy and Theory*, 31(1), 63–75.

Hase, S., & Kenyon, C. (Eds). (2013) *Self-Determined Learning: Heutagogy in Action.* London: Bloomsbury Publishing.

Hattie, J., & Yates, G. (2014) *Visible Learning and the Science of How We Learn.* Oxford: Routledge.

Hein, G. (1998) *Learning in the Museum.* Abingdon: Routledge.

Heintzman, P. (2016) Spirituality in the Outdoors, in Humberstone, B., Prince, H., & Henderson, K. (Eds) *Routledge International Handbook of Outdoor Studies* (pp. 388–397). Oxon: Routledge.

Hemming, J. (1978) *Red Gold: The Conquest of the Brazilian Indians.* London: Macmillan.

Hills, D., & Thomas, G. (2020) Digital technology and outdoor experiential learning, *Journal of Adventure Education and Outdoor Learning*, 20(2), 155–169.

Hodge, D., Baxter Magolda, M., & Haynes, C. (2009) Engaged learning: Enabling self-authorship and effective practice, *Liberal Education*, 95(4), 16–23.

Holman, D., Pavlica, K., & Thorpe, R. (1997) Rethinking Kolb's theory of experiential learning in management education, *Management Learning,* 28(2), 135–148.

Hooper-Greenhill, E. (Ed) (1999) *The Educational Role of the Museum*, 2nd edition. Oxford: Routledge.

Hooper-Greenhill, E. (2007) *Museums and Education, Purpose, Pedagogy, Performance.* Oxford: Routledge.

Hughes, C. (2011) Pleasure, change and values in doctoral pedagogy, *Studies in Higher Education*, 36(6), 621–635.

Hughes, C., & Lury, C. (2013) Re-turning feminist methodologies: From a social to an ecological epistemology, *Gender and Education*, 25(6), 786–799.

242 References

Humberstone, B., Beard, C., & Clayton, B. (2013) Performativity and enjoyable learning, *Journal of Further and Higher Education*, 37(2), 280–295.

Hyerle, D. (2009) *Visual Tools for Transforming Information into Knowledge*, 2nd edition. Thousand Oaks, CA: Corwin Press.

Hyerle, D., & Alper, L. (Eds). (2011) *Student Successes with Thinking Maps®: School-based Research, Results, and Models for Achievement Using Visual Tools*. Thousand Oaks, CA: Corwin Press.

Ifenthaler, D. (2010) Relational, structural, and semantic analysis of graphical representations and concept maps, *Education Technology Research & Development*, 58, 81–97.

Illeris, K. (2002) *The Three Dimensions of Learning: Contemporary Learning Theory in the Tension Field Between the Cognitive, the Emotional, and the Social*. Malabar, FL: Krieger Publishing.

Immordino-Yang, M. H., & Damasio, A. (2008) We feel therefore we Learn, in Fischer, K. W., & Immordino-Yang, M. H. (Eds) *The Brain and Learning* (pp. 183–198). Chicago, IL: John Wiley & Sons.

Ingelton, C. (1999) *Emotions in learning: A neglected dynamic*. A paper presented at the HERSDA Annual International Conference, Melbourne, Australia, July.

Itin, C. (1999) Reasserting the philosophy of experiential education as a vehicle for change in the 21st century, *The Journal of Experiential Education*, 22(2), 91–98.

Jackson, N. (2011) (Ed) *Learning for a Complex World: A Lifewide Concept of learning: Education and Personal Development*. Bloomington, IN: Author-House.

Jackson, N. (2011) The lifelong and lifewide dimensions of living, learning and developing, in Jackson, N. (Ed) *Learning for a Complex World: A Lifewide Concept of Learning: Education and Personal Development* (pp. 1–21). Bloomington, IN: Author-House.

Jarvis, P. (2004) *Adult Education and Lifelong Learning*, 3rd edition. London: Routledge.

Jarvis, P. (2006) *Towards a Comprehensive Theory of Human Learning*. Oxford: Routledge.

Jay, M. (2005) *Songs of Experience: Modern American and European Variations on a Universal Theme*. Berkley, CA: University of California Press.

Jonassen, D. H. (2011) *Learning to Solve Problems: A Handbook for Designing Problem-Solving Learning Environments*. New York, NY: Routledge.

Kahneman, D. (2011) *Thinking, Fast and Slow*. London: Penguin Books.

Kalbach, J. (2016) *Mapping experiences: A complete guide to creating value through journeys, blueprints and diagrams*. Newton, MA: O'Reilly Media.

Kayes, C. (2007) Institutional barriers to experiential learning revisited, in Reynolds, M., & Vince, R. (Eds) *The Handbook of Experiential Learning and Management Education* (pp. 417–431). Oxford: Oxford University Press.

Keller, E. F. (1983) *A Feeling for the Organism: The Life and Work of Barbara McClintock*. New York, NY: W. H. Freeman.

Kelso, J., & Engstrom, D. (2006) *The Complimentary Nature*. Cambridge: Bradford Book/MIT Press.

Kidner, D. (2001) *Nature and Psyche: Radical Environmentalism and the Politics of Subjectivity*, New York: State University of New York Press.

Kirsh, D. (2010) Thinking with external representations, *AI and Society*, 25, 441–454.

Kitayama, S., & Markus, H. (Eds). (1994) *Emotion and Culture: Empirical Studies of Mutual Influence*. Washington, DC: American Psychological Association.

Klang, C., & Suter, M. (2019) *Learning Design: Create Amazing Learning Experiences with Design Thinking*. Germany: Createspace Publishers.

References 243

Knowles, M., Elwood, H., & Swanson, R. (2015) *The Adult Learner: The Definitive Classic in Adult Education*, 8th edition. New York: Routledge.

Kolb, A., & Kolb, D. (2017) *The Experiential Educator*. Hawaii: EBLS Press.

Kolb, D. (1976) Management and the learning process, *California Management Review*, 18(3), 21–31.

Kolb, D. (1984) *Experiential Learning: Experience as the Source of Learning and Development*. New York, NY: Prentice-Hall.

Kolb, D., & Fry, R. (1975) Toward an applied theory oof experiential learning, in Cooper, C. (Ed) *Theories of Group Processes*. New York: Wiley & Sons.

Kolb, D., Rubin, I., & McIntyre, J. (1971) *Organisational Psychology: An Experiential Approach*. New York, NY: Prentice Hall.

Kotler, P. (1973) Atmospherics as a marketing tool, *Journal of Retail*, 49(4), 48–64.

Kujala, J. (2018) From *Erä* to *Elo*, loss or gain? A brief history of Finnish outdoor education, in Becker, P., Humberstone, B., Loynes, C., & Schirp, J. (Eds) *The Changing World of Outdoor Learning in Europe* (pp. 221–234). Abingdon: Routledge.

Kull, R (2008) *Solitude: Seeking Wisdom in Extremes*. Novato, CA: New World Library.

Lakoff, G., & Johnson, M. (1999) *Philosophy in the Flesh–The Embodied Mind and its Challenge to Western Thought*. New York: Basic Books.

Lakoff, G., & Nunez, R. E. (2000) *Where Mathematics Comes From: How the Embodied Mind Brings Mathematics into Being*. New York, NY: Basic Books.

Laski, E., Jor'dan, J., Daoust, C., & Murray, A. (2015) What makes mathematics manipulatives effective? Lessons from cognitive science and Montessori education, *SAGE Open*, 5(2), 2158244015589588.

Laurillard, D. (2012) *Teaching as a Design Science: Building Pedagogical Patterns for Learning and Technology*. New York: Routledge.

LeDoux, J. (2008) Remembrance of emotions past, in Fischer, K. W., & Immordino-Yang, M. H. (Eds) *The Brain and Learning* (pp. 151–179). Chicago, IL: John Wiley & Sons.

Lee Do, S., & Schallert, D. L. (2004) Emotion and classroom talk: Toward a model of the role of affect in students' experiences of classroom discussions, *Journal of Educational Psychology*, 96(4), 619–634.

Levesque, C., Geoffroy, D., & Polese, G. (2016) Naskapi Women: Words, Narratives, and Knowledge, in Kermoal, N., & Altamirano-Jimenez, I. (Eds) *Living on the Land: Indigenous Women's Understanding of Place* (pp. 59–84). Edmonton: Athabasca University Press.

Lin, L., & Atkinson, R. K. (2011) Using animations and visual cueing to support learning of scientific concepts and processes, *Computers & Education*, 56(3), 650–658.

Linden, D. (2015) *Touch: The Science of Hand, Heart, and Mind*. London: Penguin Books.

Lindstrom, M. (2005) *Brand Sense*. London: Kogan Page.

Lipmanowicz, & McCandless (2013) *The Surprising Power of Liberating Structures: Simple Rules to Unleash a Culture of Liberation*. London: Liberating Structures Press.

Lobel, T. (2016) *Sensation: The New Science of Physical Intelligence*. New York: Simon and Schuster.

Lombard, A. (2007) *Sensory Intelligence: Why it Matters More Then IQ and EQ*. South Africa: Metz Press.

Lowan(-Trudeau), G. (2013) Considering the ecological métissage: To blend or not to blend? *Journal of Experiential Education*, 37(4), 351–366.

Loynes, C. (2018) Consider your trace: the shift from education 'in' to education 'for' the environment, in Becker, P., Humberstone, B., Loynes, C., & Schirp, J. (Eds) *The Changing World of Outdoor Learning in Europe*. Abingdon: Routledge.

244 References

Loynes, C. (2020) The legacy of maps: Breaking the link between maps and navigation in order to experience place, *Journal of Outdoor and Environmental Education*, 23(2), 137–151.

Lundborg, G. (2014) *The Hand and the Brain: From Lucy's Thumb to the Thought Controlled Robotic Hand*. New York: Springer.

Lynch and Grainger (2008) *Big Brain: The Origins and Future of Human Intelligence*. New York, NY: Palgrave Macmillan.

Mackh, B. (2018) *Higher Education by Design: Best Practices for Curricular Planning and Instruction*. New York: Routledge.

Macnaghten, P. and Urry, J. (1997) Towards a Sociology of Nature, in McDonagh, P., & Prothero, A. (Eds) *Green Management: A Reader* (pp. 6–21). London: Dryden Press.

Maguire, E. A., Gadian, D. G., Johnsrude, I. S., Good, C. D., Ashburner, J., Frackowiak, R. S., & Frith, C. D. (2000) Navigation-related structural change in the hippocampi of taxi drivers, *Proceedings of the National Academy of Sciences*, 97(8), 4398–4403.

Malinen, A. (2000) *Towards the Essence of Adult Experiential Leaning*. Jyvaskyla: Jyvaskyla University Printing House.

Mälkki, K. (2012) Rethinking disorienting dilemmas within real-life crises: The role of reflection in negotiating emotionally chaotic experiences, *Adult Education Quarterly*, 62(3), 207–229.

Mälkki, K., & Green, L. (2014) Navigational aids: The phenomenology of transformative learning, *Journal of Transformative Education*, 12(1), 5–24.

Martin, A., Franc, D., & Zounková, D. (2004) *Outdoor and Experiential Learning: An Holistic and Creative Approach to Programme Design*. Aldershot: Gower Publishing, Ltd.

Marton, F. and Säljö, R. (1976) On qualitative differences in learning. 1–outcome and process, *British Journal of Educational Psychology*, 46, 4–11.

Maslow, A. (1954) *Motivation and Personality*. New York, NY: Harper.

Maslow, A. (1968) *Toward a Psychology of Being*, 2nd edition. Princetown, NJ: D. Van Nostrand.

Mayer, R. E. (Ed) (2014) *The Cambridge Handbook of Multimedia Learning*, 2nd Edition, New York, NY: Cambridge University Press.

Mayer, R. E., & Roxana, R. (2003) Nine ways to reduce cognitive load in multimedia learning, *Educational Psychologist*, 38(1), 43–52.

Mayes, C., & Williams, E. (2013) *Nurturing the Whole Student: Five Dimensions of Teaching and Learning*. Plymouth: Rowman & Littlefield Education.

McGilchrist, I. (2009) (expanded edition) *The Master and His Emissary: The Divided Brain and the Making of the Western World*. New Haven, CT: Yale University Press.

McWhaw, K., Schnackenberg, H., Sclater, J., & Abrami, P. (2003) From Co-operation to collaboration: helping students become collaborative learners, in Gillies, R., & Ashman, A. (Eds) *Co-operative Learning: The Social and Intellectual Outcomes of Learning in Groups* (pp. 69–86). New York: Routledge.

Megginson, D. (1994) Planned and emergent learning, *Executive Development*, 7(6), 29–32.

Mezirow, J., & Associates (2000) *Learning as Transformation: Critical Perspectives on a Theory in Progress*. San Francisco, CA: Jossey-Bass.

Mezirow, J., & Taylor, E. W. (Eds). (2009) *Transformative Learning in Practice: Insights from Community, Workplace, and Higher Education*. John Wiley & Sons.

Michelson, E. (1998) Re-remembering: The return of the body to experiential learning, *Studies in Continuing Education*, 20(2).

Michelson, E. (1999) Carnival, paranoia, and experiential learning, *Studies in the Education of Adults*, 31(2), 140–154.

References 245

Mies, M., & Shiva, V. (1993) *Ecofeminism*. London: Zed Books.

Miller, J., & Nigh, K. (2017) *Holistic Education and Embodied Learning*. Charlotte, NC: Information Age Publishing.

Moon, J. (2004) *A Handbook of Reflective and Experiential Learning: Theory and Practice*. London: Routledge/Falmer.

Moore, S., & Kuol, N. (2007) Matters of the heart: Exploring the emotional dimensions of educational experience in recollected accounts of excellent teaching, *International Journal for Academic Development*, 12, 87–98.

Moreno, R., & Mayer, R. E. (1999) Cognitive principles of multimedia learning: The role of modality and contiguity, *Journal of Educational Psychology*, 91, 358–368.

Mortlock, C. (1984) *The Adventure Alternative*. Cumbria: Cicerone Press Limited.

Mortiboys, A. (2002) *The Emotionally Intelligent Lecturer*. Birmingham: SEDA Publications.

Moseley & Whitton (2019) Introducing playful learning events, in Whitton, N., & Moseley, A. (Eds) *Playful Learning: Events and Activities to Engage Adults* (pp. 3–7). Abingdon: Routledge.

Mullins, P., Lowan-Trudeau, G., & Fox, K. (2016) Healing the split head of outdoor recreation and outdoor education: Revisiting indigenous knowledge from multiple perspectives, in Humberstone, B., Prince, H., & Henderson, K. (Eds) *Routledge International Handbook of Outdoor Studies*. Abingdon: Routledge.

Murdoch, S. (2007) *IQ: A Smart History of a Failed Idea*. London: Wiley.

Nicol, R. (2003) Outdoor education: Research topic or universal value? Part three, *Journal of Adventure Education and Outdoor Learning*, 3(1), 11–28.

Nyal, N. (2014) *Hooked: How to Build Habit-Forming Products*. London: Penguin.

O'Dell, T. (2005) Experiencescapes: Blurring borders and testing connections, in O'Dell, T. & Billing, P. (Eds) *Experiencescapes: Tourism, Culture, and Economy* (pp. 11–33). Frederiksberg: Copenhagen Business School Press.

O'Neil, J., & Marsick, V. (2007) *Understanding Action Learning: Theory into Practice*. New York: Amacom.

Ormrod, J. (2018: 346) *Human Learning*, 8th edition. Upper Saddle River, NJ: Pearson.

O'Sullivan, E., & Spangler, K. (1999) *Experiential Marketing*. State College, PA: Venture Publishing.

Paivio, A. (1986) *Mental Representations: A Dual Coding Approach*. New York, NY: Oxford University Press.

Palmer, G. (2020) Pot throwing: An investigation into the real-time cognitive and physical processes involved in craft performance. Unpublished doctoral thesis, Loughborough University.

Palmer, J. A. (2006) *Environmental Education in the 21st Century: Theory, Practice, Progress and Promise*. London: Routledge.

Palmer, J. A., Bresler, L., & Cooper, D. (2001) *Fifty Major Thinkers on Education*. London: Psychology Press.

Palmer, M., O'Kane, P., & Owens, M. (2009) Betwixt spaces: Student accounts of turning point experiences in the first year transition, *Studies in Higher Education*, 34(1), 37–54.

Paradis, C., & Eeg-Olofsson, M. (2013) Describing sensory experience: The genre of wine reviews, *Metaphor and Symbol*, *28*(1), 22–40.

Parkin, M. (1998) *Tales for Trainers*, London: Kogan Page.

Pavlovich, K. (2007) The development of reflective practice through student journals, *Higher Education Research & Development*, 26(3), 281–295.

246 References

Payne, P. (2002) On the construction, deconstruction and reconstruction of experience in 'critical outdoor education, *Australian Journal of Outdoor Education*, 6(2), 4–21.

Pekrun, R., Goetz, T., & Titz, W. (2002) Academic emotions in students' self-regulated learning and achievement: A program of qualitative and quantitative research, *Educational psychologist*, 37(2), 91–105.

Pepper, D. (1984) *The Roots of Modern Environmentalism*. Beckenham: Croom Helm.

Pine, B. J., Pine, J., & Gilmore, J. H. (1999) *The Experience Economy: Work is Theatre and Every Business a Stage*. Cambridge, MA: Harvard Business Press.

Pink, D. (2010) *Drive: The Surprising Truth About What Motivates Us*. Edinburgh: Canongate Books.

Pinker, S. (1989) *Learnability and Cognition: The Acquisition of Argument Structure*. Cambridge, MA: The MIT Press.

Pizam, A., & Tasci, A. D. (2019) Experienscape: expanding the concept of servicescape with a multi-stakeholder and multi-disciplinary approach (invited paper for 'luminaries' special issue of International Journal of Hospitality Management), *International Journal of Hospitality Management*, 76, 25–37.

Plutchik, R. (1980) *Emotion: A Psychobioevolutionary Synthesis*. New York, NY: Harper & Row.

Porter, T. (1999) Beyond metaphor: Applying a new paradigm of change to experiential debriefing, *Journal of Experiential Education*, 22(2), 85–90.

Prinz, J. (2013) Foreword: Hand Manifesto, preface, in *The Hand, An Organ of the Mind* (pp. ix-xvii). Cambridge, MA: The MIT Press.

Radman, Z. (Ed). (2013) *The Hand: An Organ of the Mind*. Cambridge, MA: MIT Press.

Randall, R., & Southgate, J. (1980) *Co-Operaitve and Group Dynamics*. London: Barefoot Books.

Ratcliffe, M. (2013) Touch and the sense of reality, in Radman, Z. (Ed) *The Hand, An Organ of The Mind: What the Manual Tells the Mental* (pp. 131–157). Cambridge, MA: MIT Press.

Richards, G., Marques, L., & Mein, K. (Eds). (2014) *Event Design: Social Perspectives and Practices*. Abingdon: Routledge.

Richter, J., Scheiter, K., & Eitel, A. (2016) Signaling text-picture relations in multimedia learning: A comprehensive meta-analysis, *Educational Research Review*, 17, 19–36.

Ringer, T. M. (2002) *Group Action: The Dynamics of Groups in Therapeutic, Educational and Corporate Settings*. London: Jessica Kingsley Publishers.

Ritchhart, R., Church, M., & Morrison, K. (2011) *Making Thinking Visible: How to Promote Engagement, Understanding, and Independence for All Learners*. Hoboken, NJ: John Wiley & Sons.

Rizzolatti, G., & Sinigaglia, C. (2008) *Mirrors In The Brain: How Our Minds Share Actions And Emotions*. Oxford: Oxford University Press.

Roberts, J. (2012) *Beyond Learning by Doing: Theoretical Currents in Experiential Education*. Oxford: Routledge.

Robinson, K. (2001) *Out of Our Minds: Learning to Be Creative*. Chichester: Capstone Publishing.

Rogers, C. R. (1969) *Freedom to Learn*. Ohio: Charles E. Merrill Publishing and Co.

Rossman, J., & Duerden, M. (2019) *Designing Experiences*. New York: Columbia University Press.

Rowe, A. D. (2013) *Feedback in higher education: Personal, relational and emotional dimensions*, Unpublished PhD thesis, Macquarie University, Australia.

Rowe, D. (2001) *Friends and Enemies*. London: HarperCollins.

Rowland, S. (2000) *The Enquiring University Teacher*. Milton Keynes: Open University Press.

Russell, J., & Barchard, K. (2002) Towards a shared language for emotion and emotional intelligence, in L. Feldman Barrett & P. Salovey (Eds) *The Wisdom in Feeling: Psychological Processes in Emotional Intelligence* (pp. 363–382). New York: The Guildford Press.

Sadoski, M., & Paivio, A. (2013) *Imagery and Text: A Dual Coding Theory of Reading and Writing*, 2nd edition. New York, NY: Routledge.

Salovey, P. and Mayer, J. (1997) What is emotional intelligence?, in Salovey, P., & Sluyter, D. (Eds) *Emotional Development and Emotional Intelligence: Implications for Educators*. New York, NY: Basic Books.

Scheff, T. (1997) *Emotions, the Social Bond, and Human Reality*. Cambridge: Cambridge University Press.

Schon, D. (1983) *The Reflective Practitioner*. New York: Basic Books.

Schultes, R., Hofmann, A., & Ratsch. C. (1998) *Plants of the Gods: A Sacred, Healing, and Hallucinogenic Powers*. Vermont: Healing Arts Press.

Schiffman, H. (1990) *Sensation and Perception: An Integrated Approach*. New York, NY: John Wiley & Sons.

Schlosberg, H. S. (1941) A scale for the judgement of facial expression, *Journal of Experimental Psychology*, 29, 497–510.

Schwetman, J. D. (2014) Harry Beck's London underground map: A convex lens for the global city, *Transfers*, 4(2), 86–103.

Seaman, J. (2008) Experience, reflect, critique: The end of the "learning cycles" era, *Journal of Experiential Education*, 31(1), 3–18.

Seaman, J., Quay, J., & Brown, M. (2017) The evolution of experiential learning: Tracing lines of research in the JEE, *Journal of Experiential Education*, 40, 1–20.

Seligman, M. (2006) *Learned optimism: How to change your mind and your life*. New York: Pocket Books.

Seligman, M. (2011) *Flourish*. London: Nicholas Brealey Publishing.

Sepp, S., Howard, S. J., Tindall-Ford, S., Agostinho, S., & Paas, F. (2019) Cognitive load theory and human movement: Towards an integrated model of working memory. *Educational Psychology Review*, 1–25.

Schull, N (2012) *Addiction by Design: Machine Gambling in Las Vegas*. Princetown, NJ: Princetown University Press.

Sheets-Johnstone, M. (1990) *The Roots of Thinking*. Philadelphia, VA: Temple University Press.

Sheets-Johnstone, M. (2009) *The Corporeal Turn, An Interdisciplinary Reader*. Exeter: Imprint Academic.

Sheets-Johnstone, M. (2010) Movement: The generative source of spatial perception, in Dolins, F. L., & Mitchell, R. W. (Eds) *Spatial Cognition, Spatial Perception: Mapping the Self and Space* (pp. 323–430). Cambridge: Cambridge University Press.

Siegel, D. (2007) *The Mindful Brain: Reflection and Attunement in the Cultivation of Well-being*. New York: Norton.

Siegel, D. (2012) *The Developing Mind: How Relationships and the Brain Interact to Shape Who We Are*, 2nd edition. New York: The Guildford Press.

Silberman, M. (2007) *The Handbook of Experiential Learning*. Big Sur, CA: Pfeiffer.

Simon, N. (2010) *The Participatory Museum*. Big Sur, CA: Museum.

248 References

Skulmowski, A., Pradel, S., Kühnert, T., Brunnett, G., & Rey, G. D. (2016) Embodied learning using a tangible user interface: The effects of haptic perception and selective pointing on a spatial learning task, *Computers & Education*, 92, 64–75.

Smit, B., & Melissen, F. (2018) *Sustainable Customer Experience Design: Co-creating Experiences in Events, Tourism and Hospitality.* London: Routledge.

Sogen, O. (2019) *Introduction to Zen Training: A Physical Approach to Meditation and Mind-Body Training.* Tokyo: Tuttle Publishing.

Southgate, J., Randall, R., & Tomlinson, F. (1980) *Co-operative and Community Group Dynamics.* London: Barefoot Books.

Sperry, R. (1968) Hemisphere disconnection and unity in conscious awareness, *American Psychologist*, 23(10), 723.

Stanton, P. (2018) *Conscious Creativity: Look, Connect, Create.* Brighton: Leaping Hare Press.

Stapley, L. (2004) Introduction, in Gould, L., Stapley, L., & Stein, M. (Eds) *Experiential Learning in Organisations: Applications of the Tavistock Group Relations Approach* (pp. 1–10). London: Karnac Books.

Stein, M. (2004) Theories of experiential learning and the unconscious, in Gould, L., Stapley, L., & Stein, M. (Eds) *Experiential Learning in Organisations: Applications of the Tavistock Group Relations Approach* (pp. 19–36). London: Karnac Books.

Sterling, S. (2001) *Sustainable Education: Re-visioning Learning and Change.* Devon: Green Books.

Stigler, J., & Miller, K. (2018) Design and expert performance in teaching, in Ericsson, K. A, Hoffman, R., Kozbelt, A., & Williams, M. (Eds) *The Cambridge Handbook of Expertise & Expert Performance* (pp. 431–452). Cambridge: Cambridge University Press.

Stone, M., & Barlow, Z. (2005) *Ecological Literacy: Educating Our Children for a Sustainable World.* San Francisco, CA: Sierra Club Books.

Stonehouse, P., Allison, P., & Carr, D. (2011) Aristotle, Plato, and Socrates: Ancient Greek perspectives on experiential learning, in Smith, T., & Knapp, C. (Eds) *Sourcebook of Experiential Education: Key Thinkers and their Contributions* (pp. 13–25). New York, NY: Routledge.

Stoten, D. (2020) Practical heutagogy: Promoting personalized learning in management education, *Adult Learning*, 31(4).

Swaab, C. (2014) *We are Our Brains: From the Womb to Alzheimer's.* London: Penguin.

Swan, E. (2007) Blue-Eyed Girl? Jane Elliott's experiential learning and anti-racism, in Reynolds, M., & Vince, R. (Eds) *The Handbook of Experiential Learning and Management Education* (pp. 202–220). Oxford: Oxford University Press.

Sweller, J., van Merrienboer, J. J., & Paas, F. (1998) Cognitive architecture and instructional design, *Educational Psychology Review*, 10(3), 251–296.

Tangen, J. M., Constable, M. D., Durrant, E., Teeter, C., Beston, B. R., & Kim, J. A. (2011) The role of interest and images in slideware presentations, *Computers & Education*, 56(3), 865–872.

Taylor, H. (1991) The systematic training model: Corn Circles in search of a spaceship? *Journal of the Association for Management Education and Development,* 22(4), 258–278.

Thayer, R. E. (1989) *The Biopsychology of Mood and Activation.* New York, NY: Oxford University Press.

Tolle, E. (1997) *The Power of Now: A Guide to Spiritual Enlightenment.* Vancouver: Namaste Publishing.

Trewavas, A. (2014) *Plant Behaviour and Intelligence.* Oxford: Oxford University Press.

References   **249**

Tuan, Yi-Fu (1974) *Topophilia: A study of Environmental Perception, Attitudes, and Values.* New York, NY: Columbia University Press.

Tuan, Yi-Fu (1997) *Space and Place: The Perspective of Experience.* Minneaplois, MN: Minnesota Press.

Tuan, Yi-Fu (2005) The pleasures of touch, in Classen, C. (Ed) *The Book of Touch* (pp. 74–79), Oxford: Berg Publishing.

Tugade, M., & Fredrickson, B. (2002) Positive emotions and emotional intelligence, in Feldman Barrett, L., & Salovey, P. (Eds) *The Wisdom in Feeling: Psychological Processes in Emotional Intelligence* (pp. 319–340). London: The Guildford Press.

Turner, T. (2005) *Video games as education and literacies: What we have to understand about video and computer learning and technological environments to accomplish learning and literacies.* A workshop presentation abstract at 'Design for Learning', The Twelfth International Conference on Learning, Granada, Spain, July 11–14.

Tversky, B. (2016) Spatial schemas in depictions, in M. Gattis (Ed) *Spatial Schemas and Abstract Thought* (pp. 79–112). London: MIT Press.

Ulrich, R. S. (1984) View through a window may influence recovery from surgery, *Science*, 224(4647), 420–421.

van Kesteren, M. T. R., & Meeter, M. (2020) How to optimize knowledge construction in the brain, *Science of Learning*, 5(5).

Varlander, S. (2008) The role of students' emotions in formal feedback situations, *Teaching in Higher Education*, 13, 145–156.

Veevers, N., & Allison, P. (2011) *Kurt Hahn: Inspirational, Visionary, Outdoor and Experiential Educator.* Rotterdam: Sense Publishing.

Verschaffel, L., De Corte, E., De Jong, T., & Elen, J. (2010) *Use of Representations in Reasoning and Problem Solving: Analysis and improvement* (pp. 2–8). London: Routledge.

Vince, R., & Reynolds, M. (2007) Introduction: Experiential learning and management education: Key themes and future directions, in Reynolds, M., & Vince, R. (Eds) *The Handbook of Experiential Learning and Management Education* (pp. 1–18). Oxford: Oxford University Press.

Vygotsky, L. (1978) Interaction between learning and development, *Readings on the Development of Children*, 23(3), 34–41.

Walker, R. (1999) Fire in the Sky: From big bang to big money. *Horizons*, 4, 5–7.

Warren, K., Sakoffs, M., & Hunt, J. (1995) *The Theory of Experiential Education.* Denver, CO: Kendall Hunt.

Watson, D., & Tellegan, A. (1985) Towards a consensual structure of mood, *Psychological Bulletin*, 98, 219–235.

Wattchow, B., & Brown, M. (2011) *A Pedagogy of Place: Outdoor Education for a Changing wWorld.* Melbourne: Monash University Press.

Wenger-Trayner, E., & Wenger-Trayner, B. (2020) *Learning to Make a Difference: Value Creation in Social Learning Spaces.* Cambridge: Cambridge University Press.

Werner, E., & Smith, R. S. (1992) Overcoming the odds: High risk children from birth to adulthood, in Feldman Barrett, L., & Salovey, P. (Eds) *The Wisdom in Feeling: Psychological Processes in Emotional Intelligence.* London: The Guildford Press.

Whitton, N. (2014) *Digital Games and Learning: Research and Theory.* New York: Routledge.

Whitton, N., & Moseley, A. (2019) *Playful Learning: Events and Activities to Engage Adults.* Oxon: Routledge.

Wiking, M. (2019) *The Art of Making Memories: How to Create and Remember Happy Moments.* New York: Penguin.

250 References

Wilcock, A. (1999) Reflections on doing, being, and becoming, *Australian Occupational Journal*, 1(46), 1–11.

Wilson, E. (1984) *Biophilia*. Cambridge, MA: Harvard University Press.

Wilson, F. R., (1998) *The Hand: How its Use Shapes the Brain, Language, and Culture*. New York: Pantheon Books.

Winston, R. (2003) *The Human Mind and How to Make the Most of It*. London: Bantam Press.

Woodall, A. (2016) Rummaging as a strategy for creative thinking and imaginative engagement in higher education, in Chatterjee, H., & Hannan, L. (Eds) *Engaging the Senses: Object-Based Learning in Higher Education* (pp. 133–155). Oxon: Routledge

Wood, E, & Masterman, G. (2006) *Innovative Marketing Communications: Strategies for the Events Industry*. Oxford: Butterworth-Heinemann.

Wu, H. K., & Puntambekar, S. (2012) Pedagogical affordances of multiple external representations in scientific processes, *Journal of Science Education Technology*, 21, 754–767.

Wundt, W. (1897) *Outlines of Psychology* (Trans. C. H. Judd). Leipzig: Wilhelm Engelmann.

Wynn, T. (2010) The evolution of spatial cognition, in Dolins, F. L., & Mitchell, R. W. (Eds) *Spatial Cognition, Spatial Perception: Mapping the Self and Space* (pp. 213–236), Cambridge: Cambridge University Press.

INDEX

Page numbers in *italics* indicate a figure and page numbers in **bold** indicate a table on the corresponding page.

3H model 63
5H model 64–65, *64*
5H-7M 64–65
7H-model 69
20 seconds of fame 161

addiction 121–122
adult learning 31, 73
agency 121, 149, 151, 154, **226**, **230**;
    see also human agency
andragogy 31, 155
animation 49
arousal 101, 103, 107, 108, 112
atmospherics 10, 169
attachment 153; attachment to place and
    space 167
attention 94, 121

Baddeley A. 51, 77, 144
Beck, Harry 144
being 29, 39, 60, 62, 180, 202–203, *203*;
    being in the now 204–205; influenced by
    conditioning 205–207; three C's model
    205–207, *206*; transformation 202
belonging 62, 153, 168
body-brain interaction 53, *54*
brain 124–125, 133; evolution of 132,
    138; hemisphere functionalities 137,
    138; increase in capacity 135; integrative

processing 139–140, *140*; mapping 136;
    memory, recall, and reflection 140–141;
    processing speeds 128–129

co-creation of learning 166
Coffee and Papers 33, 172–173
cognitive dissonance 131
cognitive load 142
colours 47
communication 212, *213*
competences, 21st Century 213
conceptual metaphors 23, 46, 74
conditioning 205–207
conduct 206–207
congruence 46–47
content 27, 94
cues and signals 49, *50*, 77, *145*, 153

design 14, 26, 32; construction and
    reconstruction 88; curriculum design
    28; design changes 157–158; design
    frameworks 12, 32, 130, 184, *185*;
    design language 26; learning design
    14, 15; principles 107; rewriting
    texts 158; *see also* congruence;
    experiential learning design; external
    representations; structural designs
Dewey, J. 9, 12, 19, 20, 25, 27, 58, 60,
    78, 217

252 Index

digital games 86, 92
digital learning 92, 94
digital memories 186
digital space 94, 174–175
doing 69, 70, experience of 71; as a co-creative design process 91; as moving 71–74; as playing 86; as the real thing 83; and sensing 69–71; sports coaching 87; tools and technology 94; touching and manipulating objects 80
dramaturgy 41–42, 91
Dual Coding Theory 107

educators 126
edutainment 158, *159*, 184, 217–218
Extended Mind Theory 148–149
Emile 155
emotions 103, 107, 109, 110, 126, 129; emotional intelligence 120; influence on the developing mind 123; negative emotions 112, 115, 130; positive emotions 106, 115–116, **117–118**, 129, 130–131; range of 112, relating to touch/body 113
equations 56
etymology 4
European Union 214
experience: mapping 38–39; meaning of 12–13; three modes of 77
experience economy 38, 62
experiencescape 29, 168–170, 218, 224–225
experiential education 16, 18, 19, 28, 156–157, 205
experiential learning 15, 23–24, 60, 166, 180; core philosophical foundations 18–20; core principles 18; cycle 103; definitions 16–17; three core traditions 156–157 typical features *22*, *24*
experiential learning design 14–15, 18, 189, *226*; aims and objectives 30–32; emotional experiences 110, 115; complexity 225; key features 28
experiential waves 40, **41**
expertise 13
external representations 14, 15, 27, 46, 136, 144, 230

fear 112, 113
feelings *see* emotions
flourishing 130

gamification 86
gaming; addictive design 122; impression of reality 87; for teaching and learning 27, 86, 175; simulation 174; *see also* gamification
Gardner, Howard 93
gates of perception 188
General Intended Learning Objectives 32
gestures 52–53, 82, 83, 89, 90
getting 204
graphics 33, *49*
group learning 152

habits 121
habits of mind 204–205
handling sequence code 97, *98*
hands, role in learning 78–83, 94
happiness 103, 130
HELM *see* Holistic Experiential Learning Model (HELM)
hemisphere dominance 159
heutagogy 155
higher education 27, 166, 170, 221
Holistic Experiential Learning Model (HELM) 39, 63–65, *66*, *67*, *215*, 218, *223*
human agency 21, 121, 122; *see also* agency
human beings 201, 203
human connection 178, 180; *see* also gates of perception; knowledge; nature; outdoors
Human Development Index 213
Human Experience Mapping (HEM) 39
human thinking 133

icons *36*, *49*, *50*, *51*
imagination 89
Imagineering 26
Integrated self 207–208
interpretation 89
intelligence, erroneous beliefs and ideas 137

jigsaws 57

Kadoorie Farm and Botanic Gardens 177–178
kindness and compassion 207–208
knowing 141
knowledge 166; indigenous knowledge 182–183, 194; spatial knowledge 74
Kolb D. 7, 19, 58–59, 61, 69, 70, 154, 201

language 47–48, 83, 89, 107
Lao Tzu 60, 206
leadership 152, 194–195

Index **253**

learning 7, 59, *61*, 107, 201; combination lock 65, *68;* complexity of 61–63; cycle 69; emotional process 110; journey app 38; learner-centred learning 154; lifewide learning 166–167; meaningful 92; multimedia learning 92; the pleasure of 115, *117–118;* politics of 155; the role of the moving body in 73; rote learning 69, 92; transfer of 201; transformative learning 28, 131; by walking 54; *see also* experiential learning design

learning environment 167, 173; experiencescape and 168–171; virtual 175

LED *see* experiential learning design

liberating structures 128

life experience 12

London Underground Map 35–36, 47, 57, 144

macro and micro design 28, 219, *233;* design illustration 220–223; structure and sequencing 33–35

maps 35–38, *162*

mathematics, teaching/doing 74

meaningful learning 92

media 92, 107; *see also* multimedia

memories 13, 102–103, 141–142, 219; *see also* digital memories

metaphors 45–46, 48, 202

mindfulness 202

Modality Principle 107

modes of experiencing 23

movement 51–52, 76, 78, 202; *see also* space

multimedia 92, 107, 108

multimedia learning 92

Multiple Presentation Principle 107

museum experience 10–11

naming 191

nature 179–181, 189

navigational tools 96

negotiating 88

non-verbal communication 82

Object-Based Learning (OBL) 80

objects 49, 80–81

online learning *see digital learning*

ontology 201

outdoor education: activities 187, 188–189; designs 198–199; women's contributions 196; *see also* Coffee and Papers

Outward Bound Hong Kong 178

Parchure, Vishwas 205, 206

Paivio, A. 107

pedagogy 155, 165

perception 93, 102

physical activities 70

physical intelligence 93

place 167–168, 170, 171, 181

plant awareness 190–191

play 86

pleasure 72, 102, 115, 121

private spaces 173

problem solving designs 31, 144

racism 9, 143

reflection 7–9, 59

relational pedagogy 111

representation designs 58, 229–232

rigidity 202

Rogers, Carl 110, 154

secure and insecure patterns 151

self-authorship 163–165

self-awareness 205

semantic memory 102

semiotics 47

senses: describing sensory experiences 108; influence on learning 102; sensing 69; sensory requirements when designing experiences 105; sensory design vignettes 106

sensing~feeling 101–103

sensory dulling and sensory focus 93

sensory focus 93, 103

sensory gating 104–105

sensory intelligence 94, 113

sensory systems, receptors 101–102

serotonin 71–72

service learning 167

signs and symbols 47, 49, *50*

Signalling Principle 107

sign language 82

simulations 83, 87, 88

sketching 27, 29–30

smartphones 121, 186

social bond 89, 113, 153–154

social capital 156

social media 121

social relationships *see* social bond

sound and film bites 56

space 76, 168, 170–171, 173–174; *see also* digital space

spatial memory system 77

steps or stages 56

254 Index

stories 56
structural designs *34–35*, 35, *43*, *45*, 226, *226*, *233*

teachers 28, 57, 72, 110, 127, 216, 229
technology 94, 184, *185*, 186; *see also* digital space
T-Group method 20
thinking aloud 55
Titanic Museum 11
touch 53
touch cards 53, *53*, 162, *163*
transfer 201
transformative learning 28

unpacking 147, 159, 179
user experience 26

verbalisers and visualisers 107–108
verbs as design clues 6–7
voice 163

wanting 204
waves *see* experiential waves 40
Widgets 51, *51*
women 196; Barbara McClintock Nobel Prize winner 125, 190; Donella Meadows 177; Women and the outdoors 196

Printed in the United States
by Baker & Taylor Publisher Services